ARE WE THERE YET?

Rosie Whitehouse studied International History and then Russian Government and Politics at the London School of Economics. She had a successful career at the *BBC World Service* until she became a mum. She then spent five years as a housewife in the war-torn Balkans, married to the correspondent of *The Economist*. Back in London she continued developing her ironing skills as she built a new career as a freelance journalist. Rosie has written on parenting and family issues for a wide range of newspapers and magazines and is the author of *Take the Kids: South of France* (Cadogan, 2003). Rosie lives in Shepherd's Bush with her husband, the frontline reporter Tim Judah, and their five children.

ARE WE THERE YET?

travels with my frontline family

Rosie Whitehouse

All the best
Rosie Whitehouse

REPORTAGE PRESS

REPORTAGE PRESS

Published by Reportage Press
26 Richmond Way, London W12 8LY, United Kingdom.
Tel: 020 8749 2731 Fax: 020 8749 2867
e-mail: info@reportagepress.com
www.reportagepress.com

British Library Cataloguing in Publication Data.
A catalogue record for this book is available from the British Library.

ISBN-13: 978-0-9555729-0-6

Cover design and layout by Joshua Haymann, Paris.
www.joshuahaymann.com

Cover photograph of Slobodan Milošević © Reuters

Printed and bound in Great Britain
by Antony Rowe Ltd, Chippenham, Wiltshire.
www.antonyrowe.co.uk

For my children Ben, Esti, Rachel, Jacob and Evie.
Travel broadens the mind. Mine has been stretched, bounced and
trampled all over by them as they have ripped open my eyes and
shown me a whole new world.

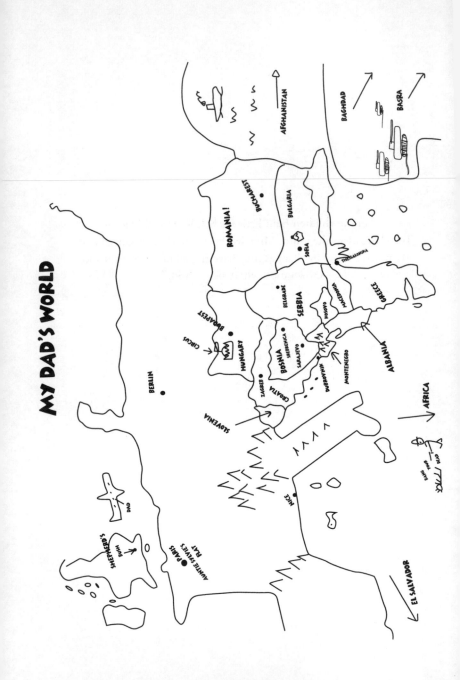

ACKNOWLEDGEMENTS

After my long suffering family, I need to thank Mark Brayne, Tamsin Cottis, Charlotte Eagar, Janine di Giovanni, Paulette Farsides and Ivan Mulcahy who thought I could do more than just change nappies. I am also indebted to Cindy Polemis who suggested that I write this book and Geoff Cooke of Warminster Barracks for finally firing the shot that rocketed it into print.

1 - Things Fall Apart

It's late on a Sunday evening in early March 1992 and Esti has finally fallen asleep in her cot. Ben is reclining in the middle of our double bed, wide awake. He's almost four-years old and over excited about staying in a yellow hotel that looks like one of his latest Lego creations. We've spent the evening eating exotic chocolate cakes in the café, inspecting the mini-bar and riding up and down in the glass elevator. Now he's on a sugar high. He's decided that the Holiday Inn, Sarajevo is the classiest place in Bosnia. Fortunately he doesn't yet know that it isn't the architecture, or the chef, that is about to make it world famous. I grope my way around the room in the half-light and climb into bed next to him. There's a crackle of gunfire outside the widow. He sits bolt upright in bed:

"Hey! What's that? Guns? Wow!"

I pull him back down and switch on the radio. It isn't the first time he's heard gunshots, and in his opinion, they add to the general excitement. Outside the people of Bosnia have been voting in a referendum that will decide if the country will break away from Yugoslavia and become independent. On the *BBC World Service*, we hear that the polls have just closed and there are reports of barricades going up all over the city. I retell the story, *Newsround*-style as the battle lines are drawn up. While we lie in the dark room listening to the TV crew next door spooling and rewinding their tapes, there's more sporadic gunfire outside the window.

"Where's Dads?" asks Ben in a whisper. Tim, his dad and my husband, is out there somewhere, but exactly where I have no idea, so I decide to say nothing. I hold Ben close.

When Tim finally comes back, I jump out of bed to greet him. Ben leaps into his arms. Other people's husbands are guaranteed to come home from work in one piece. Mine is not. It makes him more precious. In a few days he will come within moments of losing his life.

So what are we all doing here as the country descends into anarchy? Well, yes - that's a good question. I know it's *exactly* what my mother would like to know, but since I haven't called her, she hasn't had a chance to ask. I don't feel like making excuses, even if the story is actually quite simple. It's half term. Tim had to go away for work and we came too but somehow I know she won't buy that story this evening.

When I met Tim Judah, the man who was to become my husband, he was the arts correspondent on the student newspaper and spent his time writing reviews of incomprehensible, arty French films. I was the news editor, plotting with a friend how we could both get a job at the *BBC* and become world famous. Tim went home and told his flatmate that I was the most ambitious person he had ever met. Now he's a foreign correspondent covering a conflict that has already claimed the lives of a long list of journalists. How did that happen? Did I corrupt him? Leave him slightly unhinged? The moment we graduated, he left the country. Maybe it's living with me? As for my career – well, I'm a housewife and in the past few years I have come to accept that, if sometimes things are a bit crowded in our marriage, that's because I've had to learn to share my husband with the world's frightened and starving masses. I can't compete with the allure of somewhere far away, especially if it's in deep political chaos, preferably at war. That why I'm in Sarajevo. It's the only way of getting a family holiday. I can hear you thinking: "God, she's an irresponsible mother! What are you doing, you fool?" Thank goodness tonight neither my mother nor Tim's father are here to pass judgement on me. Okay, I admit maybe I am a little bit irresponsible and Tim is slightly crazy but as for who is to blame – there is only one candidate. It is Ben, that angelic looking little boy who is now curled up in his father's arms fast asleep. He brought us here. If he hadn't been born, life might have been very different.

Let's just rewind the clock two years. It's a grey November morning in 1989 and I'm late for work as usual. As I grab my handbag and bend down to kiss Ben goodbye, the hem of my coat brushes across the tracks of his wooden train set and derails a coal truck. He looks up expectantly but instantly realises that I am about to go out without him. He stares up accusingly, clutching an engine in both hands. He's almost two. The babysitter scoops him up in her arms and starts stroking his hair. I want to snatch him back but all I do is give him a quick hug and then slam the front door of the flat in his face. I can see out of the corner of my eye that there's a large blob of snot on the smart astrakhan collar of my coat but I haven't got time to wipe it off. I run down the stairs as quick as I can. I can hear him crying as I slam the main front door.

On the other side of the road, I turn around to wave at him. He's at the window. I knew he'd be there. I can only see his head. He gives me a mournful smile and a little sad wave. His sandy coloured hair is sticking up in a tuft. I hover around on the edge of the pavement grinning and waving pathetically for a minute or two in apology and then trudge off to the tube station with a heavy heart. I'm twenty-eight.

When I met Tim he had a black leather jacket and in his pocket was a bunch of little badges that he had collected in African tin-pot dictatorships. I thought he looked rather Italian. He was exotic and irresistible. In order to get him to ask me out, I set up a magazine on Soviet and East European affairs and made him the arts editor. Then I organised two complimentary tickets to a film about the French Revolution. He was supposed to ask me along. He did. To my surprise he spoke fluent French and slumped in the back row. I snuggled down next to him and had no idea what was happening on screen. He wasn't Italian at all but half French.

After I met Tim something extraordinary happened. The world that had seemed so huge and far away suddenly shrank. It was almost as if I could hold it in my hand and look at it. My parents had grown up in the same village but Tim had relatives scattered across the globe. The Britain where I had been brought up was traditional and closed. Having

Irish blood was suspect enough let alone anything else more danger-ously foreign. It was a country where the shops shut on Wednesday afternoon and having a wooden, Habitat dining table was the cutting edge of chic. It was 1984. We had fallen in love and he left to spend two years at graduate school in America. Most people assumed it was all over – long distance relationships don't last. Rubbish! Tim could speak three languages beautifully, had travelled all over the place and recognised the flags of countries I didn't know existed. I spent all my money on tickets to the States, determined to prove them wrong. We partied in New York and went to Florida for the weekend. Then I was given a place on a prestigious *BBC* training course and when Tim came home we moved in together. I was convinced that a glittering career in London awaited me. I would do what all young women were supposed to do in Mrs Thatcher's Britain; have a career, a family and look like Princess Diana.

Everything was fine until Ben arrived unannounced.

I first realised something was up when I started feeling sick and kept nodding off. At first I thought I must be ill, so I went to the doctor, something I only ever do in dire emergencies. When he told me I was six weeks pregnant, I was frozen in panic. I took days to thaw out but once I warmed up I just knew it was a boy called Ben. I had to have this baby. A warm rosy future lay ahead. I would have a beautiful baby then return to work and be promoted. I'd never felt so focused in my life, so sure of myself. So I called Tim, who was in Congo where there had been a revolution or something like that, I didn't care what exactly. As far as he was concerned this was the important thing going on in the world and the first big break in his journalistic career.

It was 4am. I was on a night shift. The news took an unnervingly long time to travel to the heart of Africa. I could feel mile upon mile of empty nothingness and I could make out dark palm trees silhouetted against the night sky as I sat with the receiver in my hand waiting for him to say something. The space between us felt dangerous and im-mense. Eventually, he stammered:

"Are you sure?"

"Of course I'm sure. Don't be ridiculous. I've never been more sure

4

of anything in my life."

Why wasn't he? Unfairly, I had forgotten the paralysis that the news had induced in me.

Tim wasn't alone. The world isn't as modern as it pretends to be. The next day I marched into the office to tell my boss the good news. He's a small, middle-aged man with gold-rimmed spectacles.

"Don't you think you might be better off having an abortion?" he asked. I was shocked by his audacity.

"You're being very headstrong. You need to build up your career first and have a life."

I couldn't believe it. I heard this from nearly everyone.

"You'll find it difficult to manage this job and a baby," he added ominously. There was a general consensus that as an unmarried mum, I would be a failure. It was deeply insulting. I argued back.

"My father was an obstetrician. His motto was: 'Everyone should go home with a prize.' I can still hear him starting the car in the middle of the night to rush to the hospital to make sure a baby was delivered safely. Babies are something to be treasured. I want my prize and I want my job. I'll prove you wrong."

My boss looked at me sadly and shuffled the papers on his desk.

There was something much nastier in the air though. There was also general agreement that if Tim and I got married the union would be a disaster as he was Jewish and I was not.

"I'm an atheist and the last thing I want to do is get married," I told my mother.

"Mixed marriages can be difficult," she replied.

"That's old fashioned rubbish. What about love and friendship? Anyway what about you? Gran wasn't too pleased after she brought you up as a Catholic and you went and married a Protestant. I'm only having a baby." It was rather as if I was having teenage tantrum but I could see my mother was genuinely worried.

"But what will the child be?" she asked me. "You need to think about these things, dear."

"Who cares?" I said.

"An awful lot of people, I'm sure," she added forebodingly.

"My baby will work it out for himself," I replied petulantly although I did glance down at my stomach and wonder what he would finally decide he was. Then I dismissed it as totally irrelevant. That was a mistake.

Let down, defiant and above all disgusted with Tim, who was still floundering about in a sea of shock and uncertainty, I packed my bag and left the unmarital home to lick my wounds and plan my next move at my sister's house in Birmingham. I was going to bring up this baby alone, whatever everyone thought. To my delight, at 3am one morning, Tim arrived and drove me back to London. He spent most of the time looking at me and smiling rather than watching the road. Six weeks of dithering had left him a new man who couldn't be bossed around - not even by me. He'd decided to ignore the ripples of disapproval in the air and take a chance. In fact, I think he quite likes doing things that other people don't. He told me that he loved me and told my sister that that meant everything would be "fine". She looked a little unsure and thought he had no idea how complicated life could be. I thought everything was very romantic. Most people thought things were off to a shaky start as we'd challenged the conventions of everyday life. I didn't think about what was going to happen next. Neither of us did. Ben seemed to have taken over, although at this stage Tim thought our lives could be in the hands of a daughter called Miriam. I wonder if she would have taken me to Sarajevo?

Once he had installed me back in our flat, Tim immediately left for Paris, where his sister lives, to hunt out stories other reporters had missed - among them one about a man from Mali (most of which is in the Sahara), who designed pullovers. Then, at the beginning of January, he discovered some more eccentric Africans across the Atlantic and bought a ticket for New York.

"Don't worry, I'll be back at the weekend," he assured me as he stuffed a change of clothes into his knapsack and rummaged in the top draw for his passport. I didn't see him until March 28th.

"Do you think he is ever coming home?" joked my mother anxiously.

He did, but he took the long way round and caught the last of the civil war in El Salvador. When he got back I was surprised that he had started putting sugar in his coffee. Three days later Ben was born.

Almost two years have passed since then and here I am standing in the Tube station getting into a muddle shovelling coins into the ticket machine. I feel slightly wobbly, as if I've got a permanent hangover. Life has been a bit blurred at the edges since Ben arrived. I've been working back-to-back shifts with Tim, as we don't have enough money for a full-time nanny. The key to having it all and managing work and life in a harmonious balance is cash. We don't have any and if we are lucky we get to spend one evening together once a week. Tim is caged in and restless. His "fine" seems some kind of distant, heavenly goal. As if that wasn't bad enough, Ben wakes up constantly at night to see which of us is at home. Last night he woke up every hour, on the hour. I've been so run down that I've even been back to the doctor who has sent me to the hospital to have tests for all kinds of terrible diseases. I have none of them. It isn't just that I'll do anything for a good night's sleep or that the money for a nanny would solve my problems. I've simply got a son called Ben and so this is my last day at work. He's won.

It's been painful and I've cried a lot as I've changed from the most ambitious person in the world into a mother who wants to bring up her baby herself. I loved the way my mother was always there for me. I'm sure I would never have wanted to be left with a nanny. Most of the nannies I've met are mind-bendingly boring. The odd thing is, yet again, my mother is horrified and thinks I'm throwing away my education. I don't care, because I am not. I am escaping a dead end. I have no intention of dumbing down. Ours will be a two-way relationship. I am going to be spending time with Ben and he will be spending time with me. It'll be the two of us against the world. Whoops! It's the three of us. I forgot Tim! As the train pulls into Lancaster Gate with a lurch, I think: "Yes, I'd love another baby." As the doors shut, I wonder what is wrong with me and so does everyone else but Tim.

By the time I wander into my office, I'm feeling far guiltier about leaving my job than I do about leaving Ben with the babysitter. That's one life. I've left that one at home and I have just walked into the other.

In this one I am supposed to revel in the long hours and the low pay. I'm an editor of the *BBC World Service* programme, *Newshour*. Everyone here thinks I'm crazy and throwing it all away for dirty nappies and mountains of ironing. All I know is that somewhere out there is real life. I want to go out and find it - with Ben. It's a world full of bright, vivid colours, deep passions and overflowing with ideas - not cluttered up with people like my colleague who commutes to Brighton, has a bottle of whisky in his briefcase and is so bleary-eyed after three days at work he can't utter a coherent sentence.

The office is a filthy, tatty, unkempt place with old wooden desks and grey telephones. I sit down gingerly. It's odd but I feel as if I no longer belong here. The programme doesn't go on air until 10pm and there isn't much going on in the world. The afternoon slips by as I alternate between worrying about what to fill the airtime with and about how Tim and I will make ends meet. I dig about in the box of tapes where we store reports that correspondents have filed but were deemed too boring to play. Maybe there's something in here that can fill five minutes? I don't care anymore. Rifling through the box, I wonder if I really will be as broke and bored stiff as my boss predicted when I handed in my resignation.

"You won't have much intellectual stimulation stuck at home," he said knowingly. "You could feel cut off from the world and short of money. My wife has found it very hard."

A vision of his wife and children in a Dickensian debtors' prison shot into my mind and I asked him rather rudely:

"Do you think your children are boring and not worth your time?"

He looked lost behind his spectacles, as if he was trying to remember what they were like. But the scariest bit of all is that he still might be right. What if I do turn into a lonely, depressed housewife? He was, after all, right about me not being able to have Ben and hold down this job but I'd rather not think about that now. So what, who cares?

This job isn't very exciting. All I do is phone up people and ask them what is going on. I don't *do* anything. There's a whole world out there but I experience things at long distance. I'm too tired to get to grips with it all but am saved from facing up to life's dilemmas by yet another phone call.

For months, while I have spent my spare time cooking up homemade baby purée and doing Fireman Sam puzzles, demonstrators in communist East Germany have been demanding the freedom to travel abroad. Last summer the Hungarians opened their border and thousands of East Germans fled to the West. I put down my coffee and pick up the receiver. It's Matt Frei, our correspondent in Berlin. He's just been at a press conference and is in a state of high excitement. The East German official fielding the questions was asked when new laws permitting freedom to travel would be introduced and he has answered that, as far as he could see, they came into force immediately. I am so dopey that I can't grasp what is going on.

"Rosie, thousands of East Berliners are storming through the crossing points in the Wall!" he shouts down the line. I wake up with a jolt.

All my life Europe has been divided in two. If you lived in the West you rarely visited the East. Those left on the other side of the Iron Curtain were prisoners. Now the walls of the gaol have suddenly collapsed. I never thought I'd see such a thing. It's as if politics has suddenly gone zero gravity for a night.

By 11pm when the programme finishes, the Iron Curtain has fallen and I have had a wonderful evening. Soviet domination of Europe is a thing of the past. How can Ben compete? Perhaps it's not such a bad job after all. I pick up my handbag and walk out of the office. No one bothers to wish me well or even say a proper "goodbye". I'm a write off. When I get home Tim and Ben are cuddled up in bed, fast asleep. There's no room for me. I feel left out and think that I've just done something rather reckless. I've become a rebel. I won't live by Thatcher's rules.

Unfortunately, communism in Europe doesn't disappear overnight. It isn't immediately clear either what difference the collapse of the Berlin Wall will actually make. The ripples of change spread slowly eastwards and just before Christmas protests against the Stalinist regime of the dictator Nicolae Ceaușescu break out in Romania. They are brutally suppressed. Hundreds of people are shot, bludgeoned and stabbed to death. The West holds it breath. The Cold War seems far from over.

Indeed, it may have just entered a new, far more dangerous stage, but my main problem is not chasing an opposition spokesman for a quote but finding a man to fix the washing machine.

While Ben and I hang around at home waiting for the engineer to come we have our first serious fight. I want to watch the tyrannical Nicolae Ceauşescu address the crowds in Bucharest but he wants to watch *Fireman Sam*. As soon as I press stop on the video he reaches over and presses the play button. Things aren't going Ceauşescu's way either and the crowd starts heckling him, just as the engineer rings the bell. Twenty minutes later and £75 poorer I make it back into the sitting room and find, to my surprise, that the news is still on and Ben is glued to the screen. A helicopter is hovering over the great big grey building from where Ceauşescu was speaking and is trying to whisk him to safety. There are running battles in the streets below. Ben turns round with an impish grin on his little, round face. We sit down together and watch quietly.

No one knows much about what's been going on in Romania. It's been a police state and a virtually closed country until today. The few journalists who've been allowed in have come back with Orwellian tales of Romanians sitting huddled in their kitchens with their coats on, warming themselves in front of the gas cooker wondering who in their family is the police informer about to have them arrested for telling an anti-government joke. As Ben starts running his fire engine up and down the coffee table in front of the TV, I tell him how the people are angry because they have nothing to eat. I wish he would say: "Wow! This is a dramatic event in post-war history," or something similarly profound but he's too busy with his toys and I don't know enough about Romania to keep his attention. I switch off the TV and we go to the park.

A few weeks later the boiler breaks down. We haven't got the money to fix it. I was the one with a full-time job. Tim is a freelance with an uncertain income that has virtually dried up. We are broke, unemployed and carried away by the romantic idea of having another baby. This is the only exciting thing going on in our lives or, maybe, there is just nothing else to do. We are stalled at a dead end and I think that I am probably to blame. It is time for some clear thinking and decisive action so Tim goes to meet the foreign editor of the *Times*. I idle away the afternoon playing toy cars and worrying what will become of us. About 5pm he comes bounding back up the stairs, his eyes shining with excitement.

"You'll never believe it! He pointed at a map of the world and said I could go to Khartoum, Santiago or Islamabad or, maybe, then he paused for a minute and said 'Do you fancy Bucharest?' It was just like a scene out of *Scoop*! I couldn't believe it. I almost fell off my chair!"

Here is my husband standing in front of me reeling off a list of exotic places. South America sounds fun but I already know where we are going. The bloody revolution in Romania is a massive story. The whole of Britain turned on their TV sets after Christmas dinner to watch the pictures of Ceauşescu's summary execution. Thousands of Romanians have been left dead or injured. One foreign journalist has lost his life. Tim is as good as packed already, although I still have my hand on the front door to let him in.

He has dark brown hair and a handsome face that reminds me of the Mediterranean. He believes that you can go anywhere and do anything. He is convinced that anything is possible and, thanks to Ben, I am to be a stay-at-home mum in a communist tower block in post-revolutionary Romania. I can't believe my luck!

Tim is gone within the week. On the way to the airport I tell him he had better make a go of this because I'm pregnant. He grins and, fired up, disappears into the terminal. A few weeks later he finds a flat and tells me to book a flight as soon as I can. The odd thing is that every time I try to call him to tell him when we are arriving, an elderly lady answers the phone. She doesn't speak a word of English. I can't imagine Tim has moved in with a Romanian granny, so I assume I must keep getting the wrong number as she's always there, even late at night.

Since Christmas the revolution has turned sour and it appears that it wasn't really a revolution after all but a *coup d'etat* in which Ceauşescu's cronies toppled him and took control. It's not at all clear that communism is dead and buried. It might be about to seek its revenge. Romania is the new frontline in the battle against the "Evil Empire". When I tell my oldest friend we are off, she takes a deep breath and looks horrified.

"I hope you know what you are doing, Rosie? You can't take Ben there, can you?"

"Don't worry. I'm pregnant," I add sounding slightly manic.

"Oh my God! You're crazy," she says as she puts down her coffee cup with a sharp clatter.

Maybe I am a bit, but I am not going to pack Ben in cotton wool and hide him at home in case seeing something out of the ordinary traumatises him. Who cares if there's nothing to eat? All I want is for the three of us to spend time together and Bucharest sounds fine to me. There are more toys than anything else in my suitcase. In fact I haven't been too sure what to pack. What is the weather like in Romania?

2 - Welcome to Romania

The aircraft is almost empty, dilapidated and shabby. The vacant seats flap back and forth as we take off and there's a horrible shudder from the undercarriage. I hate flying. I just want to get to Romania, but what I haven't realised yet is that I'm already there. This is *Tarom*, Romania's national airline.

"I wanna drink nowwh!"

Ben's whinges echo in the dreary void. A man in his early forties looks round with a surprised expression on his face as I force Ben back into his seat and strap him in.

"Sssh! Let's read this book, again. The one Granny Marion gave you."

I pick *Going on a Jumbo Jet* up off the floor.

"No! Drink nowwh!"

I look around wildly, in the hope of spotting a glass of water floating past. No such luck. No one has bothered to switch on the lights in the cabin, which couldn't look less like the brightly coloured jet in Ben's book. He pokes the front cover and looks aggrieved. I don't blame him. We've read *Going on a Jumbo Jet* five times since take off and he's right. On page six, there's a picture of a pretty stewardess handing out a can of Coke. We've been in the air almost two hours and our stewardesses have spent the entire journey gossiping in the galley at the back. Ben shouts over the back of the seat towards the crew, waving his fist. As I pull him back down one of the stewardesses tugs the dividing curtain closed with a sharp yank.

I studied Soviet politics at university and often travelled to the claustrophobic and controlled Eastern Bloc but now I'm heading to a new, wild, dangerous world where anarchy rules. It's erupted out to take the place of the crumbling Soviet Empire. I wish I had done some more forward planning. I wonder what I will do if there's no milk. Ben drinks gallons of the stuff.

"I want Daddy nowwh!" he shouts. "Daddy!"

So do I. I think he expects Tim to fly past the window with a Coke, like Superman. I gaze out hopefully as I stroke his sandy hair and he flops on my shoulder. He's like a wind up doll. He suddenly collapses in a crumpled heap when his batteries run out. We're flying into the unknown. A delicious tingle of apprehension shimmers on the surface of my skin. I've gambled everything on Tim and a new life in a place I know nothing about. I start digging around in my bag, hoping there is a leftover Smartie somewhere at the bottom. It might help calm our nerves. I'm in luck. I find two, and even if they are a bit chipped at the edge, they'll do. Ben dribbles chocolate down the front of his t-shirt, and as the plane lands, he falls asleep.

Tim meets us at the airport. There are birds flying in and out of the broken glass in the roof of the terminal. He's with Mihai, his translator, Mihai's brother and their father, who have all come in his tiny, blueywhite Trabant to collect us. This car is one of the things that set East and West apart. No one in the West would drive one but Mihai's father is very proud of his. It was made in East Germany but I couldn't care less. I'm furious. I was fancying a romantic reunion, not a reception committee.

"Why do we need so many people to pick us up?"

Tim looks at me and laughs. How dare he laugh at me? I have just come all this way to be with him. His expression reminds me of Ben who is gazing down at me from his father's arms with a slightly superior air. I feel irritated. He's still laughing as he says:

"Foreigners don't just fly in everyday, Rosie. Most people here haven't met someone from abroad in decades. They want to meet you."

That makes me feel like a curio to be gawped at and I can't see what's

14

so funny.

The suitcase is too big for the boot, so it has to go on Mihai's brother's lap, in the front. The rest of us squeeze into the cramped backseat with the remainder of the luggage. It feels surprisingly warm and cosy. The car bounces down potholed roads, and past endless, tatty apartment buildings. The flat Tim's found is not far from where Mihai's family live, in a suburb called Balta Alba, on the very edge of town.

"How far out is it?" I whisper.

"It's about a twenty minute drive."

I make a face. Tim puts his arm around me. I feel a bit suspicious. One look at these tower blocks and I am sure the apartment will be terrible. I was fancying something central. I have a sneaking suspicion that he hasn't looked at any others.

"Look Rosie. It's difficult to find places that haven't got some connection with the secret police, the *Securitate*. This is the best I could do."

He gives me a hug and adds with a wicked grin:

"The *Securitate* are still in business and now they are moving into real estate."

"What's so funny about that?"

He has a rather black sense of humour.

"They're keeping an eye on the small number of foreign aid workers and journalists, who've arrived in Bucharest, by renting them flats." Then he adds smiling: "That's us."

All of a sudden the city feels incredibly spooky. The Romanian secret police killed hundreds of people during the revolution. I move closer to Tim, although in the back seat of the Trabant that's a shift of about two millimetres.

"This place Mihai has rented for us is safe," he says, giving me another hug. I wonder how everyone knows that and how he knows that the *Securitate* hasn't just stitched us up. I've only been in the country forty-five minutes and everyone looks so friendly that I wonder how am I supposed to know who works for the secret police and who doesn't. Maybe no one does or maybe they all do. I decide it's better not to think about it for too long.

The Trabant putters up in front of a crumbling tower block. We climb out of the car. Ben is jumping up and down with glee. Tim looks at me:

"Do you like it?"

He has his arm around my shoulders. He seems to have grown six inches since I last saw him and is more vibrant than before.

"Yay!" shouts Ben.

All five of them turn to face me. I feel like saying:

"What! Is that it? It's terrible. I don't want to live here!" But Tim looks so pleased with himself that I mumble, "great!" and try to sound as convincing as possible.

The apartments are in a small, unpaved side street, in a sea of other soulless, tumble down blocks. Many years ago someone started to plaster the building but gave up half way through the job.

"Good," says Tim picking up the suitcase. "As I said, it's the best apartment we could find. I'm sure you'll like it."

I tap his shoulder.

"Hey, what were the other places like?"

He doesn't answer. He's clearly decided that we are living here. I've never seen him so decisive.

Our flat is on the tenth floor. It's decorated in different shades of beige and brown. It's a colour scheme that is set off by strips of worn out green carpet. It's cluttered with other people's knick-knacks and photos of relatives and friends of all ages. Most of these people, I learn later, are dead. Many of them were carried away prematurely either by terrible diseases or the secret police.

As soon as I step in the front door, a small, elderly lady pops out of the kitchen. She embraces Ben excitedly. He beams as if he knows her. Mihai kisses her hand with a flourish and bows. He's excessively formal and old fashioned but there is nothing cold or reserved in his politeness. He's effervescent, relaxed and friendly. This doesn't seem to fit with the Stalinist tower blocks and informers. Mihai behaves as if he's Prince Charming arriving at Versailles. I follow his example and forget about the filthy, shabby stairwell.

"This is *Doamna* Elena, Rosie."

Doamna is the equivalent of "Mrs", although it loses something in translation. *Doamna* Elena has a pot of stew cooking on the stove. It smells unappetising and I can see out of the corner of my eye that it's a nasty, dark brown colour. She clucks around while we unpack. Elena is about sixty-five. She has thinning, orangey, dyed hair and wears two woolly bobble hats indoors.

"Who is this woman, Tim?" I whisper.

She is hanging up his shirts in the wardrobe.

"Oh, didn't I tell you? The flat comes with housekeeper cum resident mother-in-law."

"What! Have you gone mad? I've already got one mother-in-law in London."

He has indeed moved in with a Romanian granny.

"Don't look so worried. She has her own place, with her husband Mitica. Her daughter used to live here."

At least, that's something.

"*Doamna* Elena will care for children, cook, shop, clean, wash. Everything!" adds Mihai.

He is tall and thin with lanky brown hair that could do with a trim and looks slightly greasy. This sounds like a terrible idea. This is what I want to do but I can see that he thinks that this is the height of luxury. It's all stitched up. He and Tim are delighted with the deal. Tim adds that Elena's food is quite good. What? He doesn't like stew. I've only just arrived and I am beginning to realise that I know nothing at all about Romania and perhaps not as much about Tim as I thought I did. He, as ever, exudes self-confidence. He is the most optimistic person I have ever met. He says things are "fine", so I believe him. What else can I do?

"Mummy! Where you are?"

Ben's voice breaks through the two men's self-satisfied round of handshakes and back patting. Ben always gets the grammar of this question, which is really a command, mixed up. I rush into the living room obediently. He's already unpacked his toys and settled in, as if he has lived here all his life. The apartment couldn't look less like our modern Habitat furnished flat in London. Tim lived there when we met and furnished it himself but, oddly, he seems far more at home here.

Elena arrives at breakfast time and after an hour of her incessant conversation my head is spinning. She doesn't seem to care that I don't understand a word of what she is saying. She used to be a peasant farmer and raised chickens until they built a tower block on her land. She clucks around me. I have to get out. Everyday about midday Ben and I go downtown. Elena finds my fascination with the city centre quite baffling and radiates disapproval. When we go out, she is usually waving her hands muttering, "*Centru, centru*" and "*De ce centru Doamna?*" which I realise means roughly: "Why are you going to the town centre?" It's clear that she thinks that we should be happy to spend our days pottering in the local park. I don't believe it! Now I am being harangued because I am not stay-at-home enough - but I don't care what she thinks. Ben and I are off to explore the world.

When we walk out of the block's main door, a boy leaps out of the spindly bushes. He's waving a stick and going "rattatatat" at his friend, who is lurking behind the lamppost. It's an ambush.

"Get him! He's in the *Securitate*," he shouts, as I strap Ben into his red pushchair with white polka dots on.

"Wow! They are playing revolution! Isn't that funny?" I say to Ben as I struggle with the straps. "I've never seen anyone do that before."

He puts his hand up and firmly pushes my head out of the way so he can see better. It's a mad violent world.

All the boys have knitted, woolly hats. It isn't just Elena. Romanians are obsessed with headgear. When she goes out Elena puts a third hat on top of the two she already wears inside. The kid, who's just leapt out of the bush in front of me brandishing a long twig, has a grubby off white hat with blue stripes on and a matching sweater. They are made out of such thin, cheap wool that the cold wind must go right through them. The kids look washed out and pale, especially next to our red pushchair. It's like a beacon of glowing capitalism in a sea of Stalinism. Ben puts two fingers together and shoots back at the boy crouching in the bush. I stride off determinedly to the taxi rank.

The taxi drives past an endless stream of apartment blocks and bumps along the half built street that was to have been Ceaușescu's triumphal way. The whole place is covered in a thick film of builder's dust and debris. Then the taxi turns at his enormous palace to drive up the main boulevard that runs through the centre. It's really no accident that Romania was Europe's North Korea. Ceaușescu made a visit to its capital Pyongyang and was so impressed by the way that Kim Il Sung, the North Korean leader had managed to design the city to glorify his rule, that he came home and simply razed the heart of Bucharest's old town. He was, I tell Ben, going to build his way into the history books. He was a monumental megalomaniac, in the true sense of the word. Ben is impressed and I resolve to take him to Pyongyang one day and see if it looks anything like Bucharest. I pay the driver the equivalent of a dollar for the twenty-minute ride. The truth is that I can only afford to spend all my time with Ben at the moment because the currency, the *leu*, is basically worthless and a small amount of hard currency goes a long way here since there is absolutely nothing to buy. Ben has a stay-at-home mum thanks to the exchange rate. I am sure we would have been bankrupt by now had we stayed in London.

The taxi drops us in the main square. The buildings are riddled with bullet holes, as there was fierce fighting here only a few months ago. Ceaușescu made his last speech from the headquarters of the Central Committee of the Communist Party on the far side, while we watched him on TV in London in another life. Next to it is the shell of what was once the elegant neo-classical university library. It was gutted by fire during the fighting. The revolution in Romania has been quite unlike the unfolding collapse of communism elsewhere. In Prague people thronged into the main square to party but in Bucharest there were running street battles. Across the road is the old royal palace. It's closed and what's left of its collection of treasures that survived the street battles intact are hidden behind locked doors. My western guidebook, which was written long before the revolution, describes the place as packed with patrols of *Securitate* agents whispering into their radios and prophetically announces that; "this large square seems to be waiting for a coup". Today it feels dead and lifeless. Events have moved on and left it behind. It used to be called Piața Gheorghe Gheorghiu-Dej after the first communist leader of Romania but I expect it is about to get a new name. It's in a sort of no man's land.

We walk across to the Athénée Palace Hotel. I'm not in a hurry so we dawdle along in the hot sun looking at the bullet holes. Ben shoves his fingers in the crevices. I can see that he is fascinated. So am I. We are at one with each other. This is the real life I was looking for. The whole façade is riddled with bullet holes. It's wonderful if slightly scary. We're touching history. Ben moves on from one to another inspecting them carefully. The hotel is dilapidated and run down although, in the 1930s, it was the place to be seen and a hotbed of political plotting and intrigue. Today it looks dirty and uninviting. It never enters my head to go in.

For me the market in Piaţa Amzei is the focal point of life in the city centre. When we first arrived, there were only a couple of bunches of spring onions and a few bitter tasting white carrots on sale. Luckily, today the sun is shining. It's late April and the metal stalls are starting to fill up. It is beginning to look like a proper market at last - pungent, alluring, rich and full of promise. What food there is seems full of life.

"Let's see the old ladies with the cheese. Come on!" shouts Ben as he darts out of the pushchair and into a smelly covered hall, where they sell heaps of yellowy looking curds, which are akin to feta. They are covered in flies.

The old women with their long black skirts and headscarves beckon him over and offer him little crumbs. He watches their lips and toothy grins with fascination. They look unnerving, like witches with scrunched up dirty teeth, but he doesn't run away. He has come deliberately to stare at them. He studies an old lady's face carefully as she says something he can't possibly understand. He is like his father, never frightened of anything and intrigued by the smallest thing. He loves the bizarre and the quirky.

We stroll over to the Intercontinental Hotel. It's a large, characterless tower block that is the hub of political activity at the moment. It stands on the main crossroads in the city, Piaţa Universitaţii, where there's a permanent demonstration against the new government and Ion Iliescu, the president, who was one of Ceauşescu's henchmen. The university is just over the road and the students are angry and frustrated that the revolution has changed so little and they expect the forthcoming elections will be rigged. This is usually where I'll find Tim, talking to the protestors. If things turn nasty he's told me this could become the next Tiananmen Square. People here are frightened that the communists could still fight back, and that's not just here but right across Eastern Europe. It is still unsure what the Soviets will do. Will they send in the tanks? This revolution isn't over yet. It's very confusing trying to work out exactly what is going on. Romania will be the test case for democracy, Russia and for us.

On the edge of the hotel car park, is a heap of builder's sand, where Ben likes to play with his toy cars while Tim and I catch a few moments together. In the hot spring sunshine it all seems magical, rather like we're on the honeymoon that we could never afford to take. The whole of Bucharest is crumbling and in need of repair or has been knocked down by Ceaușescu and is now only half rebuilt. It's like living in an enormous building site. It's bursting with chaotic energy. It's a new beginning. It's like a cold shower on a hot day. Everything seems possible. Ben loves it. The demonstrators are chanting in the background. He pulls at my skirt.

"What they shouting, Mummy?"

"*'Jos Iliescu!*' It means: 'Down with Iliescu!' They think he's a bad man. He was a friend of Ceaușescu but now he's president. He tells everyone what to do. Things won't get better until he is gone."

I kiss Tim goodbye:

"Ben's tired. It's time to get home."

Just as we are leaving, a colleague of Tim's walks over. He's called Chris Stephen and he writes for the *Guardian*. I've met him once before. He has brown hair and an elfish expression. The small group of journalists who are based here are all single. Tim has told me how shocked they were when he told them that he had a two-year old son and another baby on the way. Although a reluctant recruit to fatherhood Tim is delighted by the cachet it has brought him. He likes being different. Chris eyes my stomach suspiciously as he congratulates me on the good news. He has strings of girlfriends and doesn't seem the type to settle down. He and Tim will stay here until late in the evening just in case something nasty happens. I would like it if Tim came home now but I have no desire to hang around here all evening either. I have discovered that I can learn just as much about Romania (if not more), at home with Ben. Maybe Elena was right all along.

Back in Balta Alba, evenings work to a strict timetable.

"Hurry Ben! Get undressed or we'll miss the water," I call from the bathroom.

I've worked out that there are about ten minutes, not long after six, when you can get some hot water. If you miss this, the tap runs dry and then later, there'll only be cold water. As a consequence, the radiators never heat up and, at best, they are lukewarm. The crazy thing is that, while in winter there's no hot water, in summer there's no cold. You have to let it cool, so you can wash a lettuce.

Elena dons her extra hat and heads off home with the washing. There's no washing machine and hardly any washing powder so she boils the clothes, then scrubs them on a washing board. I feel rather embarrassed about this even though I pay her. She is the same age as my mother but, if I try to hide the clothes so I can wash them, she gets offended and chides me in a singsong voice.

"Right, out of the bath!" I shout. "Quick, or, we'll miss the cartoon."

Ben leaps out and dashes into the sitting room stark naked. I run behind with his pyjamas. He's already in the big brown chair, by the huge TV with wood veneer surrounds. I wonder why they have such a big model? Under Ceauşescu there was nothing to watch but him. The set reminds me of one we had when I was a child. It's a bit like it's been waiting all these years to show something worth watching. I feel guilty about the hours I've wiled away in front of *EastEnders*. Elena is very proud of her television and dusts it every day, while she is glued to one of the endless programmes of Romanian peasants singing.

"Hurry Mummy!"

Ben is struggling into his trousers as fast as he can. Our viewing highlight of the day, like the water, only lasts ten minutes. It takes time for the set to warm up. It's almost ten to eight when we get a picture. I switch over quickly to Bulgarian TV. Bucharest is only an hour's drive to the border. The reception is good in our area although the picture is still fuzzy. The Bulgarian station is marginally better than the Romanian one, but it isn't any use, as the programmes are incomprehensible, since I can't speak a word of Bulgarian. Ben doesn't care. His favourite show is *Leka Nosch*, which is Bulgarian for "goodnight". It's a short cartoon before the news.

"Sit!" he barks at me.

He's getting good at issuing orders. I sit down. At the moment, they are showing a Russian cartoon about a war in space. The rockets with little hammers and sickles on the side are winning.

"Will there be a war in space, Mummy?"

He is wriggling about on my lap. I'd like to say "no" definitely but that would be a lie. I don't want to lie to him.

"Maybe."

"Why do you always say 'maybe?'" he asks.

"There are some things I'm not sure about," I answer. He is certain about everything.

It isn't just the picture that's blurred. As I guide Ben to bed, he puts his hands together, as if he is trying to cut through the yellow haze. At night the air is thick and heavy.

"Why is it foggy?"

"Low voltage, I expect. Electricity must be like water just trickling into the house."

He's not interested in the answer. Obviously he isn't a budding scientist.

Outside Ben's window, there's a rumble of trams and packs of wild dogs barking. It feels so good to be somewhere so different from London. I feel like a new woman.

"I'm not gonna sleep," Ben announces.

"Oh yes you are boy!"

I turn off the light defiantly, while he is still jumping up and down on the bed.

"*Jos* Mummy! *Jos* Mummy! *Jos* Mummy!"

He's chanting at the top of his voice. He's catching on fast. I was right to take the time to explain what was happening at the demonstration. But get rid of me and things will be better! How ungrateful can you get?

I fall into bed and read descriptions of Bucharest on the eve of the Second World War in Olivia Manning's *Balkan Trilogy*. There is page upon page about mountains of fruit heaped on carts and endless streams of teashops and pastries. I skip the story and re-read these passages again and again in disbelief. When Tim comes home I am half asleep, dreaming about cakes. It must be the new baby. The odd thing is that Ben rarely wakes up more than once at night these days.

3 - A Communist Education

On either side of the small stretch of motorway that runs north-west from the Romanian capital, flat uninspiring countryside slips away into to the hazy horizon. It's 8pm on a warm evening in early May. We are heading north to tour the country on the eve on the first elections since the revolution. In fact Tim is touring the country. Ben and I are here for the ride. Tim is sitting in the back seat. His hair is sticking up in tufts that constantly rebel against the order imposed by his comb and his pink shirt is crumpled. It's the end of a long day. Ben is sitting on his lap as there are no seatbelts in the rear. I'm happily driving along at sixty miles an hour when all of a sudden, in front of me, there is a wall across the two lanes on my side of the road.

I slam on the breaks and swerve onto the half-built hard shoulder. There is nothing to warn drivers that it's there and it seems to have no function whatsoever. My hands are shaking and I don't feel capable of driving any more. Tim can't understand what is the matter with me. I think I'm living in a madhouse but he's totally unflustered. Don't get me wrong. This madhouse is the most riveting place I've ever been. It's just I can't believe he can stay *so* calm. Ben asks cheerily:

"Are we there yet?"

Then Tim gets in the driving seat and drives calmly round to the other side the wall and puts his foot down.

After the motorway stops, the road winds on through the mountains. The journey drags on for hours. I lie down with Ben and try to sleep on the back seat. I'm beginning to feel like the Virgin Mary en route to Bethlehem. I can feel the baby kicking. It feels incensed. At 2.30am, I'm jolted awake when it's Tim's turn to slam on the brakes. There's a large flock of sheep asleep on the road and they won't budge.

"Rosie, Wake up! You have to do something to get them to move while I drive behind you."

What, I wonder? I stand in the pitch black waving my hands and shouting "yah!" at a bunch of totally disinterested sheep who stare back blankly. In Romania shepherds still wear coats made out of sheepskin and carry large menacing crooks. They look like the grim reaper. The sheep don't think much of me and eventually I have to literally push them out of the way. I'm not sure pregnant women should be doing this kind of thing but we can't wait as Tim has a deadline to meet. He's calling the shots now. I feel that I've been reduced to some sort of press groupie.

"If you weren't up to it you should have stayed at home," he snaps.

I've hardly seen him since we moved to Bucharest. Our Balkan honeymoon is over. Or rather my Balkan honeymoon is over. I was the only person on it, happily wandering the streets of Bucharest as if I was on holiday. Tim has been working all hours and looks exhausted.

It's mid-afternoon when we finally arrive in Cluj and check into the hotel. Tim leaves immediately to start doing interviews. I'm left to unpack and deal with Ben who moans like a buzzing bee.

"Mummeee! I hungreee! Mummee! Listen Mummeee!"

It's depressing. I'm tired and he is trying my patience.

"You have to wait. The restaurant is shut."

I try to reason with him but it's no good. On the way here, he threw up his breakfast all over my new, flowery, summer dress. It's now covered in congealed sick in the sink. I can't stand the nagging any longer, so I take his hand and decide to go and show him that the restaurant is actually closed. I lock the bedroom door and check it carefully as I don't want anyone to get in.

"You know Ben, that if the restaurant is shut, there's nowhere else in town where you can get something to eat, so you'll have to wait."

I can tell he's not listening. He is more interested in pressing the button for the ground floor:

"Where's 'puh'?"

I point to "puh" for *parter*, ground floor in Romanian.

"Wow! I can reach 'puh'!"

He's delighted. So am I. When we arrive at "puh", we are feeling upbeat and optimistic. Once you can reach "puh" anything's possible - but as soon as the lift doors open I can see the restaurant. Its huge, brown, wood panel doors are firmly closed.

"Mummeeee! Open it nowww!"

I realise that I am supposed to achieve the unachievable. In desperation, I give the kitsch glass door handles a shake and to my amazement a grumpy waitress sticks her head out and asks me what I want.

Ben, immediately, puts on a plaintive look and starts moving from one foot to another and looks needy, as he puts his head on one side. It's a trick he's learned from Mihai who uses it to cadge a beer off me. The waitress's hair is dyed a reddy, copper colour and her face is white and angular. She wrinkles her lips tight, as I gesture at Ben, and tell her he's hungry. She breaks into a smile and opens the door. As we walk in, a chef in a dirty, white coat pops his head out of the kitchen door and waves cheerfully as she ushers us to a table by the window. The white tablecloth has some dirty splodges on it and the odd hole. Her high heels clatter on the brown parquet, as she runs to the kitchen to get something for Ben to eat. He's wriggling around on the cheap, plastic imitation leather seat and swinging his legs, humming. I can see he's going to grow up to think most things are possible if you just ask.

Within minutes the waitress reappears with an off-white plate on which sits a lump of grey mashed potato and a charred, dry piece of meat. Ben grabs the first chunk I can cut. It's so tough he can hardly chew it, but he reaches out to shovel in the next one all the same. I warn him to slow down, but he's not listening. Those hidden flaps in his ears that automatically come down when I'm telling him something he doesn't want to hear have been activated and, within minutes, the meat has disappeared. Now, I'm trying to spoon up some mashed potato, when he leans over the plate and vomits the whole thing up over my hand. I am furious and before I can stop myself, I say:

"Oh my God! Ben! What will the waitress say? Can't you just try to eat it again? You can't waste food here."

Ben looks at me out of the corner of his eye, uncertainly. I can see that he's sure that I've finally flipped. I grab the napkin and frantically I start spooning the regurgitated food into it. With a bit of luck, I can hide it in my handbag before the waitress comes back to the table and she won't realise what has happened. I can dispose of it in our room later.

At this moment, a man appears at the table asking if he can help. I look around wondering how he got in as the waitress locked the door behind us. I can see a cup of coffee, at what must be his table behind us. He wasn't there when we arrived. He is tall, well-dressed in a beige suit and sports a bushy moustache. He's well-fed and has a rather sinister air that's confirmed when, he says, he knows my name and that my husband works for *The Economist*. Tim is also the magazine's Romania correspondent but I'm surprised that he knows this, as the publication has no bylines and the writers are always anonymous. I assume he must be some sort of secret policeman or government official. I can't think of anything to say as I hold the last spoonful of vomit hovering over the napkin. He's very charming. I'm not sure if he is trying to intimidate me, or simply being a gentleman. I decide that I'd rather not think about it. He fetches Ben a glass of water.

"I'm sure I could get him something else to eat," he says with a dismissive wave at the plate. I have a feeling that he could do just that, but I certainly don't want to be indebted to him, so I lie and tell him Ben is ill. He adds:

"If you need anything just ask."

He goes back to the table behind me and starts reading the paper. I can't believe he is holding it up to partially cover his face. I feel like we are in a movie but the scene is robbed of its sinister, dramatic edge by the napkin full of congealed vomit I am still holding in my left hand. This kind of thing only works if the secret police make you feel frightened. I don't, but then I could just get in my car and drive over the border and never come back if I felt like it. I feel foolish and incredibly lucky. I think he has a bum assignment. I feel sorry for him. He pops up everywhere over the next few days.

The waitress comes over, as soon as he has left the table, and I get my purse out ready to pay her.

"No! No! No, charge, not for him."

She smiles at Ben, and ruffles his hair. I realize that she has probably fed him her lunch and I'm carrying it out, freshly vomited, in my handbag.

"Why didn't you get more food?" demands Ben, outraged that we are leaving the restaurant.

"I didn't like that man," I whisper.

I can see him picking up his paper and paying for his coffee.

"Why?" he asks, mystified as I hustle him out of the door.

I think he deserves some sort of explanation. I hated it as a child when I was fobbed off, so I say honestly that I think he might be a spy.

"What's a spy?"

"A person who watches you to find out what you are doing."

"Why?"

"Why, indeed?" is all I can say to that, but then I have to admit it's quite nice that someone thinks we are worth following.

Back in Bucharest however, something truly sinister happens. One day I answer the phone. It's a secretary from the foreign ministry. She wants to talk to Tim about a press conference.

"Ah! Mrs Judah," she says slowly. "Ah! Your name, Judas you know what it means? You know Judas?"

I am horrified.

"Yes, thank you. I'm not Jewish. Goodbye!" I say quickly in a clipped voice and hang up.

Nothing like this has ever happened to me before. It feels like a horrible echo from the distant past. Maybe this was what worried my mother. There's a dark side to Romania that I don't like at all, although it doesn't make we want to run away - quite the opposite. I do feel guilty however about saying that I'm not Jewish and hanging up. We've decided to bring Ben up as Jewish. I agreed to do this to please Tim.

At the time I wasn't sure that this was a good idea. My mother despises religion. Suddenly it all seems very significant and I've reacted to this anti-Semitic insinuation not by defending my son and husband but by separating myself from them. I won't do that again. I'm not going to let other people's hatred drive us apart. On this one I will stand by Tim even if I feel like I have just been transported back in time to the 1930s. The knots that bind us together tighten and I have an overwhelming desire to put my arms around him. This would probably never have happened if we had stayed in London where you don't get these types of phone calls. Perhaps I should call her back and say "thank you." I do feel resentful though about something completely different. I don't think of myself as Mrs Judah at all but there's no one in the entire country that knows I'm called Rosie Whitehouse. What happened to her?

On a more mundane level, getting something to eat is becoming an obsession. It must be pregnancy. Unfortunately for me there have been food shortages all over Eastern Europe and the Soviet Union but in Romania the problem has reached crisis point. Ceauşescu, who was a maverick in the Soviet camp, did what he pleased. He ruled his country as if it was his own fiefdom and had a whim that he wanted to pay off the national debt. As a result everything that was produced was exported. It didn't matter if the population went cold and hungry. Even though there's been a revolution, just how much is still being sent abroad is a mystery. Conspiracy theories abound as Romanians have a tendency to exaggerate, dramatise and ignore the fact that the whole economy is collapsing and less and less is actually being manufactured. The shelves of the supermarket next to our flat are completely empty. I have a Romanian friend, Oana, who is also pregnant and is constantly picking off the paint on the wall and eating it. She fascinates Ben and I try to explain to him that I think she has a vitamin deficiency. He stares at the wall. It doesn't look very appetising. It's a dirty, light beige and increasingly chipped at the edges as Oana has been to visit quite a lot recently. Luckily for the two of us an election is imminent and to sweeten up the voters, some luxuries, which I used to consider boring basics, have been imported.

One day Ben and I come back from a trip downtown with a box of oranges. I'm addicted to ferreting around the city centre and for a western shopaholic, living in an ex-communist dump this is the equivalent of winning the pools. We burst through the front door.

"Elena!" shouts Ben charging down the corridor to get her.

She lets out an excited gasp as I wave the box triumphantly under her nose.

"*Vi! Doamna!*"

Vi! is her favourite expletive. I'm not sure what it means but it's some terrible, dire warning and it's always followed by a wild waving of hands. Sometimes, she crosses herself, mid-sentence. Today it sets her off on her favourite topic: "*Cînd Ceauşescu...*" or "When Ceauşescu was around". She has a rather ambivalent attitude towards the former dictator. A lot of Romanians still admire his nationalist politics and the way he stood up to the Soviet Union, by refusing to join in with the crushing of the Prague Spring in 1968 and by flirting with China. Ceauşescu also nurtured the most phenomenal cult of personality. I watch her. It's difficult to shake off years of indoctrination. Ben is obsessed with Ceauşescu too, even though he missed the propaganda. Now, although the man is dead, people never stop talking about him. He still dominates politics here, just as his palace dominates the skyline. When we visit his grave in a Bucharest cemetery it takes ages to find since it's just like all the others. It's a mound of earth marked by a simple wooden cross. I take a picture of Ben beside it. When the photograph is developed, I notice he looks crestfallen as if big men from history, even tyrants, shouldn't end up in an ordinary hole in the ground.

To be honest most children in England Ben's age wouldn't give any of this a second thought but politics matters more here. It's that real world I was looking for where ideas matter. It's fascinating and I have no one else but Ben to talk to about it. Tim was so busy he forgot my birthday. Anyway I'm going to show him the world - the good and the bad. I'm not going to talk down to him but nor will he have to talk up to me. We'll find our own level, although my mother thinks I'm taking it all too far. She's even accused me of hot-housing Ben and making him precocious. It's true, he speaks in a way other children don't but I like to think it's proof that you don't know what children are capable of talking about until you give it a go. Anyway there isn't much else but politics to talk about. The shops are empty, there's nothing on TV and there are no comics and hardly any books. Shortages of everything from milk to hot water dominate our lives and lead to riotous excitement over a simple orange. There are no fictional goodies and baddies at hand to distract us so we talk about Ceaușescu and the *Securitate* in the way my nephews in Britain discuss the Ninja Turtles or Action Man. In Ben's head Ceaușescu must be Action Man's arch enemy, Dr X.

Ben pushes past me to get into the kitchen. He's desperate to eat an orange. He hasn't seen one for months. Elena hasn't seen one for years. Just imagine someone gave you a kilo of the best caviar for free – that'll give you just a hint of how we feel today. Elena cuts the fruit in quarters and ceremoniously puts it on the table. Only children and pregnant women get to eat anything as nourishing as this. Elena refuses a slice. When Ben has finished, she wraps the peel carefully in a piece of paper and puts it in her string bag that she always carries, just in case something materialises. She says she is going to boil the rind up to make a tasty cup of tea for her husband. She'll serve it up after supper as a surprise. Ben's rubbish will be an evening treat for Mitica. When I tell Ben what she has done, he rifles through her bag to check that it's true. At which point Elena gets confused and thinks we want the peelings back. It takes ten minutes to convince her that I don't. Later we sneak a few oranges into her bag.

"I'm Santa," says Ben.

While she is tenderly arranging the fruit in a bowl, she proudly tells Ben how the shops were full of oranges and pineapples back in the 1970s. In those days, Romania was the most liberal country in the Soviet bloc. I translate. Thanks to Elena's endless chatter I've begun to pick up the language. I explain what she is talking about. Ben looks perplexed. It's surely no coincidence that I have developed a craving for pineapple juice. I tell Elena and that only starts her off again. We hear all about the pineapples for a second time. Just the thought of them makes her laugh. Ben watches her carefully. By now he is looking seriously confused.

"But wasn't Ceauşescu bad?" Ben says quietly.

He fixes his gaze on me as if the answer lies in my face. I sit down next to him.

"Well that's right but, at one time, things were better here than in other communist countries."

Elena hears the word "communism".

"Ah…" she lets out a strangulated sound. "Communism! It's terrible!"

It doesn't quite square with the rosy picture that we have just been painted. She gestures with her finger at her throat, as if she is about to slit it. She adds viciously:

"That's what communists do to you."

She shudders. Then she puts two fingers to her forehead.

"Bang! That's what he got. He deserved it."

Ben watches her antics with a bemused grin then turns to me and asks:

"What's communism?"

I have a three-year old who wants to know what communism is. I'm delighted. I'm more than delighted – I'm ecstatic. This is even better than the box of oranges! I knew he had it in him. I knew he would catch on if I just kept talking to him. Maybe I am rather like Elena. I launch enthusiastically into a fairytale version of the Communist Manifesto although Ben probably thinks communism is some terrible affliction that only someone like Action Man can save us all from. I spin a tale of oppressed workers in factories and toiling peasants. My story stops in 1917. I don't get any further because Elena interrupts. She's back in "*Cînd Ceauşescu*" mode. Before the revolution we are told, the Great Man organised for the rubbish to be collected and dealt with the rats.

She lurches back across the kitchen and schizophrenically changes track again, as she gestures at the gas cooker. She shows me how her husband drilled holes in the pipes on the top of the stove, so that before the revolution, when the gas was turned on, it would actually heat something. The pressure was so low, the flame hardly burned otherwise. At least that's one thing that's better now. The gas leaps up when it's lit, as if it wants to singe your eyebrows. Elena is delighted and keeps the rings burning all day to heat the kitchen. I think we might all blow up. This place is fascinating. Even making a cup of tea is a challenge. Ben and I are having the time of our lives but that's because we have the luxury of being outsiders. I'm revelling in someone else's misery. Ben opens the oven door and gawps at the holes in the gas pipe at the back. I love him. When Tim gets home he suggests they read Beatrix Potter together.

When we follow Tim on assignment to Bulgaria, Ben gets even more confused. Things are better in the capital Sofia than back in Bucharest, even though they are themselves still in the grips of an anti-communist revolution, but since they have ten minutes of cartoons a day that does not surprise Ben. Nothing, however, has prepared him for the cake display in the exclusive Sheraton Hotel. He stands transfixed, in front of a chocolate gateau and a selection of pastries that only foreigners and the elite can afford to buy, but at least this is one step in the right direction. He strokes the glass cake cabinet and wets his trousers in excitement.

Then we go to Greece, to do some shopping, and he discovers a land full of crisps and ice creams that everyone can afford. He stands in a packed supermarket, lost and bewildered.

"Why are there lollies here?"

His nose is peeping over the edge of the freezer. He's staring at the brightly coloured packets and I can see he has forgotten what life is like in London. He looks so worried that I can't just dismiss his question so I attempt a storybook version of Stalinism. Words like "capitalism" and "markets" waft across the frozen pizzas. I'm not sure he understands a word I'm saying but what matters is that I'm saying something. I love these kinds of conversations and so does he. I can see Tim laughing at us out of the corner of my eye.

Back in Sofia, Ben's communist education continues apace. We are amongst the last visitors to see the embalmed body of Georgi Dimitrov, the Bulgarian communist leader, who is remembered chiefly in the West for having been accused by the Nazis of setting the Reichstag on fire in 1933. He was acquitted of the deed in a high profile court case and then fled to the Soviet Union. After the war he masterminded the communist takeover in Sofia but died mysteriously in Moscow in 1949. He lies in state in a mausoleum in the main square. We buy a ticket in the shop across the road and sprint back quickly to the entrance. I'm scared this morbid attraction might close early since it's his last day on the job. I know that gazing at a glass-encased corpse is not what most people, especially my mother, think that we should be up to - but I don't care.

"You must be quiet inside, ok? It's a tomb," I whisper in Ben's ear.

We are the only people inside the mausoleum, besides the guards, standing at the corner of the big platform on top of which he is laid out. It looks like a rather uncomfortable bed. Ben holds my hand tight:

"Is he asleep, Mummy?"

He obviously thinks Dimitrov is a sort of a communist Sleeping Beauty. He might wake up and make a comeback.

"No! He's dead."

"Why's he in a bed, then?"

There are small potted cypress trees at each corner.

"He was once a hero but, now, he is going to be closed down and buried."

"Killed like Ceaușescu?"

I'm delighted. My boy is catching on faster everyday. I adore him; he's a challenge. How could I ever leave him with anyone else?

Now we've been in Sofia for some weeks, the hotel bedroom has come to resemble a gypsy encampment. I've bought a small, one-ring, portable electric stove and whisk up scrambled eggs for Ben's dinner. One day when I am boiling a corn-on-the-cob, I manage to fuse the electrics in the entire room. I hide the stove and look as innocent as possible when I report the problem to the reception but I fail to keep a straight face when the engineer arrives. Although the Sheraton has an extensive, luxurious menu it's pricey and Tim is nervous about his expenses appearing abnormally high. I save room service for the evening. Once Ben is asleep and work is over, Tim and I have a romantic meal for two sent up which we usually eat in the bathroom so as not to wake Ben.

Everything is idyllic until President Iliescu calls in twenty thousand miners to break up the demonstration outside the Intercontinental Hotel in Bucharest. Waving cudgels and hammers, they are busy beating up the student protesters and anyone else they come across. It looks as if the revolution is lost. Communism is fighting back. It's a huge story but Tim is in the wrong place. In the midst of the tension, Ben, somehow, manages to tear a large strip of bedroom wallpaper off with a toy car. Already panicked that his career is going down the tubes, Tim envisages the final nail in his coffin being the moment a bill for the re-wallpapering of the bedroom lands on his editor's desk in London.

Not that popular, we set off in search of a tube of glue. This is Bulgaria, so we are back in an hour. In Romania, we would have been gone two days. By the time we get back, Tim has found a taxi driver brave enough to drive us back to Bucharest *and* we have a tube of glue. Things are definitely better in Sofia. Who cares that it smells foul and leaves a horrid brown mark around the edges of the torn paper? Tim does.

"Is that all you could get? It's going to show," he says in disgust.

I wonder when he last went to the shops. I hastily patch up the wallpaper and we leave. This isn't the moment to pick a row, although I am sorely tempted.

Six hours later, we arrive in Bucharest. It's a sinister scene. Although I try not to show it, I'm frightened. There are armed soldiers on every street corner and the roads are deserted. The only people out are gangs of miners looking for someone to beat up. It's overcast and surprisingly cool for June. I wonder what has happened to Oana and her husband. They were both regulars at the student protest. Ben is mystified that the taxi driver is so nervous about lingering in the city that he won't even come in for a coffee. He dashes upstairs and down the hall to the toilet. Having relieved himself, he runs back downstairs. He doesn't wait for the lift and is gone.

"Why's he in a hurry? Doesn't he like it here?" asks Ben.

He takes this as a personal insult. He's back home. How can someone not like your home? I'm glad to be back although Tim has a tough time convincing his father that we shouldn't catch the next plane back to Britain.

In July, my mother comes to visit. We bomb around the country in an ancient, white, rented car. It's rather like old times. We often used to accompany my father when he went abroad lecturing and teaching in countries that most people didn't visit, like communist Poland and Saddam Hussein's Iraq. We reminisce about how, once in Warsaw, my mother bought a bottle of what she thought was mineral water - when she took a huge swig, it turned out to be white vinegar. Then she laughs about the dead horse that was left festering for days on the steps of the hospital in Basra. But, while we are off having fun, Tim is sent to the Yugoslav-Albanian border, as it looks as if Stalinist Albania is about to collapse. He wants to be one of the first journalists in when it happens. God knows what will happen when the regime there finally crumbles.

Eventually, my mother leaves to fly home to Britain at 6am on a brilliantly sunny morning. She gets into a taxi at the crossroads by the metro station *Titan*, just around the corner from our flat. I wave her "goodbye" as the taxi speeds off bouncing over the holes in the road. Ben and I are utterly alone. Besides Elena, Oana and Mihai I know no one else in the entire country. The only friends we have made are the small group of journalists based in Bucharest and they have all gone to the Albanian border with Tim. Oana is hiding out in the countryside somewhere. History hangs on a knife edge. If the revolutions of the past few months collapse and the Soviets return triumphant, what would the West do then? I hold the white handlebars of the buggy and stare at the sea of grey tower blocks that stretch off in orderly rows down the two large, dusty boulevards. Ben is slumped in the pushchair munching on a slice of stale bread. A cold wave of panic runs through me, followed by an overwhelming rush of excitement. In the meantime, we are free to do whatever we fancy. It's exhilarating. There is no one but Elena to tell us what they think we should be doing and so I can simply pretend that I don't understand what she is saying if I feel like it.

4 - At Home in Bucharest

"Wow! Calippo lollies. Is it Greece?"

We are standing in a newsagent in Shepherd's Bush. We have come back to Britain, to have the baby. The hospitals are so appalling in Romania that giving birth there is not feasible. Ben gives me an odd look. In eight months, he has developed amnesia, as far as England is concerned. Romania is the real world now and Greece is his benchmark for excellence. London fails to impress.

We kick about aimlessly for weeks, waiting for the magical day. The baby is due on October 20th. Tim is flying home on the 18th. He is convinced the baby will wait for him to arrive.

He gets home at 10pm. I'm so excited to see him again, I can't wait to make love to him and as a result the contractions start at midnight. The labour is horrendous. The pain is unbelievable and there isn't a doctor available to give me any serious painkillers. I can't believe it! I have come all the way from Bucharest for this. Tim is so exhausted that he falls asleep while I roll around in agony. I want to hit him.

All the sweat and screaming however produce the most beautiful baby with truly enormous eyes. I am sure there is a direct correlation between the two. Esther is tiny, just two and a half kilos. I put that down to being pregnant in Romania. Moments after she is born, someone lets off some bangers in the street outside and Tim rushes to the window with Esti in his arms. I mutter under my breath that they are fireworks but I know he is hoping for something more dramatic.

Ben was longing for a sister and is ecstatic. It adds to his belief that he will always get what he wants out of life. I take one look at her and decide, for Esti's sake, that I must get a job. Now I am a new woman. I'm a role model. I decide that, when she is six-months old, I'll do something about it. Life's old dilemmas are back to haunt me. Some sort of compromise seems the best idea. But how can I work and look after them at the same time?

Unfortunately, Bulgaria is still in a state of revolutionary turmoil and Tim can't stay to discuss it or, as he keeps on telling me, he'd be sacked. Secretly though, I think he's more than happy to be off. So, yet again, Ben and I are left alone. We cross the days off until Esti has her first round of inoculations and we can fly home to Bucharest triumphantly. Clean, sterile needles are hard to find in Romania and AIDS is a big problem. Having any jabs there is out of the question. I try not to think about how much I miss Tim.

Stocking up in the supermarket for our return keeps us entertained. "Esti needs this!"

Ben has selected a packet of instant egg custard baby food. He pops it in the shopping basket and darts off into the next aisle.

"I need these!"

He's waving a packet of mini chocolate Santas. They go in the basket. Esti is staring at the Christmas decorations.

"Let's get Esti some tinsel, Mummy! She needs it! Then she won't cry, when I want my story."

"That's a good idea. Anything to keep her quiet."

She wails from early in the evening to the moment the credits role on my favourite TV programme *Newsnight* at 11.15pm. I've no idea what is going on in the world. When Tim phones, she is always asleep and he can't understand why I'm near to tears. I end most days feeling angry and resentful that he is in a fancy hotel in the middle of a revolution and has spent the day meeting interesting people. It's a bad case of envy. I wonder if love is really enough to keep a marriage going when he is always in one country and I'm in another. Perhaps long distance relationships don't work after all. One reason I gave up work was so we could spend more time together - not less. In goes the tinsel. It's followed by a bib with a reindeer on.

"Ben! I'm the one doing the shopping," I snap. "Not you! Take it out! I'm trying to work out how many tins of baby milk and packets of nappies I have to buy. These are the things we really need for Esti. Just give me a moment to think, will you?"

"I know Esti. I know what she needs. You don't." He argues back but doesn't wait for an answer and sticks his head in the pushchair.

"You'll like Bucharest, Esti."

He glances up at me.

"Can we go home now?"

Waiting for the weeks to pass is an ordeal. I don't feel at home in London anymore. I feel like we are floating in limbo. We will only be saved when Esti can have her jabs and we get back to where the action is.

At last, not long before Christmas, Esti finally becomes the only baby flying into Romania. The plane is packed with couples searching for orphans to adopt. I'm bursting with excitement but feel rather guilty about having a baby of my own. In 1984 Ceauşescu launched a campaign to increase the birth rate. Contraceptives were banned and every woman of childbearing age was forced to undergo a monthly examination to see if she was pregnant. If not, the *Securitate* would want to know why. As a result, thousands of children have been born and given up for adoption and have subsequently spent their lives in the most appalling conditions in Romania's orphanages. They are Ceauşescu's little ghosts and they're a big story back in Britain. Many of them have never been lifted out of their cots and are unable to walk or speak, even though they are four or five-years old.

At Bucharest airport, there's the usual reception committee waiting for us: Mihai, his brother, his father and his mother, who has also come along this time, to see the new baby. Mihai's brother goes home on the bus so we can all fit in the Trabant. The pushchair is rammed in between my legs and Esti is perched on top of a suitcase on Tim's lap. It would have been easier to get a taxi but in Bucharest the logic of that doesn't come into it. It's wonderful to be back.

Elena is waiting at the lift door to greet Esti. She lets out a frenzied shriek as we emerge:

"*Prinţesa!*"

She grabs her and covers her with a flurry of kisses. She has renamed my baby. Esti is now called: Princess. The excitement reaches orgasmic levels when we unpack a bag of satsumas, which sit glowing bright neon on the off-white kitchen table, next to Esti's packets of baby rice and egg custard. Ben is dancing round the kitchen. The fruit looks so wonderful that I can't believe that there are heaps of satsumas sitting in supermarkets just a couple of hundred miles away. Elena claps her hands.

"*Vi, Doamna!*"

She inspects the plastic baby bottles with teddy bears on and lets out a gasp. I feel triumphant. Romanian babies still have glass ones, shaped like horns. She peers at every packet of food carefully. She turns the egg custard around to look at the back suspiciously.

"Why did you buy this?" she asks accusingly. "Princess will have soup, when she grows big enough, not that. She'll eat real food. I will make it."

Ben looks horrified and pulls a face.

"Poor Esti. I don't like her soup. It's disgusting."

The Romanian for soup is the unappetising sounding word *ciorbă*. Elena never calls her concoctions the alternative *supă*, probably because super they certainly aren't. Luckily Elena can't understand what Ben has said but I still signal to him to be quiet.

"Don't worry, Esti can have instant egg custard when Elena goes home."

In fact Esti will always love soup and dislike egg custard.

The day after we arrive back in Bucharest, Tim and Mihai buy an enormous Christmas tree in the market. As soon as she sees it, Elena scurries off and re-appears with a little box of tatty decorations.

"For Princess," she announces with a flourish.

Ben looks put out and he eyes his sister suspiciously as Elena wraps some tinsel round the handle of Esti's car seat, which doubles up as a baby chair.

For Christmas dinner, we have a miniscule chicken about the size of my fist and some roast potatoes, which we eat on the coffee table in the sitting room. Everything seems perfect - just us. The kids even fall asleep after lunch so, we too, can spend the afternoon in bed. Then in the early evening, the elderly, exiled former king flies in unannounced and Tim and Chris spend the night running around after him. He is the last person Iliescu wants to join the celebrations. I agree. I feel let down by life. Why did this man have to mess up my Christmas? When Tim gets home at three in the morning we have a terrible row. Although maybe I have a row, I don't think he says much.

One rainy day, not long after the New Year, a van selling eggs pulls up in the courtyard in front of the flats. Elena grabs her coat and extra hat and is off into the scrum below to get something tasty for her Princess. About two hours later, she returns, almost in a swoon. Her extra hat drops to the floor as she staggers in with an incredible mountain of 96 filthy, unappetising looking eggs balanced precariously on layers of soggy cardboard trays. How many omelettes can we possibly eat? As I take the trays off the exhausted Elena, I realise, before she sees my confusion, that there would be no point of queuing for all that time just for half a dozen.

Once she's recovered, Elena puts some of the eggs in the fridge door and stashes the others on the back balcony next to the petrol canisters. Ben, who's been keeping an eye on Esti in the sitting room, can't contain his excitement any longer. He runs into the kitchen and throws open the fridge door with a crash - one of the eggs falls to the ground and breaks on the old, green, kitchen carpet:

"*Vi, Doamna!*"

Elena shrieks as she drops to her knees, almost in tears, in front of the fridge.

Ben freezes, with his hand on the door, and watches in disbelief as she scrapes every part of the anaemic yolk and jellified white bit off the carpet with a knife. She then places it all, carefully, in a cup and puts it back in the fridge. Ten years later, he'll still open the fridge door with a careful glance at the egg tray.

The lift in our apartment block hasn't worked for weeks on end, so we have to climb up the long flights of stairs with whatever vegetables we have managed to get hold of in the market. The day after the miraculous delivery, there's a broken egg on the steps leading up to the seventh floor. The yolk is congealing in a sea of coagulating white. It's outside *Doamna* Colan's flat. Ben stares at it with a serious face and nods knowingly:

"Poor *Doamna* Colan! She dropped an egg."

He stands shaking his head from side to side. He repeats this reverently every time we walk past. *Doamna* Colan is an elegant chemistry teacher, who is married to a civil servant and anywhere else in the world wouldn't think twice about a broken egg. What is really extraordinary though is that no one thinks it might be a good idea to clean the mess up. It stays there for weeks until it's worn away to dust. Romania is seriously dirty - the perfect place for someone like me who hates tidying up.

The egg, however, turns out to be the light entertainment. It's a hard cold winter. Tim has spent most of it in Bulgaria. My father was away a lot when we were small children, either at the hospital or abroad, so it doesn't seem odd to me that we are alone. Ben and I are just coming back from the market with a bag of potatoes. The metal on the edge of the door at the entrance to the apartment block is icy cold. It hurts my hand as I push it open. Ben runs past me:

"What's that Mummy?"

He darts over to a huge, ornate, black coffin lid, which is propped up by one of the front doors, on the gloomy ground floor. It is decorated with a big, silver cross that looks out of place in the concrete entrance hall.

"It's the top of a coffin," I say in surprise.

"What's a coffin?"

"The box they put you in to bury you when you die."

"Why's it here?"

"So everyone knows that someone has died, I guess."

"Why?"

"So they can say they are sorry. Anyway, you should come away. It might fall on you. What would the owners say if we broke their lid?"

I redirect him up the stairs. We start the long climb.

"Whose is it?" asks Ben.

"I don't know," I answer somewhat unnerved.

We have flights to discuss this. Without Ben I would have scurried past and forgotten about it. He is, I'm realising, my key to finding out what makes this place tick. Elena fills us in, when we get home:

"Oh, he was only a cripple, who never went out".

He's dismissed, but in Ben's mind, this recluse is a man of mystery. Every time we walk past his flat he asks:

"What was wrong with him? Why couldn't he go out?"

I have no idea. The ground is frozen and it takes a long time to bury the poor man. It's so cold, that they can't dig a hole to put him in. The corpse seems to be there for an eternity waiting for its funeral. Oddly, Ben isn't interested in the coffin on the third floor. The top of this one, which is a plain brown, belongs to the mother of the administrator of our block, who just a few weeks earlier had given Ben a boiled sweet. She was a very nice lady but her son is unnerving. He has an arrogant, smarmy air about him and I wonder if he was an informer for the secret police.

One cold, windy morning, Ben charges into the kitchen, his eyes gleaming.

"Mummy! Come quick! They're taking a dead person away. I'll get Elena. Elena! Come!"

He runs off down the corridor to find her. Whenever there's a funeral in our block of flats, everyone gathers on the balcony to watch the hearse leave. I'm glad we live on the top floor. According to my mother Ben is developing an unhealthy obsession with burials. Maybe I shouldn't have taken him to stare at Dimitrov. I, however, am terrified of real death – not the embalmed version. Since my father died suddenly a few years ago I have felt my own mortality hanging over my head like the sword of Damocles but, for Ben, death is just part of the entertainment. He is bursting with life. Unfortunately, we miss the departure of the cripple and I have a sneaking suspicion that Ben thinks he is still there, inside his flat, not allowed out, even at the bitter end.

A few weeks later, we walk over to Mihai's house for lunch. Tim is off interviewing someone important. His Bucharest is a world of political intrigue. Ours is more down to earth. We stroll past a row of garages. As I turn the corner, I see a horse and cart with an open topped coffin on it. It's all on its own. There's a dead woman of about fifty, who is a nasty grey colour, lying inside it. I wonder where everyone has gone and who she is.

"Pick me up! I want to see!" shouts Ben. "Daddy saw a dead baby in the river. He told me."

I pick him up and quickly carry him, kicking and screaming, in the opposite direction. Although I feel like going over and having a closer look, I think my mother might be right. Perhaps there are limits to what children should see.

"Why's she parked there?" he asks wriggling about in my arms.

"I have no idea."

Some things here are completely baffling and rather unnerving. That's what makes Bucharest such fun - you either love it or hate it.

When we get to Mihai's, we discover that the family fish has jumped out of its tank and committed suicide. Apparently fish do this when they feel cramped and depressed by their surroundings. This is too bizarre for words. I feel for the fish. Mihai came home yesterday and found it lying on the small rug that covers the concrete floor in his room. He feels that the fish has insulted him. His flat wasn't good enough for a pet. Ben wants to see the body but, fortunately, his mother has already put it down the rubbish chute.

The New Year hasn't only brought a rash of funerals. The other big event is that Ben has started school. He is going to the French Lycée. Tim's mother, Granny Marion, is French, so Ben has dual nationality. This is one of these chance moments in life. We went first to the American school, to see if they had a place for him, but Ben was too young. If we had stayed in Shepherd's Bush, we would have sent him to an English nursery. Now, by a quirk of fate, he's signed up at the French Lycée. I have always longed to be bilingual. It infuriates me that Tim slips so casually from French to English. I am delighted that the kids will grow up being able to do this. I know nothing about France and have yet to realise what an effect this decision will have on my life and that the question of who Ben is has been complicated further.

At the moment, however, I'm more concerned that it's now time for Esti's next round of inoculations. For most people this requires an amble round the corner to the GP. We however have to fly across Europe. Ben doesn't want to go and he's still sulking, when we get to the airport:

"Can't I stay with Daddy?" he says as we climb out of the taxi. The reception committee doesn't do send offs.

Tim takes us right up to the passport control desk, to say "goodbye" and, as I hand over the three passports, I turn to kiss him. The policeman in the booth shouts angrily:

"What are you saying 'goodbye' for?"

He waves the three passports at Tim in an officious manner. Tim laughs:

"No! I'm not going. There are three of them," he says as he pulls back the lapels of my coat and gestures at Esti, who is huddled in the sling inside. It's the same old coat, the one with the astrakhan collar. Tim is brimming with pride.

"What! The baby already has a passport? How? How come?"

He just can't believe that Esti has her papers in order, since the only babies flying out of Bucharest are orphans, who've just been adopted and only have transit documents. He finds this so amusing, that he looks at her passport twice, laughing and shaking his head.

"A British baby! How nice!" he says, grinning as he hands back the papers. I wonder if he is beginning to think there are no children in Britain.

The departure lounge is crowded with couples and their newly adopted children. The older ones stand quietly, looking bewildered. Their new, western clothes don't fit properly and they show a detached indifference to their new mothers and fathers, who coo around them. I try to cheer Ben up by getting him to watch what I think is the Lufthansa plane that has just boarded, taking off. I bend down next to him:

"Look! There it goes."

As we watch it move down the runway, there is an enormous explosion and the aircraft blows up right in front of our eyes.

"Oh, my God," I mutter under my breath. How can this have happened? I have told him to watch! How can life be so cruel?

Complete panic breaks out inside the waiting room. People run screaming to the departure gate. They clearly want to get out of Romania as soon as possible, which is rather strange since flying is obviously dangerous. On the runway there is an eerie calm.

Ben stands transfixed watching quietly, his hands in his pockets. My son has seen something I never wanted him to see but he just accepts it and studies the scene. Everything all around me is grey, except the tail fin of our Swissair and the shell of the burning plane. Outside there is complete silence and only an airport bus, driven by a man with a large fur hat, sets off in the direction of the carnage. I hate flying at the best of times. I bend down in front of Ben and start doing up the buttons on his coat:

"Daddy will be back in a minute, if a plane's exploded. It will be a big story. Perhaps we should go home."

Then we stand silently in the corner of the room gazing out of the window at the wreckage and the bus, which is now parked next to the heap of burning metal. All of a sudden a middle-aged man shoots up and grabs Ben, while shouting at me:

"Come on! We have to get out of this crazy place. I can't stand it any longer."

He runs for the doors of the departure lounge, where another airport bus, also driven by a man in a big fur hat, is collecting passengers for our flight. I run after him in a panic. People are fighting to get on board. He's already on the bus by the time I get there. I think I'm about to lose Ben in the scrum. Esti, in the sling on my chest, is almost crushed in the automatic doors. When we finally clamber in, Ben is wailing in the man's arms further down the aisle. He must be a lunatic to hijack someone's child like this. Perhaps he wanted an orphan and couldn't find one. No one notices Ben's screams. This is a busload of people who just want to get away. I feel as if I'm on the wrong bus. I want to go home to Balta Alba. I shout loudly at the man with my child. He is put out and was clearly expecting to be thanked. With a furious expression on his face he passes my son back through the crowd. Ben is crying and worried about Esti whom he has seen sandwiched in the door. He still hates automatic doors but has never been frightened of flying.

When my father-in-law picks me up at Heathrow, I relate the story. He is every inch the English businessman in a dark pin-stripped suit. He takes a deep breath:

"I bite my lip. I won't say what I think. I just hope you know what your doing bringing up my grandson."

I glance at Ben and then back at my father-in-law whose face has fine, dark foreign features. I look back at Ben and I can't imagine any of this will have a profound affect on him.

I learn later, that it wasn't the Lufthansa plane that had exploded but the government jet, which was on a test flight, as it was due to fly the president to Moscow the following day.

Back on our Swissair, no one knows this yet and the engines are revving for takeoff. Once we are in the air, there is a complete shambles, with adults calling the air stewardesses to bring them yet another stiff drink. All the orphans are crying and their new parents can't calm them down. I can see the shell of the plane burning on the runway below. Ben stands up on his seat, when the seat belt sign goes off and starts playing with the boy behind. He pulls out his black plastic rat. He scurries it along the top of the seat and disappears.

"*Unde este șobolan?*" he shrieks. The boy laughs. He and Elena play "*Unde este șobolan?*" or "Where is the rat?" for hours on end. Ben hides it, while Elena runs round the flat, gleefully waving her arms and shouting: "*Unde este șobolan?*"

The boy's adoptive parents ask me what he's saying and I'm struck by the fact that they don't know their child at all. I foolishly assume I know mine. They can't even speak the same language as theirs. I wonder if they will ever understand the country he comes from. I certainly don't and I've been living there for over a year. The only baby not crying is Esti. The woman next to me, who just happens to be the wife of one of Romania's leading opposition leaders, leans nosily over and asks me, peering into the sling, if she is sedated. There's always an element of duplicity in the air, as things are never, in a Romanian's eyes, as simple as they seem. Although she's English, I think she's obviously been around

Romanians too long.

I have begun to think the same thing of Ben. Last week we were invited to have tea with two women in their forties, who had come from Canada, to adopt a couple of babies. I decided to leave Esti at home with Elena and just take Ben. Esti is so perfect that I didn't feel it would be fair to show her off. As we bumped along the misty pot-holed roads to the city centre, Tim explained to me that these two women effectively bought their babies by giving the families money with which they could buy land, when they agreed to the adoptions. One of the children was already with them. She was a girl of Ben's age, who had spent the previous three years in an orphanage.

The flat was small and gloomy. In the corner of the room, I was surprised to see a cot. So was Ben.

"Let's go and say hello," I suggested and guided him over to what appeared to be an overgrown, six-month old baby.

I have never visited an orphanage, as I am sure I would bring a child home. It's cowardly but I don't go with Tim, although he has been to lots of them. I think he is made of stronger stuff than I am. He limits and guards what he allows himself to feel so that he can get on with his job. Ben held the little girl's hand and offered her a bit of chocolate. He was very affectionate. It was the first time she had ever eaten anything like this. She sat rocking backwards and forwards. Although she couldn't talk, Ben tried to play with her. Without us knowing, he had overheard our conversation on the way and was, obviously, expecting someone of his own age to be like him. After ten minutes, he walked across the room to the new mother and asked:

"Why'd you buy *this* baby?"

He gestured towards her new daughter like a lawyer. Tim and I were mortified. It was probably my fault. I am bringing up a little monster. Flustered she offered us more tea and bustled into the tiny kitchen. I spent the journey home drowning in self-doubt, and to make matters worse Tim pointed out that, what was really shocking, was that Ben wasn't surprised that someone could sell their baby and someone would be willing to buy it. What had horrified him was that this woman had bought, what he considered, an inferior model. What will my mother say?

5 - The Only Tourist in Town

It's the middle of an overcast afternoon in late January 1991. We are speeding down the motorway towards Dover, listening to *Spot the Dog* on the car stereo, heading back to the Balkans and Tim. Esti is next to me, in her pink car seat with giraffes on. She's asleep and pretty, little milky bubbles are resting on the corner of her lips. She's beautiful and, more to the point, fully inoculated. Ben is in the backseat gazing out across the dank countryside, with a serious expression on his face. He's wearing his new, green hat with a furry inside and earflaps. He is strangely quiet. It starts drizzling. I wonder what he is thinking. He doesn't want to talk to me. I can't stand the silence and am longing for a conversation. I try to think of something outlandish to say that will grab his attention.

The road is nearly empty and, as we reach Kent, the rain turns to sleet. I can hear my mother's voice:

"I don't like to say this dear, but do you think it's a good idea to drive the children to Bucharest? There must be easier ways of getting there?"

The sleet starts to turn to snow. I'm annoyed with her. Why couldn't she just say: "That's wonderful dear. Have fun!"

Now I'm left with a horrid, nagging feeling. A cloud of self-doubt hovers over my head. By the time we get to the dockside, huge flakes of snow are floating down and the wind is icy.

There are a few minutes to spare before we board the boat. I'm not missing the opportunity to have one more shopping fix. We blow our last bits of change on a reduced price *Fireman Sam* Christmas annual and a yellow tractor before we run back across the dockside to the car. I feel like I'm bunking school. There is nothing tempting me to stay in England.

"Get in quick! Ben, hurry! We can't miss the boat."

As I open the door of our black Fiat Uno, three tins of Esti's favourite chocolate pudding fall out with a clatter onto the freezing tarmac. Clambering in and out of the car is a nightmare. It's so tightly packed, that there's hardly room to move. It's stuffed with Esti's bottles, her nappies, endless jars of baby food and Ben's toys. In the boot there's six months supply of SMA baby milk and a stash of ready to pour formula in miniature cartons, which I plan to tear open, as I speed them eastwards. It took days to work out exactly how much Esti drinks in a week and even longer to stow the cans away. I've counted every gram carefully, as I can't afford to run short. There is no baby formula in Romania so, without this SMA, Esti can't survive.

The shop assistant at Sainsbury's gave me an odd look when we went to buy a trolley load of formula. I felt like shouting at him; "there's no baby food within a five hundred mile radius of where I live," but decide against it. I tried breast-feeding but, just when I really needed to make it work, it was a total failure. Still I can't imagine breast-feeding would have been as satisfying as that trip to the shops.

"Why's that man looking at us?" asked Ben. "Doesn't he know what Esti needs?"

"No, he doesn't," I explained under my breath as I stacked the thirty-two large bucket-sized, yellow-lidded tins on to the checkout conveyor belt.

In Calais, we put the Fiat on a sleeper train heading for the Alps. It's the only car train that operates at this time of year. I just booked it, regardless of where it went, as anywhere closer to Bucharest than London would do. When I told Granny Marion where we were going, she said, with a surprised expression that it must terminate somewhere near Val d'Isère, in the middle of the mountains. She asked me why I was going there, as it was quite out of the way and if I had snow chains for the car.

Of course I didn't and I felt a sudden panic at the thought of ending up in the middle of the Alps but pretended I knew exactly what I was doing even though I had no idea where Val d'Isère was.

"It's great! I won't be tired and we'll arrive refreshed and ready to go," I said to her, sounding deliberately positive.

"But what about the snow, Rosie?" she asked looking worried.

Why are old people always so negative about everything?

Ben is now as surprised as I was, to discover that we have ended up on a ski train heading for the Alps. He looks around carefully and asks, as any sensible three-year old would:

"Where these people going?"

The tone of my voice implies that that should be obvious. And now, it's time for me to sound knowledgeable.

"The Alps." I quote Granny Marion at him: "It's going somewhere near Val d'Isère. That's a big resort in the mountains."

He looks horrified. He's going to Bucharest and hasn't factored this in on his mental map of Europe. He's never heard of the Alps before.

"The Alps are mountains," I explain patiently.

"What do they do there in the snow? It's so cold isn't it?"

"They're going on holiday."

"Holiday?"

"Yes! Just like those people, you've seen at the airport, buying sunglasses and wearing brightly coloured hats."

I'm incredulous that he can sometimes be so stupid, forgetting that my mother and mother-in-law think the same thing about me.

"They're tourists. Most people aren't as lucky as you and they only go abroad for a few weeks every year. They don't live there."

"But, what do they do there?"

"Just have fun, Ben. What do you think they do?"

I'm getting a bit exasperated. When he gets hold of a question, he just won't let it go. Later in life, it'll be just the same. He'll bore the family stiff discussing obscure topics like Mingrelians in Georgia, but now it's tourists that are on the agenda. It's obvious to everyone else what tourists are, but not to him. The odd thing is that two weeks on a package tour, in his mind, is far more exotic and exciting than his life in post-revolutionary Romania. He is sitting on the bunk in our compartment swinging his legs off the edge of the bed.

"Can I be a tourist, Mummy?"

I say nothing.

Most people I talked to in London have either lost interest in what is happening in Eastern Europe or assume that after the peaceful, positive transition in Poland and Czechoslovakia that everything is dandy. In our corner of Europe things are not going so well. A bunch of desperate, former communist politicians are trying to hang on to power by whipping up the crowd with nationalist rhetoric. The civil wars that raged during World War Two look like they are about to be re-ignited. There are no tourists where we are going.

With some premonition of Ben's desires, Granny Marion has bought him *Topsy and Tim go on Holiday* as a parting gift. We read it as the train rattles across France. When we get to the final page, where there is a picture of the two of them digging on the beach, Ben asks to read the whole story again. Then we have to discuss where tourists go on holiday, if it's not to the Alps. I tell him about the Mediterranean, as I cuddle him to sleep. He goes into a deep slumber. I don't. The real tourists on the train decide to party late into the night. As if this is not bad enough, we only have two bunks and I'm too terrified to tuck the kids in together in one, in case Esti falls out. I lie along the edge to keep her safe and she spends the night kicking me in the back.

Once we finally get to the Alps we have to wait half an hour on the freezing platform, as a car load of young skiers have gone off to enjoy a strong coffee in the café leaving their car, which is in front of ours on the train, blocking us in. I'm desperate to get some formula out of the boot to feed Esti. I am not feeling too enamoured with Ben's tourist idols.

As soon as we do get the car off the train, I stop in the first lay-by to hunt for some breakfast for Esti. I can't believe what has happened.

"Oh Ben!" I gasp as I open the boot.

"What, Mummy? What?" he asks breathlessly.

I'm rummaging desperately among the luggage.

"All Esti's ready to serve stuff is frozen solid!" I shout back in desperation.

There are no shops anywhere to be seen and the only way to defrost it is to sit on a carton, as we drive towards Geneva, where we are to meet Tim. He is doing an interview with Michael, the former King of Romania, who lives there. I still haven't forgiven the King for messing up Christmas but I can't wait to see Tim. It's two weeks since we flew out of Bucharest. I check my make up before we set off. I am so tired that I have trouble focusing on the road. Thankfully the icy carton between my legs stops me from dropping off to sleep. I can see Ben in the rear view mirror, looking bored. I start chatting:

"You know Ben, when King Michael lost his throne, he became a chicken farmer."

"Good idea," he mumbles.

I'm stumped. I wasn't expecting that reply.

"What do you mean, good idea?"

"He'd have his own eggs," he mutters.

While in Geneva, we stock up on French books to practice with when we get home. When we come out of the bookshop, it's snowing heavily. Other cars are stopping to put on chains. I point this out to Tim, who impatiently bundles the three of us into the car. There is no time to stop and wait for the weather to improve, as we have to get to Sofia, where Tim has to interview the president of Bulgaria. He has been ordered by his editor to get there as quickly as possible, and you don't argue with that. You just go or get left behind. I don't mind. It's fun and it was like that when we travelled with my father. Things were always a little chaotic. Once we ended up sleeping on the platform of Cracow station. I don't remember why this happened but only that my mother was furious and I thought it was wonderful.

As we wind our way up to the Mont Blanc tunnel, I do begin to feel a little anxious. We are the only car on the road. In Italy, huge snowflakes, the size of golf balls drift slowly past the window. It looks like an Arctic landscape. The snow just keeps on falling as we drive across Yugoslavia. By the time we get to Sofia, I am exhausted and have cystitis, which I put down to sitting on too many frozen SMA cartons. Ben is delighted to be heading back home via Bulgaria.

"Are we going to the Japanese hotel?" he asks chirpily.

"Yes! Of course," says Tim.

"Yey! Esti you'll love it. They planned to murder the Pope there."

Incongruously, Sofia has a hotel with a Japanese garden and a Japanese restaurant. It's earned its place in world history as there's a bar on the top floor where the plot to assassinate the Pope was hatched. Soviet agents hired a hit man here to gun down John Paul II, whose election in 1978 as the head of the Catholic Church was stirring up nationalist, anti-communist feeling in his Polish homeland. His appointment coincided with a series of events that undermined communism and, finally, brought us to the Balkans.

A week later, it still hasn't stopped snowing and the water features in the Japanese garden are hidden under more than a metre of snow. Tim's job is done and it's finally time to drive the last leg of the journey, home to Bucharest. As we set off early, we have the road, unsurprisingly, yet again to ourselves. We skid into two ditches before it gets dark. But, by nine in the evening, we are getting close to the border, when we come across a traffic jam. A policeman taps the window and tells us that a blizzard has blocked the road. Ben screeches in glee:

"Wow! A giant lizard is blocking the road!"

He leaps up and peers across me, towards the stern looking officer. I pull him back:

"What? Sit down! What are you talking about?

I can't stand the way he thinks that some of the things that worry me are a huge laugh.

"Sssh! It's a policeman!"

Ben has seen too many cartoons about jolly policemen; if he doesn't show some respect for the Balkan variety, he's going to get us all in trouble.

"Has the policeman seen the lizard, Mummy?"

"What lizard? What would a lizard be doing out in this weather? What are you talking about?"

I can't follow this at all.

"The policeman said he's blocking the road," says Ben excitedly.

This is just too much! All I can think of is a huge, fat lizard basking in the snow, when in reality, if we don't get Esti somewhere warm, she could freeze to death.

"There's no lizard, you idiot! He said 'blizzard' Ben, that's lots of snow."

I don't know why I bother, as he is lost in space and thinks we are starring in some return of the dinosaurs movie.

Tim gets out to ask for help and comes back in couple of minutes with two young men in black leather jackets. He's smiling and looking triumphant:

"These guys will help us. They know where we can get a room. We've got to be quick, though."

"Is the lizard coming?" asks Ben.

Tim isn't listening. He is, I'm beginning to realise, a survivor by instinct. Only he could pull this off.

"Hey, Ben! You'll never guess what these two men do for a living?"

He turns round grinning, while I think, in the circumstances, he should really be watching the road.

"They're circus performers, on the way to show off their motorcycle act in Bucharest."

Ben clicks back into reality, or at least his father's version of it, as he was just in the big top in Bucharest at Christmas.

"Wow! Where's their bike?"

The circus boys do as they have promised and take us to a nearby town, where they help us to get the last room in a truly filthy hotel. They tell us tales of their life, while we drink red wine. The bad news is that the hotel has a communal bathroom. I ask foolishly:

"Is it clean, Tim?"

"Don't go unless you have to," he replies, still smiling.

Ben is humming on the bed. I don't want to sit on the bed, let alone get under the covers. At least Esti seems to agree. She has a look of distain on her face, as she glares at her father and big brother.

"You're too fussy," says Tim. "It's a great adventure, isn't it Ben?"

He nods wildly. They have teamed up against me. The two of them settle down between the sheets, laughing and giggling at us, while I stretch out in my big black coat. I have to admit, grudgingly, that it's been a great evening. Although she has been saved by a circus duo, Esti isn't impressed, probably because she missed out on the red wine and spends the whole night awake. A church bell tolls the hours. She doesn't cry but lies next to me wriggling around, her huge eyes searching around the room with a furious expression on her face.

Back home in Balta Alba, in the weeks that follow, the tape that came with *Topsy and Tim go on Holiday* is constantly on the cassette player that I've brought from London. Every day is grey and snowy. We watch women sweeping frozen clods off the top of the block opposite. They don't bother to look and see if anyone is walking underneath. Tim is away for weeks, first in Moldova and now in Albania. The days slip by in a monotonous haze of broken nights and trips to the market. I always seem to be waiting for Tim but I really can't imagine what it must be like to be married to someone who is always there. I don't think it would suit me at all. I quite like being alone but even I have my limits. We stayed in Bucharest so Ben could go to school. I think that was a mistake. It's time for some truancy. I can understand why Ben finds the picture of the beach at the end of the *Topsy and Tim* book so alluring.

It's Easter by the time Tim has finished his assignment. He has interviewed entire families, who have spent the past forty years as political prisoners in a mini-Albanian version of the Gulag, living in an isolated village, which they were not allowed to leave. Some of them were betrayed by Kim Philby, the British spy who worked for the KGB. I'm impressed, impressed enough to forget how long he has been away and at the same time amazed there is somewhere worse off than Romania. I have difficulty imagining this. I'd love to go. We have arranged to meet in Sofia and to take Ben and Esti to Greece on holiday. Ben is packing his backpack with essentials; a few Lego bricks, his fire engine and some cars. He looks up excitedly:

"Will I be a tourist Mummy?"

I bend down to help.

"Yes, why not?"

We head for the nearest Greek island, Thassos, which is off the coast of northern Greece. The weather is overcast and out of season it's incredibly dull. Most of the place is still closed up for winter and we have to drive around the entire island looking for a hotel. Ben starts moaning.

"Don't worry, now we don't have to do any sightseeing," quips Tim who's driving. His idea of a holiday is to do nothing at all. Ben who is sitting next to me in the back seat looks aghast.

"I want to be a tourist!" he groans. Sightseeing is exactly what he has in mind. It's what tourists do. Esti is on my lap. She turns to him with a definite expression on her face and utters her first word:

"Buh!"

It bursts out loud and strong. She looks at him hard and repeats herself:

"Buh!"

This means, I think:

"Ben! Just, shut up!"

It brings him up short. She has interrupted him, and put him in his place, for the first time. Amazingly, he doesn't see this. He is simply, egocentrically delighted that the honour of being the subject of her first comment has been bestowed on him.

"Don't forget your first word was 'dog,'" adds Tim from the front. He's clearly peeved that he hasn't been chosen for the accolade, yet again.

Eventually, we find a hotel that is open. It's a brand new holiday complex and we are, in fact, the only guests. Indeed, I think we are the only tourists on Thassos. The weather is cold and wet and the hotel has no heating. Worse than that, it doesn't have any hot water either. Tim is furious and demands a reduced rate. Then in the space of a few hours, I discover that my mother has had a stroke and Tim finds out that his cousin has died and an old friend has committed suicide. The hotel is spookily quiet. The rain rattles the windows. I have a dream that the dead are outside waiting to say "goodbye". We aren't up to much holiday fun. I make us a meal of cold, tinned sweetcorn and sliced chicken. The restaurant is closed.

"Are you sure this is Greece, Mummy? I wanted to be a tourist," says Ben as I hand him a paper plate.

"Yes, definitely, this is Greece," I say passing him a plastic fork. I glance at the window, praying nobody dead is lurking outside. "Although, I think, I've gone off it. What about you?"

Greece slips down the rankings in his list of the top ten countries, never to recover the top slot. We leave early and head somewhere new.

By mid-May we are in Yugoslavia. It's late on a Friday night as we drive around the corner of a dark road. Tim brakes fast. Parked in the middle is a huge red fire engine. Ben points excitedly at the machine as a man armed with a rifle walks up to the car window. Ben watches him carefully, and so do I, while Tim shows him his accreditations and our passports. He lets us pass. We have arrived in Knin, a non-descript Croatian town that is just about to become the capital of the breakaway rebel Republic of Serbian Krajina.

The hotel is a converted old people's home built in the 1970s. I plug in my portable electric cooker and whisk up fish fingers and peas, which I bought earlier in Bosnia. Tim goes out to a midnight rally. I am so delighted to have found something so easy to cook that the sinister nature of events outside passes me by. It is only when the kids have fallen asleep that I stop to think about it. The next day, in a Stalinist -style referendum, the local Serbian population will vote to remain in Yugoslavia with Serbia. Not to vote in the poll would be to identify yourself as not being a Serb and hence you would have no right to carry on living here. It would put your life in danger. Knives are drawn. War is looming. The dark feels dangerous. I long to know what is going on outside. I wish Tim would come home.

While the Sunday morning ballot takes place, we walk downtown to buy some bread and cheese to make sandwiches. Ben is holding Esti's pushchair as we wheel into a small shop, which is covered in Serbian flags. They are playing traditional, rousing nationalist songs. The assistant passes me a loaf that is identical to every other loaf in the country. It's fat, white and elongated. In fact it's a fatter, fresher version of the loaves on sale in Balta Alba. Ben pulls my sleeve:

"Why's the window of that shop broken, Mummy?"

"Sssh! Wait! I tell you in a minute."

"It's been looted and belongs to Croats who have fled," I explain under my breath once we have left the Serbian shop.

"What does 'looted' mean?" he asks.

I could ignore him and dodge the issue but he needs to build up his vocabulary if he's going to understand his new world. I tell him.

We walk back up to the hotel and start packing the car. It's so filthy, that I decide to give it a bit of a clean. I sit in the front seat wiping the dashboard with a baby wipe, while I wait for Tim to file his story to London. A Scottish colleague of his sticks his head in the window and says:

"A bit of Sunday morning car cleaning? How civilised!"

I feel a compete idiot. The world is collapsing, war is about to break out, and I am tidying the car like a suburban housewife. Tim thinks this is a huge joke. I worry that it is in fact true.

We drive towards the coast through villages where some houses stand empty. They have broken windows. A few have been set on fire. Outside others, elderly neighbours sit watching the traffic.

"Cor! Who are they?" Ben points at a Japanese television crew, who are recording the scene. "Where are they from?"

They look completely out of place. An old Croatian lady is shelling peas, on a bench outside her house. They film her carefully. She is completely oblivious to their presence, as if this happens everyday. I don't feel so bad about cleaning the car. A few months later she and the rest of the Croats in the village have been driven out.

Two hours drive down the road is the balmy, warm, Dalmatian coast that was, until a few weeks ago, a mecca for package holidaymakers. Ben is at last standing on a Mediterranean seafront under the palm trees. It's late spring 1991. Behind him is the old part of Split, which is built into and around the palace of the Roman Emperor Diocletian. Further along the seafront there's a market full of luxuries like artichokes and dark green courgettes, vegetables that simply don't exist in Romania. Ben wants to see what's around every corner and in every shop. I finger the clothes; the kids admire the toys. Ben is entranced. Esti and I bask in the warm May sunshine. It's too perfect.

"Take my picture, Mummy!" he calls.

He's got a plastic camera hanging round his neck, that shows tacky, touched up photos of the old walled city of Dubrovnik and the famous, arched Ottoman bridge at Mostar, when you look through the viewfinder.

"I'm a real tourist!" he announces, brimming with pride.

But, he isn't. The place is deserted. We are here because a young Yugoslav soldier, a Macedonian, has been lynched trying to keep the crowds under control in a demonstration. He was killed after being yanked out of his armoured vehicle by angry protestors, who see the army as a symbol of Serbian domination of the Yugoslav federation. At least that is what I understand has happened. It is very confusing trying to work out what is going on. The upshot is that Yugoslavia is a country that's falling to bits. Croatia is about to break away and bid farewell. Civil war is imminent.

The atmosphere is heady. You can almost smell it in the air. It makes you feel light-headed. Tim has been sent to talk to the last few tourists, who've stayed on in Split, but the main problem is finding them. We are the only three left. Tim has to resort to interviewing Ben, as he buys him an ice cream at a stall, where they have flags for the foreign visitors who are supposed to be buying the cornets. There's a whole array of them from all over the world sitting, waiting for the tourists to return.

On the eve of war, Ben, Esti and I have a truly wonderful time drinking Coke and wandering around the ancient alleyways. I want to indulge them. He wants to be a tourist on a package tour. I don't feel guilty – there are plenty of Yugoslavs doing exactly the same.

"I feel like Nero, Ben," I say as I tuck him into bed.

"Who's that?"

He snuggles up to me.

"He fiddled while Rome burned. We are having fun, while war is breaking out."

He is asleep in moments. The excitement is enough to make anyone feel tired.

We head for Zagreb, the Croatian capital. On the way, we pass by the famous lakes and waterfalls of the Plitvice National Park. It's closed. As we drive through the town where many of the local Serbs who work in the park actually live, Tim is craning over the wheel.

"That must be his butcher's shop."

"Whose shop?" I ask, confused.

Tim may file knowledgeable articles but he often forgets to tell me what he has written and we only get the paper in the post weeks later.

"The Serb who was killed when the Croatian police tried to get the park back under their control," he says slightly exasperated.

In fact this butcher is one of the first casualties of the Yugoslav wars. I feel that I really should have known this as my grandfather was a butcher and I'm embarrassed by my ignorance.

Last year, 800,000 tourists came to the Plitvice park. Today, the place is deserted.

"Wow tanks!" shouts Ben, as we slow down near the park gates.

Tim gets out to talk to the soldiers. He's picked up some Serbo-Croatian in such a leisurely fashion I didn't notice him doing it. They are young Yugoslav army conscripts. They are happy and smiling. One of them, who must be about eighteen, gives Ben a biscuit. Then we drive on, up the deserted road.

"What were they doing, Dads?" asks Ben as he finishes the last bite.

"Carving out this bit of Croatia for the Serbs," answers Tim stretching his arms straight against the wheel.

They looked far too innocent to be doing any such thing, but it's true. The battle lines are being drawn. Ben stares out of the window. There are old ladies on the side of the road with small stalls of cheese. They used to have a good business selling to tourists, but now their living has gone. Tim stops to buy some. It is dry and not very good. Perhaps it has gone stale. Ben throws his slice out of the window. Tim asks for another one. He can't possibly like this stuff? He must, single-handedly, be trying to keep the old ladies in business.

It's the evening of Friday May 17th 1991. I'm cuddling the children to sleep in a dark hotel room, while a crowd of young men march past the hotel singing a fascist song from the Second World War. The Croats are just about to vote in a referendum to leave Yugoslavia. It's creepy and frightening. When I was five we came to Croatia on holiday. All I can remember is how blue the sea was and how warm the sun felt. I was a real tourist. I have a photo of myself smiling in a psychedelic, 1960s sundress. Tim is out filing his story. I wish he would come back. I have a romantic birthday supper laid out in the bathroom and a bottle of Croatian wine we can drink in the bath. It's a night to forget it all and have some fun.

"Why do people use fire engines to block roads, Mummy?" asks Ben.

"It's my birthday, Ben. It's a big one – I'm thirty. Can't we talk about something else for a change?"

He knows the answer to his question but has this irritating habit of continually checking that what he has understood is right.

"Because fire engines are the biggest vehicles in most towns. They are the best things to block roads with," I mutter under my breath.

"What going to happen next?" he asks excitedly.

"I don't know. Now, you must sleep."

"Does Dads know?"

"Yes, ask him, maybe he knows," I say, although I am not sure anyone knows what will happen next.

6 - Late Night Lightning like Artillery Fire

A few weeks later, on a sunny June morning, back in Bucharest, I wake up early and listen to the *BBC World Service*. War has broken out in Slovenia. Tim is there, covering the story. I always knew Tim wanted to be a foreign correspondent but I never imagined he would be a war reporter. I feel like someone has hit me in the back. I wasn't expecting this. I stand in front of the mirror and look at myself. I feel shaky. My suntan looks pale. I haven't even had time to make a coffee, before there is a frantic ringing on the doorbell, which wakes Esti. Elena bursts in, peeling off her hats, in a dramatic swirl that seems more like a swoon.

"*Doamna!* Did you hear the news? It's a war! No! Not a war, again!"

I end up ushering her into the kitchen and making her a coffee. She's almost in tears, when she realises that she has woken her beloved Princess.

Ben appears. Fortunately, he's spent most of the morning playing with his toy railway and hasn't asked what is going on. He sets Elena off again:

"The poor children! Not a war again."

"What's the matter, Mummy?"

He knows something is the matter. His voice is soft and quiet. I can see that there's no point in fobbing him off, even if he can't really understand what she is saying. I tell him simply what has happened:

"A war has broken out in Slovenia. That's where Daddy is."

"Where's that?" he asks with a tone almost akin to defiance.

"Slovenia, the top left hand bit of Yugoslavia. They want to break away and have their own country."

His face doesn't move. There isn't a flicker. I don't know what he understands.

Then he asks:

"Will Daddy be ok?"

He has thought through carefully what I have said and his expression slowly changes from one of unnerving blankness to one of worried tension. This is one of those moments when it would help if you could just stop the clock and think carefully. Or, maybe consult a library of parenting books. Not that I have ever found any of them to be of much use. I can't imagine even one that has an entry: "War has broken out. Your husband is in danger. You explain this to your child in the following way…" I hope the best thing to do is to be honest and make sure he is fully aware of what is happening. I pray it's the best way to deal with the situation. Unsure, I put on my definite voice:

"Yes, of course, he will."

I decide not to think about what could happen to Tim too carefully. It could be tempting fate. Why didn't I look at him a little more carefully before he left? I wish I had run my fingers around his face so I could conjure him up in my mind's eye better.

"What's up with Elena?" asks Ben, staring across the kitchen at her.

It's true. She never sits down and drinks coffee. He's never seen her without a hat before, so to him it's clear that something very serious must have happened.

"She's worried that there will be a big war. Like there was when she was young," I say and then immediately regret it. That was a bit harsh.

"Will it happen here?" he whispers putting his hand out towards mine.

I see with some horror that this is a genuine question. He's actually taken on board and processed what he's seen driving around Yugoslavia. He was right to keep checking about those fire engines. I've never felt so close to him. An unbreakable bond has just pulled us together. I feel like now it's really us against the world.

"No, it won't happen here," I say definitely but add: "I hope not anyway!" just in case.

Back in my bedroom, I get dressed, while Elena coos over Esti even louder than normal. At last, they go to queue for bread. I look in the mirror again and notice my first grey hair. I'm mortified and let out a deep sigh:

"Ooh! I don't believe it!"

Ben shoots in, swinging round the doorframe. He looks as if he hasn't a care in the world:

"What's up Mummy?"

"I've got a grey hair! Look! It's your father's fault."

Ben's expression changes from expectant excitement to anger, not because I have suddenly grown old but that I could say that Daddy has done something wrong:

"What about Daddy? When's he coming home?"

"I don't know," I snap.

"Why?"

This is a stupid question, I think and shout:

"There's a war on!"

He looks at me and puts on a tense grin that I assume is supposed to make everything better. Suddenly everything has changed. I hope I'll cope. I'm not sure I'm up to this. Ben stares up at me waiting to see what I will do next.

When Tim left for Slovenia, he told me he would be back at the weekend. He flew, which is why we didn't tag along as normal. The air tickets were too expensive, just for a weekend. But two months pass by and he still isn't back. This is the second time this has happened. I resolve not to believe him next time. By now he has moved on to Croatia where the war there is gathering pace.

"Esti will start to walk before Tim gets back," says my mother down the crackly line from Cornwall.

I'm tired but she makes me laugh. I am already in bed. It's almost midnight. You can't just pick up the phone and make an international call here. You have to book it in advance. You ring, give your number and the one you want to call and then wait for the operator to call you back. Usually I fancy a chat with my mother after the children have gone to bed but by the time I get the call, it's often 2am. I suppose someone from the secret police has to listen in and there aren't enough English speakers on duty. Tonight I'm lucky; it's only 11.50pm. It's August and the heat is stultifying. There is lightning, but no thunder or rain.

"Don't be so blunt with Ben. You don't have to tell him everything. Cosset him a bit," she says. But it's okay for her to hand out advice; she's miles away. I decide to wind up the conversation:

"I have to go Mum, Tim will call when he gets back from the front. I want to know he's safe."

Ben wakes up and comes into my bed:

"Was it Dads?" he mutters, rubbing his eyes.

"No, it's too early for him. Go to sleep."

I get his teddy and he soon closes his eyes. Esti is peaceful in the cot next to the bed. I'm glad I am not alone. I wait anxiously, in the dark. Eventually, at about 3am, Tim phones:

"Are you ok?"

He sounds tired. He tells me about a German journalist, who has just been killed in Glina, a town in Croatia, and that he was one of the last people to talk to him. He was married. I'm frightened.

"How are you?" he asks.

"Fine! I'm fine. We are all fine."

There are a thousand things I would like to say but where do you start? I don't want to say anything that might worry him or make him feel homesick. Fine is the best fallback, especially at this time of night. Fine is what Tim wants things to be.

"It's odd, there is lightning but no thunder and rain. It looks like artillery fire," he says.

"It's here too."

The weather binds us together. I don't mind waiting for him. My grandmother waited seven years for my grandfather to come back from fighting in the Middle East during the First World War. It must be in the blood.

"You need to sleep. Be careful, I love you," I say softly and he is gone.

Now I do feel alone. I watch the lightning, broad sheets of it low on the horizon. All that seems to matter are Tim and the kids. Life has a new intensity I've never felt before.

And so the summer drags on, night after night. In the morning, I'm exhausted and Elena plays with the children while I sleep. Someone beating a carpet in the yard below wakes me up about noon; someone is always beating a rug. I suppose no one has a vacuum cleaner. We certainly don't. When I get up I find Elena in the kitchen feeding Esti.

"Waiting is the worst thing," she says, calmly.

When the war broke out in Slovenia, I took the children home to England, where the newspaper headlines all read: "War in Europe". There was an atmosphere of panic, whenever the topic came up. People discussed it earnestly on *Newsnight*, while the rest of the time, everyone seemed oddly removed from what was going on, as if this was just something that was happening on TV. It didn't suit me, so I came home to Bucharest where things seemed more real.

The summer is stifling. It's so hot I can't think straight. My self-imposed, six months deadline to get back to work has passed but I'm too hot, too exhausted and stressed out to think about picking up the phone and booking a call to some newspaper editor in London and trying to sell a story. None of them care what is going on here anyway.

My mother sends me something to read to take my mind off things. It's Peter Mayle's *A Year in Provence*. It's a best seller in the Europe where they have money to buy books. She has chosen it, as she knows I want to learn more about France now Ben is at the Lycée. So we spend our afternoons on the front balcony. Ben and Esti are in the paddling pool and I sit on the floor next to them enthralled by my book. I cannot put it down. Mayle does nothing but eat. I'm gripped by his descriptions. Although I'm a lifelong vegetarian I find myself reading aloud to Ben and translating for Elena details of meaty casseroles and grills. Provence sounds wonderful. Elena is not impressed. She'll make me a chicken casserole she says and suggests a slowed cooked cockerel. I panic. What's my mother done? What if she really does cook it – what will I do then?

"What's wrong with them?" interrupts Ben.

He's pointing at the elderly couple who live directly opposite us. They are both dressed in layers of black. She has a long shirt, shawl and a headscarf. He is wearing, what must have once been a smart suit and a 1950s-style hat, at rather a jaunty angle. They appear at about nine in the morning and they sit next to each other on two upright wooden chairs, staring at us without moving a muscle or saying a word, all day.

"Why don't they move?"

"I expect they say the same kind of things about us, Ben."

We by contrast, have the paddling pool, a colourful sheet tied up as a sunshade and we eat on the balcony. There's a clatter of plates at breakfast, lunch and dinner. I often have the radio on and, in the evening, I light candles. We have geraniums in tubs. Elena thinks this outdoor living, in skimpy clothes, is all very dangerous because there might be a draught. It's around 36°C and very humid. The temperature never seems to drop, even at night.

Turning the page, as Peter Mayle describes his happy encounters with rustic types, I glance up to check on the factory that I can see between the two apartment blocks on the left. Most of the time, its chimneys puff out grey or white smoke. Recently, however there has been an alarming development and bright yellow smoke has started belching out in the middle of the afternoon. Sometimes it turns pink and purple. It's a mass of colours in an urban wasteland. No one cares about the environment here, let alone the dangers of toxic waste, so I don't take any chances. Once we took a trip to two towns in central Romania. One had a factory that covered the entire town in a film of white powder while the other scattered acrid, black dust everywhere. In an hour, Ben's teddy turned a nasty grey. He still is, even though he has been washed a hundred times.

This afternoon the sky is turning a strange yellow so I hustle the kids indoors and shut all the widows in the flat. We all sit inside, until the chimneys stop spewing out something that looks like the northern lights into the atmosphere. Ben is furious:

"Why can't we go out? Esti's hot - aren't you Esti?"

In fact, Esti is always cold, even in the height of summer.

"Do you remember that electric green river we saw in Bulgaria, Ben?

It wasn't supposed to be green. Someone had put something in it to turn it that colour. It's called pollution. It's dangerous. I don't want you to breathe in those fumes," I explain. He still looks furious:

"Everyone else is outside."

"They don't know that it could be dangerous. No one has told them," I say definitely.

"How come you know?"

"I'm not from here. People in London know this but people here don't."

I feel as if I am from another planet, not just another country.

"You're making it up. I want to go out."

"I know what I am talking about," I insist.

"You're mad, you are. That's right isn't it Esti?"

Esti is trying to eat an orange, plastic giraffe. I don't think she is the person to ask.

The days pass slowly. There seems to be time for everything but little to actually do. The heat slows me down to a snail's pace. I'm beginning to think that if I stayed here for another forty years I could end up like the immobile old people opposite. I spend some evenings with my friend Sophie. She's an aid worker and came to Bucharest to join Alec Russell, her boyfriend who is a reporter for the *Daily Telegraph* - but now he's also in Croatia. The two of us are beached in Bucharest. But the evenings I spend alone are the worst. Once the children have gone to bed, the silence in the flat is oppressive. There is a limit to how many times you can re-read *A Year in Provence* or watch the ancient re-runs of *Dallas* that are constantly on TV. There is only sticky red wine to drink. I imagine that if I was in London I would have a wonderful social life but I don't want to move back. I'm in love with a disembodied voice that calls me up every evening and the only place I would like to be is Yugoslavia.

I stand in the silent kitchen and hear the neighbours throwing something down the rubbish chute. I rarely have to put out the garbage here since Elena keeps everything that might possibly be useful. The kitchen cupboards are full of old jars, empty cardboard packets and old bottles. I decide that I'll finish my bottle of wine and throw it down the chute for the sheer hell of it. I'm finding her clutter really annoying. It's time to move on. At least this little episode keeps my mind off the frontline and occupies the minutes until the news on the *BBC World Service*. I hope that if anything happens to Tim it would be a news item, so I listen religiously and so does Sophie. In reality I know that they report the injury of some journalists and not others. It depends what else is going on. I don't mention that bit to Sophie.

At last, the summer is almost over. It's the fourth time I've checked my hair in ten minutes. Elena is scurrying up and down the corridor from the kitchen, clucking. Esti is crawling along behind her. She's wearing a white cotton dress that Elena keeps immaculately laundered. She looks wonderful, just like a real princess.

"*Ah Doamna!*" Elena claps her hands in glee. "I remember the day my Mitica came back from the war. I was so excited to get him back. A husband home at last!"

It sounds like any old husband will do or perhaps I have been alone too long.

"You look wonderful! Hurry! You mustn't be late. Ben! Come I must brush your hair."

We are about to meet Tim at the airport. Elena knows exactly how I feel. War binds the generations together.

I haven't told Mihai that Tim is coming back. I don't want the reception committee today. We go in a taxi. It's wonderful to have Tim home at last although I can't get near him as the kids are jumping all over him. I look at him carefully to see if he is the same man. He is more handsome than before and has a deep, suntanned face. The job clearly suits him. That's enough for me. Ahead of us we have two weeks together at home. He has bought me a watch as a present. It's a diving watch although I can't even swim under water. It seems an odd choice but ever since I have never spent a day without it on. Despite that I'm annoyed that he bought it because he saw a similar watch on a waitress. I don't like him looking at waitresses like that. Later we will make love while I wear it. I never imagined there could be so much passion in life. That's why I'll wait for him again and again because being apart is like saving up for Christmas. When I do finally get my hands on him life is extravagantly rich for a few magical moments.

The phone rings. It's his editor. Unfortunately, there's been an attempted coup in the Soviet Union and the Moscow correspondent, who is covering for him in Yugoslavia has to go straight back to Russia. There are fears that the military will take control and attempt to regain the power and influence the Soviets have lost. I don't have time to consider the possible consequences of what has happened as Tim's editor has decided that we are moving to Belgrade for good, tomorrow morning. I'm delighted. It's closer to the front line but how can I possibly tell Elena?

7 - Autumn in Serbia

It's a blustery, dark, November lunchtime. We're coming home from school in a taxi, because the car tyre is flat. The taxi driver is hunched over the wheel, puffing on a cigarette. We're crushed in the back, on the fake brown leather seat, underneath Esti's buggy and Ben's school bag. I ask the driver to stop half way up Knez Miloša, one of Belgrade's main roads. It's a busy grand boulevard lined with dark grey, almost black, public buildings. It's the most depressing street in the city. He pulls up opposite the Ministry of Defence. I try not to look at it. The Yugoslav army are laying siege to the beautiful, walled city of Dubrovnik. Tim has been there for six weeks. Closer to home it looks as if the army and Serbian paramilitaries are just about to take control of Vukovar, another Croatian town, which is less than a hundred miles northwest of Belgrade. Everyone is expecting a bloodbath when it falls. I am praying that the outrage that the siege of Dubrovnik has caused will stop a full-scale massacre there but there is no guarantee of that. Commentators on the *BBC World Service* discuss what is going on in animated excitement. The topic makes me feel so cold inside that I wonder if I can move. They can go home and forget about it. I can't. I wanted the real world. Now I have it.

Ben stops my thoughts wandering from the task at hand:

"I'm not getting out," he grumbles.

"Oh, yes you are!" I say definitely.

I'm not in the mood for an argument although I don't blame him. I really don't like Knez Miloša either. A few weeks ago, I was going the other way in a taxi with a Yugoslav friend, who told me to watch out for the white transit vans driving up and down. She is convinced that they are full of the coffins of dead soldiers, which are being secretly brought back from the frontline. I have no idea whether it's true or not, but it's put me off this dull, gloomy boulevard, where battle plans are drawn up. I decide not to shout, but coax him out. The driver sits sullenly in the front seat, doing nothing to help lift the pushchair and the bags out.

Once we are all on the pavement, I pull a wad of banknotes out of the pocket of my new, brown duffle coat. My old black one has been eaten by moths. There are a huge amount of moths in Serbia. I start to count out the money carefully. I don't want to make a mistake. I have never been very good at maths and the hyperinflation that has just started to take hold is testing my skills to the limit. The war is eating away at the economy like a cancer and prices are spiralling out of control.

"Cor! How much is that?"

Ben's head pops up at the corner of the taxi window. I try to subtly elbow him out of the way. Will he ever learn when to keep his mouth shut? This isn't the moment for a chat. I tell the driver to keep the change, not because he deserves it, but because I just want to get rid of him and can't stand the thought of waiting, while he in turn, counts out the notes laboriously.

As he pulls off, he keeps his hand, that's still holding my change, hanging out of the window. As he accelerates, he lets it go. The money blows away behind the taxi in the wind. The bills, about ten or fifteen of them, end up bobbing in the gutter, bouncing around like leaves at our feet and around the wheels of Esti's buggy. As they flutter about, we stand and look at them. I'm flabbergasted but none of the passers-by pay any attention. Ben points down at the edge of the pavement:

"There's the one with the boy on. I like that one."

Two months ago, Ben was so delighted to earn his first pocket money, which was one of these stylised Dinar bills, with the picture of a schoolboy on that he asked to have his photo taken holding it proudly for the camera.

"Why'd he do that, Mummy? Why?"

He's still looking down at the notes, which are now settling in the soggy leaves, in the gutter.

"I don't know, maybe he didn't like me. I just don't know, perhaps he's making some kind of protest now the money isn't worth anything. Perhaps, it's because I'm a foreigner. I simply don't know Ben."

"But why?"

He knows the Yugoslav economy was in marvellous shape compared to its Eastern European neighbours. It was obvious, even to a child - there were fish fingers for sale here after all - but what he doesn't understand is the way the war has destroyed all that. This is my fault, as I don't understand it either.

"Wars do this sort of thing Ben," I say taking his hand. "You know, when Granny Marion was little, she lived in Germany before she had to move to France. It was after a big war, called the First World War and it was the same there. Suddenly, money was worthless and the government kept printing more and more, until you had to take a wheelbarrow full to buy a bag of flour. Then people just gave up using money. Once her mother traded a pair of gloves for a loaf of bread."

He stands there looking sombre, listening carefully.

"Let's hope it doesn't get that bad here," I add trying to make things sound positive.

I look down at him and feel like shouting after the driver: "You should have thought about things earlier!" but I decide not to. Who am I to judge him?

There is no escaping it; Belgrade is an unnerving place. It isn't because everyone is running around waving Serbian flags, applauding Slobodan Milošević, the Serbian president for taking them into an idiotic conflict and ruining the economy. There's an air of tired resignation that pervades everything. It seems people are slipping deeper and deeper into war without thinking about the consequences. Almost no one protests. Nobody really questions the war. Not a single person does anything about the situation. There's a blind acceptance. I can't help wondering why, if the taxi driver doesn't like the fact his wages aren't worth anything, he doesn't do something about it?

For the first time, I begin to understand what it must have been like in Nazi Germany in the 1930s. It's as if people think everything is beyond them and they are being sucked into a vortex. On the one hand I feel guilty that I am so quick to apportion blame, since I have the luck not to be born here, but then on the other hand, I think the fact that Tim is risking his life to find out what is really happening on the frontline to both Croats and Serbs does make it my business and I have the right to criticise what I see. That said, I'm often just as guilty as everyone else in this city. I push the situation to the back of my mind, as I try to get on with everyday life. It goes on even if our new home is the pariah of Europe. The banknotes are still fluttering in the gutter. Ben bends down and picks them up and we walk away to do the shopping.

Eventually inflation will hit a record annual rate of 851,000,000,00 0,000,000,000,000,000,000,000,000,000,000,000,000,000,000,000, 000,000,000,000,000,000,000,000,000 per cent. At one point, a bunch of carrots costs an annual salary. New banknotes are constantly being reissued. The biggest has a face value of 50,000,000,000 but is worthless as soon as it is printed. Life in Belgrade does indeed become like surviving in 1920s Germany. Wages have no value almost as soon as they are paid. I'm lucky - I have foreign currency.

Along the main street are rows of young men standing outside the shops, whispering, "*Devize, devize,*" under their breath. They want to change money on the black market. Ironically this is a cash economy now. I wrote my last traveller's cheque, in a scrum of people, trying to withdraw their life savings from the bank next to the flat. The panic was frightening. Ben was knocked over in the surge of people fighting to get to the cashiers. Then the bank closed and it hasn't opened since, although every day a crowd gathers expectantly. Ben gives them a wide berth.

"What are they whispering?" he asks every time we pass a moneychanger.

"*Devize,* it means they want to change money."

He's growing up to be an incorrigible opportunist and asks:

"Will they change anything for money?"

He has this live-for-the-moment streak in his character. I wonder if it has something to do with the war and what he would be like if we had never brought him here. I have never thought carefully about what effect moving to another country, especially this one, would have on him. It was an oversight.

I change our money with a man in the Press Centre, who has staked out a profitable patch all to himself. Ben watches, as he counts out a wad of notes that reaches as high as the top of my coffee cup but is only worth fifty German marks, which is less than £20. His eyes are fixed on the cash:

"Cor, Mummy! What can we get with that?"

Exactly! I feel the same elation. We may have foreign currency but I still have to get to the shops and spend this wad of money before inflation renders it worthless. It's like being a contestant in a crazy TV game show. We're on a mad dash to the shops. I stuff the money in my pocket and get up quickly. It's the fun of the chase. Belgrade may be unnerving but this live-for-the-moment atmosphere is intoxicating.

One of the receptionists rushes up to give the kids a kiss. They are a big hit in the Press Centre. A waiter pops out of the restaurant to see Esti and it's a round of saying "*dovidjenja*" or "goodbye" to everyone and waving madly to all and sundry until we get on our way. Their enthusiasm for the children is boundless.

As we dash to the supermarket, Ben starts muttering under his breath to Esti:

"Wizz ya! Wizz ya!"

It sounds unnervingly like: "Fleece 'ya, fleece 'ya!"

Esti looks at him, from under the brim of her fake fur hat, suspiciously. At the checkout, the woman in front of us leaves her change, a few crumpled worthless notes, on the plastic bags, at the end of the counter. I'm surprised how many people do this. I can hear my grandmother, my father's mother, who managed the accounts at the butcher's shop, saying: "Look after the pennies and the pounds will look after themselves." The suburban West Midlands seem a long way away from this chaos – thank God, I hate the place. Ben's voice brings me back to reality:

"Doesn't she want that money? Can I have it?"

He never misses a trick. There are no pennies to look after here any-way. Hyperinflation has made Yugoslav coins redundant. We scurry home with six boxes of French ice cream - all mint. There may be no milk but there's always ice cream. I try not to stare too long at the gyp-sies and poverty-stricken old age pensioners wading into the fountain to retrieve the notes that Belgraders have tossed in the water now that small change is a thing of the past.

As time rolls by the only coins the kids ever see are Deutschemarks as German money soon replaces the Dinar and becomes the unofficial currency of what's left of Yugoslavia. As inflation spirals out of control even Ben stops picking up other people's discarded, crumpled notes at the checkout. They are worthless. From now on, Ben only wants to be paid in German coins. It will take years to change his attitude. He'll also grow up to have no idea of the value of money and be the most extravagant member of the family. I blame Slobodan Milošević.

Despite all this, Belgrade is wonderful. Moving here from Bucharest has been like emigrating to California. We're back in the consumer-ist world, or at least, after Bucharest, war-torn, inflationary Yugoslavia seems like the real thing. Hot water flows out of the taps. We can buy fish fingers, frozen peas, pizza mixes, Jaffa Cakes and marshmallow bis-cuits. There's even a McDonald's! And guess what? We have a washing machine! Esti hasn't seen one before and holding the door and staring through the porthole, while the multi-coloured clothes spin round, is her favourite hobby. It's a dangerous one though, as the machine has a tendency to leap around the bathroom.

When the weather is good, she stands on the small, wrought iron bal-cony, looking at the traffic whizz past chanting: "*Ma-ma-ma maşina.*" It's Romanian for "car". She speaks as much Romanian as she does Eng-lish and answers not only to the name Princess, but also to "*Scumpi*", which means "sweetie" but comes from the word *scump* for expensive. It suits her perfectly. She will grow up to have chic, pricey tastes. Serbian, however, confuses our Romanian princess for a long time. Next door lives a very friendly old lady. When we go in and out, she pops her head out to see what is going on. Ben and I wave and shout:

"*Dovidjenja!*"

"Esti!" shouts Ben indignantly. "What are you shouting? Mummy, did you hear that?"

"I didn't hear anything, Ben, I'm just hoping this stupid lift will come and I don't have to wave and shout "goodbye" for the fifth time."

"She said, 'Tom and Jerry!'"

He starts saying "Tom and Jerry" very fast and it does indeed sound like "*dovidjenja.*"

"She's crazy, Mummy! Listen she's still shouting it at the old lady."

It's true, she is. I visualise Serbian paramilitaries shouting, "Tom and Jerry" at their victims, as they ethnically cleanse parts of Croatia.

The old lady next door is always there. In fact, I never see her leave the building in four years, apart from for a two-week trip in summer to see her sister, who lives in Vojvodina, north of Belgrade. She always opens her door and asks, "husband?" with a worried expression when she hasn't seen Tim for a while. She nods, when I tell her the name of the latest frontline. She lives in one room and has dyed, copper coloured hair. I never find out what she's called. We buy her biscuits at Christmas and she gives the kids little jelly bunnies, called *Zeka*.

When Tim is home the flat is a hive of activity with a stream of journalist friends coming and going. We host a lot of parties. The talk is about the war. It often turns to the death of a journalist and photographer but doesn't linger there long. There's a lot of laughter. Tonight, Matt Frei from the *BBC* has come round with a gaggle of other reporters. He's bought Ben a white plastic lorry with the letters UN stuck on the side by some opportunist sales person. They are playing a game of aid convoys on the carpet. My mother is here for a visit. She passes round a bowl of *Smoki Flips*, peanut flavoured corn puffs. There are a lot of affairs going on – the rules that govern everyday life seem to have gone out of the window. I notice that two of our guests are clearly getting intimate even though they're both married to other people. The humour is black and the wine is strong. At the end of the evening my mother is beaming and looks ten years younger:

"I haven't had such fun in a long time," she tells me.

"See. Don't believe everything you see on TV. They edit out all the fun bits and the boring hanging about," says Tim.

Although some days it can feel like we are dancing on other people's graves I suppose that's part of the fun of war.

The reporters move in a pack and roll into town all at once. Some of them boast about the dangerous side of the job. They are daredevils and have a certain glint in their eye. I can see the thrill of it is an addiction. These are the people who will take unnecessary risks when they are carried away by the moment. I check for that glint constantly in Tim's face but so far he looks just the same. I study it more carefully these days. I like watching him when he is asleep.

The excitement of the move has made it easier for the three of us to accept the main problem that our family always seems to have. We are in one country and Tim is in another. He has been in Croatia for six weeks and the flat can feel very empty at times. I miss Elena's constant chatter. I also miss her help. We have no vacuum cleaner and there are none for sale in the shops. Vacuum cleaners, which I guess were made in Slovenia or Croatia, have disappeared; so have mops. I am left to clean the wooden floors on my hands and knees. It reduces me to tears. All the frustrations and anxieties of my everyday life become centred on this single task. Did I study at university for five years to end up doing this? Maybe my boss was right. I am not cut out to be a housewife. I'm sure that this would have happened wherever we lived. Mops or no mops something would have got me down in the end. All mothers at home with small children have days like this. I need a job but I've no babysitter and my husband is besieged hundreds of miles away. I'm supposed to be being a role model for Esti but, even if I had a babysitter, I'm not sure I could leave the children. They need me or maybe I need them. I'm not sure. Anyway what job could I do? I can only think of one and I couldn't just abandon them and go off to report from a frontline, which is realistically the only job I think I could do here. We might both be killed. I'm stuck. We don't need the money - so why am I crying? I take it all out on the floor.

Then, one day I see a small ad for a second-hand vacuum cleaner. The owner is leaving Yugoslavia. We buy it for $17! A few weeks later when we get back to the flat after a trip to the shops and, just as life is looking up, the phone rings. There's a croak and then I hear a woman's voice. It's the lady who had sold me the vacuum cleaner:

"You know that vacuum cleaner, I sold you? I want you to give it back now! I've decided not to emigrate after all. Bring it back to my flat at 4pm!"

I can't believe I'm hearing this. This vacuum means so much to me, how can she take it back? It may blow dust, rather than sucking up crumbs but it beats getting down on my hands and knees with a wet cloth. There are simply no machines, even as bad as this, on sale anywhere in Belgrade anymore.

"No! I'm not giving it back! You sold it to me," I say sternly.

"I'm not emigrating anymore and I want my vacuum cleaner back," she shouts.

"You can't do that! You sold it to me. No! That was the deal. I'm sorry. Goodbye."

I hang up feeling outraged. Why isn't the stupid woman leaving? I feel a little bit guilty. I must be going mad. Ben appears the moment the phone rings. He hopes it was Tim on the line:

"Who was it?"

I tell him.

"You should give it back Mummy?"

"I'm not giving it back!" I say like a petulant toddler.

I love my vacuum cleaner. Ben wrinkles his forehead and looks a bit stern. He's imitating me.

"Sweeping the floor with a dustpan and brush was too much. It made me cry!"

He still looks stern. In these kinds of things, he is always on the Serbs' side. It may sound odd but this is a wonderful moment. I know he really knows me. Stuff work – this is more important.

Winter arrives in its usual, creepy, Balkan way. The sky has turned the colour of pewter and it looks like it might snow. When we moved in September, most of the other people in the flats were old age pensioners. Now, they've all started dying. Luckily, there are no open topped funeral carriages here but the large, grey wooden doors of our apartment block are covered in black-rimmed death notices. They are there to inform passers by of which of the residents has died.

"What's that one say?" asks Ben chirpily.

Now, I know why I have a masters degree in Russian Government and Politics. It was to prepare me to translate Serbian death notices for Ben. I start reading aloud.

"Is that the old man with the white hat, Mummy?"

"Oh dear, probably."

He was a lovely, friendly old man. I feel sorry for him.

"Who's next?"

He's so chipper; I'm horrified but admit it's entertaining. How can he possibly think he has the right to lecture me about giving back a vacuum cleaner with this attitude?

He bounds up the stairs before I can point this out.

Our flat has wooden, double doors and a parquet floor. It's white-washed and furnished with basic, brand new furniture, although the sofa is a hideous purple with swishes of grey and blue. It has two doors that open onto the bedroom and large glass ones that lead into the sitting room. It's all my own place. It's our first real home. There are no one else's ornaments and knick-knacks but mine. The kids have a huge bedroom, which looks out over the top of Marx-Engels Square. Ben, who liked my version of the Communist Manifesto for three-year olds back in Bucharest, is very proud to live on what must be the last Marx-Engels Square in Europe. This is the centre of Belgrade. Dotted around the square are a collection of large, Stalinist-style un-friendly looking buildings. Bordering the small park, along the other side of the apart-ment, there is a collection of tasteful neo-classical, turn-of-the-century government offices and the Yugoslav parliament. When we moved in, I was worried about the noise from the traffic, but since the war started petrol has been in short supply and a lot of the cars have disappeared. I have this idea that the war is outside the front door but not in the flat, which is ridiculous, but it makes me feel better.

I walk over to the video to put on *Fireman Sam*, while I cook the fish fingers we've bought for tea. On the main square, by the fountain, a row of creamy, brown coloured coaches have pulled up. About a hundred old people, with striped, plastic suitcases and cardboard boxes, get out and sit on the edge of the flowerbed. The war has never come so close to my front door.

"Who are they?" says Ben pulling his wicker chair up, so he can see better.

"I guess they've lost their homes in Croatia. They're refugees."

"What - Croats?"

"No! Idiot! Croats wouldn't come here would they? Think straight, they're Serbs from Croatia."

"What were they doing there?"

Thinking straight doesn't get you anywhere here. This explanation takes us through the bath and into his pyjamas. If you think your children are boring, it is your own fault – you can make them as interesting as you want them to be.

After the bath, he's back at the window checking on progress.

"There are still some of the old people there. Isn't anyone coming to get them? How come they are just sitting there like that?"

"They've had a shock. They've just been driven from their homes. What do you expect them to do? Go to the pizza restaurant? I don't expect they have any money either."

He doesn't answer but he does grow up fascinated by maps showing ethnic divisions.

I don't rush to put him to bed. I won't have anyone to talk to when he is asleep. I expect you think I'm a strange mother. Esti has dozed off. He turns the TV on. A black and white newsreel flickers on the screen:

"Who's that man on telly, Mummy?"

"Adolf Hitler. He was the leader of the Germans in the Second World War. He's the reason that Granny Marion couldn't stay living in Germany and fled to France. He wanted to kill all the Jews, so she had to run away."

I have worried about how, one day, I was going to tell Ben that Jews were so hated that they had been slaughtered in their millions. I was shocked when I discovered this as a child. The big difference here however is that I am telling Ben, not a simple if nasty historical fact, but that someone hated his family enough to try to murder them. To my surprise he accepts the hard facts of the Holocaust as if he knows them instinctively. There is no need to discuss it and he moves on. I feel short-changed.

"Why's he on telly?" is all he asks.

It's a fair question. This isn't just some history documentary that is on by chance. Serbian TV is an endless cascade of propaganda. In this carefully chosen clip, Hitler is meeting Ante Pavelvić, the Croatian *Ustasha* or fascist leader. By the time I come back from the kitchen with a glass of wine, there are pictures of Serbs murdered by the *Ustashas* fifty years ago all over the screen. Thank goodness the wine is good in Yugoslavia. It helps keep me sane. Ben is glued to the screen:

"Who are they, Mummy?"

I could just turn the set off and change the subject. I don't. I explain how Serbs were considered part of the sub-human Slav race, according to the Nazis and their (Slav) Croatian allies. He does indeed have an odd mother:

"One of the reasons people don't complain and make a fuss about the war is that they are frightened that it's going to be a re-enactment of the Second World War, Ben. They're scared."

He looks at me carefully. I think it is time to change channels and be a bit more normal. Perhaps I am bringing him up the wrong way. On the other side is another regular, a movie in which Farah Fawcett-Majors tries to murder all her children. It's on at least once a month and alternates with *The Third Man*. I give up and switch the set off.

The atmosphere here is one of dogged resistance against the enemy. Serbs see themselves as victims in this war. All the little boys in Belgrade wear battle fatigues. Ben is desperate for a pair. The next day when I pick him up from school, a small, white modern building in the suburbs, I ask:

"Did you have a good day, Ben?"

"Great! We played building a wall to keep the Croats out."

"What!"

"Yeah, it was great, I got to shoot over it and kill them."

"We need to get a few things straight. Your father is being besieged in Dubrovnik. That's Croatia. He's being shot at by Serbs! And you did what?"

"I was fighting for those old ladies we saw outside last night."

I'm beginning to think I'm not up to this. Life was supposed to be easier in Belgrade. There has to be more, not less, plain speaking in our house I think.

After lunch, the phone rings. It's Tim. I'm amazed. We haven't spoken for six weeks, as there are no phone connections between Serbia and Croatia anymore. E-mails and mobile phones haven't arrived yet. I can't believe it's him. It is a fantastic moment. He asks me what is going on. My mind goes blank. I can't think of anything to say. He tells me he can't stay on the line long as the switchboard at the *Times* have rigged this up somehow and the call is incredibly expensive:

"I just wanted to tell you, that I didn't get on the last boat evacuating refugees."

My mouth falls open:

"What! Why not?"

I feel like I want to kill him. He should be with me. He's now trapped in the city. There is no way in or out. He could be killed by a sniper or by the shelling. If Dubrovnik falls there could be a bloodbath.

"I saw a woman getting on board and she had a little baby in a pram and a boy just like Ben, who was holding a teddy. She made me think of you. I thought I have to stay for all the people who are left behind."

There isn't any time to discuss anything else. He's surprised me. I had no idea he was so moral and he's right. If there are no journalists left in the city anything could happen. I was always brought up to think that you should have a job that gave something back to society. Tim has certainly got that. In supporting him I hope we are making a small but positive contribution to the world. It comes at a price though. I feel sorry for Tim, he's missing out on the kids growing up and we are missing out on him. I feel like a single mother. In the meantime the three of us pull a little bit closer together and wait.

Ben decides his Dad is a big hero. At least that is a relief. Someone round here is setting him a good example at last. I'm left with the problem of explaining why he has decided to stay in a city under siege to my father-in-law.

"I think Tim is being very reckless," he says sternly.

I side with Tim and, after the moral argument, I point out that there's also the more mundane one, which is that he could get the sack if he leaves and then where would we all be? My father-in-law is a businessman. He listens, sighing deeply down the phone. He was in the army in the Second World War. I guess he knows more about battlefields than I do. I detect a sense of vulnerability in his voice. I try to be considerate and not pick a fight. We have a tendency to bicker about things.

"You can't possibly stay there," he says definitely. "It's not a place for the children."

I'm incensed. This is the most interesting place I've ever been:

"Don't be ridiculous! It's a great place for the kids. They are seeing exciting things. What are they supposed to do? Fester in Holland Park?"

He sighs:

"Well if that's what you think. Just remember the fact that just because the two of you find it interesting doesn't necessarily mean it's good for the children."

I'm so cross, he is lucky he is London.

Just like Grandpa, Esti isn't impressed with Tim either. When he finally comes home she turns her head the other way when he tries to give her a kiss. I have flu and am in a bad mood. He tells me he feels like he has come back to enemy territory. I'm furious. I live here.

Late at night, on the same day that Tim tells me he is staying in Dubrovnik, my friend Sophie calls from Bucharest. Her boyfriend is in Dubrovnik with Tim and has also decided not to leave. She asks:

"Do you get used to this Rosie? Does it get any easier?"

"Ask me in ten years time," I reply.

8 - Gunfire in Sarajevo

The February half term holidays have just started. As I bundle Ben into the car outside the school gate, I can hear one mother - the wife of a diplomat - discussing her upcoming skiing holiday in Austria. He asks expectantly:

"What are we doing, Mummy? The teacher asked us all if we were going away."

I feel bad. We have no plans. Ben always has an uncanny knack of making me feel that I'm under-achieving.

We drive home through a sea of greyness. I try to change the subject:

"Do you know Ben that Belgrade actually means 'white city?'"

"It's not white!" he grumbles sticking his chin deeper into the collar of his coat.

Whoever named this town can't have been here in the winter, when its large 1950s buildings merge with a leaden, cloudy sky. There's always a damp, chilly feel in the air too. Belgrade is built on an exposed promontory, at the point where the Sava and the Danube rivers meet. The damp is only driven out by the freezing *koşava* wind, which blows from the depths of Siberia, until it hits the old part of town, which is perched on the brow of a rocky outcrop. In the park outside our flat, the snow has turned to a freezing slush. It couldn't look less inviting.

Back in the flat, Tim is in bed with flu. The climate is really unhealthy. He's due to go to Sarajevo tomorrow, where a referendum on independence is being held. The European Community (EC) has announced that Bosnia-Herzegovina will be granted recognition as an independent state, if the majority of its citizens vote "yes". The Serbian population have already had their own referendum and they've voted unanimously to stay in Yugoslavia. I'm packing Tim's suitcase. He really looks ill:

"You can't possibly drive there, it'll take hours in this weather," I say as I roll up his grey t-shirt and stuff it down the side of the bag.

It's his lucky t-shirt, which I always put it in his suitcase. Since the war broke out in Croatia I've become more and more superstitious. Ben who is on the bed, sitting next to his father, sees an opportunity:

"Can we drive him?"

I wonder why I didn't think of that.

"Yes, Tim. Let me drive you. In this state, you'll have an accident," I say quickly.

I have a fear of car crashes. In my pop charts of fear they are number two after plane crashes and just before sinking ferries. Driving him is the only way I'm going to allow him to get there. There's talk of the war spreading to Bosnia if, as expected, the referendum gives the thumbs up to independence. But everyone knows that a war in Bosnia will be far worse than the one in Croatia. It's impossible to believe that that will happen. It's 1992 after all. But, now I am much more concerned about the ice on the road.

The journey takes us through various armed roadblocks and round plenty of icy bends. The battle lines are already being drawn up. Ben is hanging over the front seat, as we drive up to the summit of a snowy hill:

"Great! A roadblock! I like roadblocks. Look at his gun Dads! Is he going to shoot us?"

A man in military fatigues stands by the side of the road with a rifle. I slow down.

"Don't say anything," warns Tim, as he winds down the window. Ben is wide-eyed. The cold air blows straight in. He watches carefully as the man turns the pages of our passports and looks at Tim's papers and accreditations. Esti looks wary. She may be tiny but she can feel the seriousness of the moment. He waves us on with his gun. As I drive off, Ben turns around and gazes at him standing alone on the brow of the hill.

The road passes through the Drina Valley. During the Second World War there was fierce fighting here. Communist Partisans fought *Ustashas* and Muslim militias who in turn fought Serbian royalist or *Chetnik* forces. It's wild, unspoilt and rocky. It's covered in snow and looks like a scene from a fairytale.

We finally pull into Sarajevo.

"Wow! Look at the hotel," Ben shouts, as we drive into the parking lot of the Holiday Inn. "It looks like it's made out of Lego!"

It's a yellowish cube-like building, which does indeed resemble one of his creations. I notice immediately that Sarajevo is built along a narrow valley surrounded by mountains.

As I unpack the suitcase Ben jumps up and down on the bed:

"What we gonna do, Mummy?" he asks breathlessly.

"I don't know. How about a cake?"

Esti claps her hands.

"Yes! Cake! Yes, yes!"

In moments we are settled at a table in the atrium-style lobby. The two of them love hotels and revel in every moment of this, as if we are taking tea in the Ritz. After they've devoured two enormous chocolate concoctions we decide to cross the road, to see if there is anything interesting in the National Museum opposite the hotel.

It's a nineteenth century yellowy coloured building with a random collection of bits and pieces of local history. Its large, echoing rooms are full of old-fashioned, wooden display cases. It doesn't impress Esti, who falls asleep in the pushchair. Ben however, is in his element. He loves all museums, even the Balkans' most boring ones. He is riveted by the exhibits, especially of bits of rock and what, I think, are arrowheads. We spend two hours staring at what must be the world's most unimaginative displays, while I laboriously translate the little typed-up explanations that have gone brown at the corners. As usual, we are the only people in the place. People don't go on these kinds of outings in this corner of the world. The empty museum seems quite normal.

We pass the evening in the hotel bar talking and laughing with other journalist friends and colleagues, while Esti and Ben make a collection of cocktail sticks and empty peanut packets. The main topic of conversation is whether there will really be a war in Bosnia. No one is sure what will happen. There's a buzz in the air. This is a big story. Everyone is excited. Tim has just returned from the ski resort village of Pale, just outside Sarajevo. The Bosnian Serbs will soon make it their headquarters. He recounts a meeting with a group of Serb men and how he asked them if they were scared of a possible war. "We are armed up to here," they told him pointing at their necks, "why should we be frightened?" was their answer. Lying in bed in the dark, I ask Tim if he thinks there will be a war:

"I can't believe they could be so stupid. It's not as if they don't know what it will be like," he replies.

That's the logical analysis. Exhausted, he falls asleep immediately before I can get a deeper assessment of the situation.

The next day, he's up early and leaves immediately after breakfast to cover the referendum. After weeks of grey skies, the sun has finally decided to show its face. I feel really upbeat, almost as if we are on a holiday. There can't possibly be a war today. The sky is blue and the slush on the pavement has dried up in the warm sunshine by the time we get outside. We set off to explore.

"Look! Mummy, look!"

Ben pulls at my sleeve yanking the buggy round. He's pointing in the window of a tiny, dingy-looking shop. Sitting on a yellowy paper lining, among the cartons of apple and apricot drinks arranged artistically in pyramids, is a small, green, toy armoured personnel carrier.

"I want it! It'll go with the tank that Mihai gave me. Can we buy it?"

He looks so desperate. How can I possibly say no? The only problem is that I'm not sure it's for sale.

"It looks a bit like a decoration, don't you think?"

We go into the shop, which has a small selection of notepads with kittens on and coloured pens from China, dotted around the biscuits. Ben's luck is in. The armoured personnel carrier is for sale. As the shop assistant lifts the little green model out of the window, she blows the dust off and hands it over. It's a snip at roughly one mark.

Ben brumms it up and down his coat, as we walk along the bank of the river Miljacka, to see the spot where Archduke Franz Ferdinand, the heir to the Austro-Hungarian throne was assassinated in June 1914. I remember my history teacher writing "Sarajevo" on the blackboard, as none of us knew how to spell it, let alone where it was. I was captivated by the grainy photographs in the textbook and now I'm here in what I once thought was a faraway, exotic place. I feel a tremendous sense of achievement swelling up inside as I try to explain my excitement to Ben who gazes around him at the hard-faced skyscrapers and apartment blocks, singularly unimpressed. They don't look very exotic. At last they give way to faded, candy-coloured crumbling edifices with a real central European feel.

"They must have been built by the Austrians Ben, when they occupied the city in 1878. Until then it had spent four hundred years under Ottoman rule. Wow! Isn't it great!"

Although still elegant, most of the buildings are in a state of decay. Their paintwork is chipped and peeling. There's no sun on our side of the road. The bricks here look dark and menacing. He smiles up at me. I can see he is slightly amused at my antics. We stop in the gloomy shade outside the museum dedicated to the assassin, the Bosnian Serb, Gavrilo Princip. It's closed. I can't believe it. I rattle the door. I'm within yards of the spot where the gunshots that catapulted Europe into the carnage of the First World War were fired and no one is interested but me! The place is deserted.

Undaunted, I give a quick lecture, tour guide-style, on what happened here on that fateful day. To my joy Ben listens carefully as I explain that Princip was part of a band of excitable disorganised youthful assassins who wanted to drive the Austrians out of Bosnia, which they hoped would then become part of a pan-Slav state with Serbia at its heart. To my surprise Ben thinks that Princip is a hero and says:

"What were Austrians doing here? He just wanted to get his country back didn't he? I'd do the same."

I quickly add that, reflecting in prison, Princip was wracked with guilt by the consequences of his actions and it wasn't that simple. Unfortunately, the actual spot from which he fired his gun is commemorated by some rather tacky looking footprints, which mark where the nineteen-year old Princip stepped out of the crowd and fired from. The plot was in fact so badly planned it nearly went completely awry. In the end, Princip only got close enough to the Archduke because his driver took a wrong turn and stopped the car. Ben finds this hilarious. I don't think it's funny but then he has grown up surrounded by Balkan chaos and bungling so I forgive him. Personality is shaped by environmental factors, that's for sure. It makes a difference where you are brought up. Esti stares sullenly at the empty road from her buggy.

"Can we have lunch?" says Ben.

He's right. There's nothing to linger for on this sad street corner.

We head for a small, trendy pizza restaurant around the corner. It has dusky pink walls and black shiny chairs with deep purple, flowery covers. It's modern and stylish. Yugoslavs make great pizzas. The best ones have eggs on top. The man sitting next to us is reading the newspaper carefully, while the children slurp down their Cokes. I ask them to be quiet. There's a marked tension in the air. The restaurant is full but nobody is talking. Ben wants to hear more about the murder before the Sarajevo tour continues. I whisper over the lunch, filling in the details of the lead up to the bloodshed of the trenches. Words like "mobilisation" and "armistice" float backwards and forwards across the table. It's better than lingering on today's problems. It's not as if our worrying about them will change the situation. I try to push them to the back of my mind.

Sarajevo is unnervingly peaceful. Without the tourists, Baščaršija, the old Turkish market area, feels like the Ottomans have only just left. Sarajevo was the administrative centre of their western possessions and there are plenty of mosques and minarets. The maze of alleyways is full of tiny shops selling tourist trinkets. They are irresistible. I buy two small cloth dollies, a man and a woman, tied together by a piece of red string. There are lots of exotic embroidered slippers, with turned up toes. They are a hangover from when the city was run by the Turks. As I am short of cash, we decide to come back the next day to buy some for

Ben's cousin, Jo, who lives in Yorkshire. Ben doesn't want to leave:

"Can I do a drawing? I want to draw this place and send a picture to Grandma."

Esti is sleeping off the pizza, so there is no reason why not. There are so many shops selling notepads with cute little pictures on that we are soon set up with pens and paper. He draws while I write some postcards. We put them in the box outside the main post office but I can't find an envelope for Ben's picture, so I put it in my pocket.

"I'm hungry," says Ben.

He never stops eating. Esti needs waking up so I suggest that we buy some chocolate bars and eat them by the river.

At the kiosk, he selects two bars of golden-wrapped *Cipiripi*. These are the kids' favourite chocolate. They taste really sickly and have a picture of a mad looking chipmunk on the packet. They think they are called "chippy-ripi", but it's actually pronounced, "sipi-ripi". As ever it leads to confusion at the cash till. We eat the bars in a scrubby little park, on the riverbank, just opposite from where the famous assassination took place. Ben wants to hear the story again. I've just seen the Yugoslav movie of the murder on TV, so I paint a colourful picture of June 28th 1914 in Sarajevo. It's eerily quiet.

"Will there be a great big war again, Mummy?" asks Ben, while I am carefully sharing out a bottle of water.

A noisy wedding party passes by before I can answer him and within minutes, we hear the sound of gunfire. There's nothing surprising in that, as people are always firing in the air at weddings and on holidays. However, this isn't the usual madcap, repetitive firing that usually goes with celebrations, but rather a couple of sinister sounding shots. We are alone and I feel a little bit unnerved. That's enough sightseeing. I stand up quickly and put the bottle in the plastic bag on the back of the buggy:

"Let's go back to the hotel, kids."

I don't feel safe anymore. Ben doesn't argue.

The mid-afternoon sun is so warm, that even though there's still some snow on the ground, we take our coats off and walk without them for the first time in months. Soon, I've forgotten all about the wedding. On the way back a number of friendly people stop and talk to us, and in particular to admire Esti, who is pushing the buggy in a determined fashion with her huge, fake fur hat still on. Elena would be proud of her for keeping it on while everyone else is being rash enough to take theirs off. Her enormous eyes peep out from under the white fluff. The atmosphere of foreboding feels more intense by the minute. It's only hours until the polls close. I wonder what will happen. The weather is so wonderful and warm that I decide to sit down on a bench in another little park.

"What are you thinking about Mummy?" asks Ben anxiously.

"I was thinking about what Chuck said last year, when we were in Greece."

Chuck is a journalist friend of Tim's who is married to a Yugoslav.

"Do you remember that he said we should move here because there would be rivers of blood in Bosnia?"

As I repeat this story, I suddenly think:

"What am I saying? My mother would be furious if she could hear me."

I hear her voice saying:

"You'll give them nightmares."

Then I think "no" what's the point of hiding things from them? They'll process what they want and ignore the rest. They need to be prepared for what could happen. If nothing happens, they'll forget it.

When we arrive back at the hotel, the kids are starving. I call room service, without bothering to ask for a menu. Foolishly, I forgot my camping stove. The hotel food is pretty predictable. I order the regulation *pohovani sir* (grilled cheese) and a side order of grilled mushrooms. Esti loves mushrooms, which is good luck as in winter vegetables are in short supply, as they aren't imported. About 8pm, I turn off the lights and try to get them to sleep. The room next door has been turned into an edit suite by a TV crew and, through the closed interconnecting door, comes the screeching sound of respooling tape.

"What's that noise?" whispers Ben. "It's scary."

Esti is crying and wriggling around. While I walk up and down with her in my arms, I explain about how the television news is made. This seems to do as a bedtime story. Esti drops off. I can't believe my luck, since over the past month or so, at least three times a week, she has vomited before bed. I have begun to worry that she might be allergic to mushrooms. But the prime suspect is the milk. It comes in long-life packs, with a picture of a cartoon-style cow on the front. It smells and tastes foul but Esti loves it, which is good because that's all that is all there is. I just can't wean her off a bottle even though she is 18-months old. It must be something I'm doing wrong. No sooner have I got her into bed and moved across to cuddle Ben, than she starts crying and throws up all over the hotel's white, pressed, linen sheets. There's curdled milk and mushrooms everywhere. The spooling and respooling of tapes continues frantically next door.

"Wonder what they make of us, Ben, with all these wails and sicking sounds coming from our side of the door?" I giggle.

It all seems quite normal and cosy. He laughs:

"What will we do with the sheets, Mummy?"

"I'll just stick them in the cupboard and worry about it later," I whisper as I get back into bed to give him a cuddle. "At least Esti is asleep now."

In the half-light, I switch on the radio and on the *BBC World Service* I hear that the polls have just closed and there are reports of barricades going up all over the city.

While we lie in the dark room listening to the TV crew next door, there's a volley of gunfire outside the window.

When Tim comes back, he looks tired. I ask him what's going on:

"What happened? How did it start?"

"There was a murder at a Serbian wedding. It all began when the father of the groom was shot. It gave the Serbs the excuse to send out their paramilitaries and set up barricades," he explains.

Ben who is still awake leaps up from under the sheets

"Hey, was it our wedding? The one *we* saw?"

He's wide-eyed, clutching his teddy:

"So it's a new war! We heard the shots of the new war!" he shouts with glee.

When he gets bigger, his ambition will be to watch history unfold in front of his eyes. It already has.

"You need to go to sleep," says Tim, getting into bed next to him.

They fall asleep together. Everything about the bedroom looks so normal. It's hard to believe what is going on outside. I can't sleep. I lie looking at the ceiling, listening to doors opening then slamming shut in the corridor and the occasional gunfire outside.

We spend the next day sitting in the room. It isn't safe to go out. We watch developments on television. There is a live broadcast with cameras positioned all over the city. Tim is out trying to get the latest news. Ben watches the screen carefully:

"Where's Dads? Will he be on TV?"

"Maybe."

He's restless cooped up like this. The day seems to be going on forever. He walks over to the window. I lurch to grab his shirt:

"No! Stay away from there! Someone might shoot!"

But in the end I find it's very difficult to spend all day in a room with beige wallpaper and brown wooden furniture and bedspreads in different shades of tan, without peeping out. A couple of hours pass and I can't resist any longer. I pick him up in my arms and we look out. He feels heavy. He's growing fast. Adorning the Bosnian parliament building opposite there is a huge portrait of Tito and the streets are deserted except for an old man walking his dog. The sky is overcast and it looks like it might rain.

When Esti is sleeping, I take him out of the room to peer over the balcony into the atrium where there are armed Bosnian Serb militiamen sitting on the big sofas. The hotel has become their headquarters. Ben points over the balustrade:

"Look, Mummy! He's got a gun."

I pull his hand back:

"Sssh, Ben! He'll hear you," I whisper. "Come on! Let's go back to check on Esti."

Amazingly, there is room service, but it's only omelette and yet more mushrooms. I try to tell Esti not to eat them, but she does anyway. Ben looks crestfallen:

"I wanted chips!"

"Chips are off today. You're lucky to get that, idiot," I snap.

About six in the evening, I put the two of them in the bath. Just before they get in, there is a major kerfuffle outside the hotel as two buses draw up. While the kids are in the tub, washing and playing with the plastic shower hats and tiny bars of soap, Tim arrives back. He heads straight to the window to see what is going on:

"Rosie, it's the international observers getting on a bus!"

I must look blank as he adds slightly irritated:

"They've been monitoring the poll. Now they're getting out of Sarajevo as fast as they can. I'm going to see if I can get you on."

We shouldn't be here, I know that. The war that everyone was dreading is about to begin. It was probably irresponsible to bring the kids. That's what my father-in-law will tell me. Tim rushes out of the door. I feel sorry for having put him in this position. Now, he has to worry about us as well as his job. I pull the plug out of the bath:

"Quick kids, get out! Maybe, we are leaving."

"Where we going, Mummy?" asks Ben, as I rub him down.

"Maybe, we're going on a bus."

"Where's it going?"

"I don't know. Somewhere. Hurry! I have to dress Esti."

There isn't time to talk.

Within minutes, Tim is back in the room:

"Quick! Get the kids dressed!"

He has managed to get us on the bus. It's going to the airport.

"They'll wait five minutes, but no longer."

"I'll never make it!" I say in disbelief.

Getting the kids out of the house in five minutes is an impossible feat at the best of times. Four minutes later we run through the lobby. When we arrive outside the hotel, the engines are revving and we jump on, just in time. I've got Esti's milk bottle and some nappies stuffed in my pocket next to my passport and I've got the buggy. Then I realise:

"I've forgotten my handbag, Tim. My make-up!"

"Don't worry there's no time. Look after the kids!" he says, as he kisses me quickly. It's dark and cold. Now, the war is starting, I have no idea when I will see him again. I can't take it all in. I glance down at Ben. At least he has his teddy. The doors of the bus shut. He waves to Tim, happily.

Inside, it is completely full, but utterly silent. We have to stand on the steps by the driver. There is nothing else I can do. There are no seats. As he pulls away and starts to drive slowly along the big main boulevard, I press back against the window to stop myself from falling over. I hold Ben's hand tight and worry that I might drop Esti. Slowly, as we edge along the deserted street, it begins to sink in that if anyone starts shooting, we are probably in the most dangerous place on the bus. I'm in the firing line. I wish we had stayed with Tim. Esti senses I'm nervous and starts crying. Her sobs echo in the silent bus and a woman in a large black fur coat hisses:

"Sssh! Quiet!"

I turn to the Irish EC monitor next to me and shrug my shoulders. He smiles back and then I look at the woman more carefully. She is shaking and the fur on her coat is so thick that I can see each hair quivering individually. I wonder who she is. She can't be an international observer as she is clearly a Yugoslav. She looks as if she is fleeing to save her life.

Ben is trying to stand as tall as he can, even though I want him to sit down on the floor in case someone fires at the bus. He is seriously impressed that he is next to an EC monitor. He has even seen this particular one on telly. The EC monitors wear white and he is very proud of a white woolly hat he got for Christmas. He's wearing it now. Their job is to, well…monitor the situation, and if they can manage it, spread some goodwill across the frontlines. It's a tough assignment. Not having grasped the full potential of what is going on, Ben isn't frightened. He starts talking to his hero. He brings out his armoured personnel carrier, which he has hidden in his coat pocket, to show him. Soon the bus stops at a roadblock. Ben asks eagerly what's happening, as the EC monitor steps out to talk to some men with guns. A cold ripple of fear runs over my skin. I don't answer.

When the monitor gets back on, he rearranges the seating in the front, so we can sit down. It's still a bit exposed, but what can I do? The woman in the fur coat is just across the aisle. The bus stops again a few hundred metres down the road and men with rifles come up to the window and start waving their guns. The bus is in total silence. Back in Belgrade we are plagued by car cleaners, who work the traffic lights at the corner of the park near our flat. They wave their windscreen wipers in exactly the same way as these men are waving their guns. Ben pipes up:

"Oh no. Not car cleaners! Not now!"

The EC monitor winks at him and laughs as he gets out to negotiate our way through. No one else says a word. I'm not sure that the bus will be allowed to carry on to the airport. The men are angry and shouting. I'm nervous that they may insist on getting on the bus with us. It could turn very nasty.

They let us pass. We continue through a housing estate. As we drive past, more armed men come out of their back doors and start firing in the air. Ben presses his nose against the window, peering through, studying the darkness:

"Why is he doing that? Is he showing off?"

I nod "yes", as Esti starts to fall asleep.

The bus seems to take a short cut to the airport across a field but in the dark emptiness, it's difficult to tell. It could just be a potholed road.

Eventually we arrive at the airport where the EC monitor guides everyone into the check-in hall. Ben is thirsty, but everything is closed. He's getting tired and cross. After a long wait in the cold departure lounge we are ushered across the deserted runway to a JAT Yugoslav Airlines plane. No one has been issued with a ticket and that's probably why, while I walk slowly across the tarmac, other people, especially the woman in the black fur coat, sprint up the stairs pushing other people out of the way as they go. As the plane takes off there seem to be some people who don't have seats, huddled at the back. By now Ben is in a very bad mood:

"Where is the stewardess? I want my free toy!"

I just wish he would be quiet. This isn't the kind of flight where they hand out free trinkets. The plane stays dark while it flies out over Bosnia. I'm terrified but try not to think about it too much as Tim is in far more danger than I am.

"I want a drink! Where is she? I'm hungry!"

He starts to cry. I snap at him:

"This isn't the kind of flight, where the stewardess checks your seat belt, let alone serves snacks. Please be sensible!"

I try to shock him back into reality, by pointing out why they haven't turned on the lights:

"I think they are worried someone might shoot down the plane, Ben. If they had the lights on perhaps it would be easier to spot."

I feel that I shouldn't say this. Mothers aren't supposed to scare their children but he is the only person I have to talk to. Esti is calmly drinking some milk. Eventually the Swiss man sitting next to us opens his shiny brown leather briefcase and gives Ben a roll. He has saved it carefully from breakfast at the hotel, wrapped in a paper napkin. Ben is impressed and fortunately, at this point, the lights come on.

It's a short flight and we are soon in Belgrade where we are ushered into a queue. At this point, I realise that we are going to have to pay for the flight. I only have a hundred dollars in my pocket and some Dinars, worth about 20 marks. I don't have a credit card because this is now a cash economy. Credit cards don't work here anymore. I'm not too worried, as I don't expect that they will fly us back to Sarajevo although I do begin to get anxious when the Swiss man, who is now at the front of the queue, pulls out his wallet. Several blue 100 mark bills are placed on the counter. Then it's our turn. In Serbian I ask the woman in a blue uniform behind the till, how much it is and she quotes a figure in Dinars that's equivalent to about 15 marks, roughly £5. Amazed at the price difference – we had two seats after all, I assume that she thinks I am a Serb from Sarajevo and scarper before she sees she has made a mistake.

Outside, more EC monitors are waiting with a bus to take the international observers to a hotel. I ask, but they won't give us a lift into the town centre. Luckily, I have just enough Dinars left for the taxi fare. I hope that Tim left some money in the desk draw back in the flat. On the last leg of the journey home, Esti is sick in the taxi. More curdled milk and mushrooms end up on the brown imitation leather seat. I'm not sure if it's the stress or the mushrooms again. Luckily, the taxi driver is listening to loud Balkan pop tunes and doesn't notice that Esti has been sick. I try to pick up the white, soggy lumps in my gloves and pop them into a crumpled piece of paper. It's too late when I realize that it's Ben's picture for Grandma. I suddenly remember the sheets in the cupboard in the Holiday Inn and feel a bit guilty. How long it will be before someone finds them? As I get out of the cab, I notice that a couple of the Sarajevo mushrooms are still on the back seat but the grumpy taxi driver doesn't make me feel like I want to jump back in and pick them up. I wonder what Tim is doing. Although I feel miles from the action and rather jealous, all I really want to do is shut the front door and lock the war out. I want to gather the kids close and keep them safe. That said, it's been a tremendous weekend.

Next day, we take a stroll downtown. We've had to buy more warm clothes, as our entire winter wardrobe is back in the Holiday Inn with Tim. I decide it's time to treat the kids. Luckily, there were a couple of hundred Marks in the desk draw after all.

"What do you fancy?" I ask stopping in front of a toyshop, in a modern shopping centre.

There are so many bags hanging off the buggy that it tips up when Esti gets out. It's a private shop and the window is full of toy soldiers and combat gear mixed in with pink teddies. It takes ages for the two of them to decide what they want:

"That's it! There, Mummy! Down there in the corner. That's what we want."

Ben is pointing to a pastry set. I'm amazed:

"Are you sure?"

I thought it would be a fight between the panda with the pink bow and the set of tanks.

"Yes, we are, aren't we, Esti?"

She nods.

The two of them spend the rest of the day making a bakery out of homemade playdough. I'm not sure what to make of them. Are they in some sort of denial or just being totally normal? My mother calls to say that she got our postcard. To my surprise she opts for normal.

9 - At Home in Belgrade

"Where's Mr Parking? Why doesn't he find us a space?" asks Ben as we drive up and down the street outside our flat.

Ben loves Mr Parking. I can't see him anywhere. Mr Parking is the man who organises the parking lots outside Belgrade town hall. It's an elegant 1880s building that was once the royal palace and is right next to our block of flats. For a tip, he lets us park in the lots reserved for local officials. I haven't seen him for weeks and have to be careful where I put the car, or we'll be towed.

"I think he has gone back to Bosnia to fight, Ben."

"What!" Ben is horrified. "Why? I want to park the car. Doesn't he want to stay here?"

"No, I expect he wanted to go home and defend his village."

"Where is his village?"

"He's from eastern Bosnia, the bit between here and Sarajevo. He told Dads he comes from Kamenica. It's in one of the last bits there that's still under Muslim control."

It's a village close to the town of Srebrenica.

"What! He's a Muslim?"

Ben is amazed:

"But he looks like everyone else!"

"Of course, he does! You don't look different if you're Muslim. Bosnians look the same whether they are Muslims or not."

My mother has just sent him a book about the crusades.

"I thought Muslims looked like Arabs."

Ben never stops asking after Mr Parking as the months roll on:

"What's happened to him?"

"Maybe, he is besieged in his village. It's a Muslim stronghold. He's fighting, I expect."

He always asks:

"Poor Mr Parking. Is he dead?" and I answer:

"Maybe."

I can tell he thinks I'm hiding something but I really have no idea what has become of Mr Parking. The scenarios aren't good though. The fighting in eastern Bosnia is vicious.

After a ten-month siege Kamenica eventually falls to the Serbs. Not long after it has been overrun, Tim goes to watch the exhumation of a mass grave on a hill above the village. It's a sunny winter's day and the corpses steam, as they are lifted out of the frozen ground. The Serbs are looking for their dead. In this part of Bosnia, there are tales of captured Serbian prisoners being roasted on stakes and impaled. Some of the bodies in the grave have had their arms and legs tied up with wire. One has no head. Tim gets back very late at night. His boots are covered in mud from the grave. He leaves them in the bathroom. He's exhausted and falls asleep immediately. I lie next to him in the dark. When I glance across the hallway to the bathroom, I can see his boots. I get up and shut the door. I think about all the things he has seen. I can't take my eyes off him. How can he remain so calm and composed? I would be a nervous wreck. I realize that his kind of journalism is not for me.

When Ben gets up the following morning, he wants to know why the bathroom door is shut. When he opens it he sees the boots. It's inevitable he'll ask about where the mud has come from:

"Why are Dad's boots so dirty? Where's he been?"

"Nowhere special," I say trying to shrug the question off and concentrate on loading the washing machine. I think I should start to be a bit more reticent about things. It's too terrible to contemplate. Tim is still asleep. I look at Ben.

"I wanna know. Tell me!"

He looks determined. He's right. There's no point in lying. It's interesting and worth talking about after all. I close the door. I don't want to wake Tim.

"Daddy's been to see a mass grave in Mr Parking's village. The mud is from the grave. It was being dug up."

"Was Mr Parking in it."

"No. They were Serbs killed by Muslims."

"By Mr Parking?"

"Oh Ben! How do I know?"

"Where has Mr Parking gone now?"

"The Muslims who escaped have gone to Srebrenica. Dads saw their footprints in the snow. They had run away across the fields. I expect he ran off too."

I open the bathroom door and go into the kitchen to make breakfast. He runs off to play Lego. Life goes on. He isn't the slightest bit bothered. A glance inside the family photo album will tell you what our life is really like here. There are endless pictures of parties. Tables covered in pizza and *Smoki Flips*. Kids gorging on Smarties. Dotted between them are pictures of soldiers firing on the frontline and burning houses. I keep the truly gruesome ones in a box under the bed.

It's about eight one evening, when the phone rings. It's Chris Stephen, Tim's friend:

"Hi Rosie, where's Tim?"

"He's trying to get into Srebrenica. It's the Muslim enclave. Conditions are appalling inside. That's the story."

"Srebra… what? Where is it? How do I get there?"

He's in Montenegro.

"Quick Ben! Get the map. It's Chris. He wants to know how to get to Srebrenica."

Ben runs to get the map off the shelf. I can't run too fast. I'm pregnant and having morning sickness in the evening. Ben loves Chris. He plays toy soldiers with him while they discuss battle tactics past and present. Chris always seems to have a copy of the film *Waterloo* somewhere in his luggage. It is one of Ben's favourites. They watch it every time he comes to stay. Chris is one of the most affable and good-humoured people I know. Ben jumps expectantly up and down on the bed next to me:

"Will he take me? Ask him, Mummy!"

I try to stop him leaping on the map, as I search frantically for somewhere called Srebrenica.

As we all get used to the chaos, life seems to get more normal and, at last, I have found a wonderful babysitter, called Maja. Her father's Serbian family originally come from Montenegro, where everyone is fantastically tall. She towers over the kids.

"Why are you so huge?" asks Ben impertinently and nearly everyday.

"We are all tall so we can see over the mountains," she answers.

Ben is impressed. Chris has told him on the phone about Montenegro's incredible gorges and peaks. It is a mountainous, if minute place. It makes up in height for what it lacks in width which is a bit like Maja, who is incredibly thin. She is the perfect foil for Ben.

"Maja! Tell me the story of the Battle of Kosovo again."

Maja begins the epic Serbian poem that tells the story of how the heroic Prince Lazar was defeated by the Turks in 1389, at the Field of Blackbirds, outside modern day Priština, the capital of Kosovo. All Serbs know this story off by heart. Their greatest defeat is turned into a tragic drama in which defeat is turned to victory because Lazar chooses the Kingdom of Heaven rather than a kingdom on earth. He'd rather die than submit to Turkish rule. Better to be killed in battle, than live as a slave. It's the ultimate moral victory. His defeat spelled the end of the medieval kingdom of Serbia and Serbian national identity was kept alive by the continual retelling of such epic tales. Some Serbs relate the story as if it happened yesterday. Ben seems to be moving in this category too:

"Why did Lazar die, Maja?"

"He chose the Kingdom of Heaven."

This is a very symbolic story. Lazar is a sort of Serbian Christ. His death, fighting for what is portrayed as truth and justice, promises a resurrection of Serbia at a later date. This story helped keep the Serbs going as a people through centuries of Ottoman rule. It has a powerful message in modern day Serbia too. It was no coincidence that Milošević sealed his rise to power in 1989 by giving a speech at the battlefield and thus evoking the Lazar myth - but such subtleties are lacking on Ben:

"I would have fought on, what's the point of going to heaven? Couldn't he go abroad? Tell me about his chopped off head. Why didn't he win?"

This is a pertinent question. There was trickery and treachery on the battlefield. The Serbs feel that they didn't really lose the battle in military terms, fair and square. In purely tactical terms they are probably right. The film of the battle is always on TV. It's blood-curdling X-rated stuff. My little boy from Shepherd's Bush sits on the cushions in front of the TV shouting:

"Come on, Lazar, Come on, Lazar!" as his hero leads his men into battle.

I'm amazed that he doesn't need a translation. It makes him seem like a new child. He's learning fast and I realise that he isn't just from Shepherd's Bush anymore.

A few days later, we are walking down the main shopping street, Terazije, to the supermarket.

"Can we go to McDonald's?" asks Esti from the pushchair.

"No point Esti. There aren't any chips," says Ben in a know-all fashion before he turns to me to ask:

"Why aren't there any chips, Mummy?"

"Sanctions, that's what they said," I reply.

"Sanctions, Esti, no chips because of sanctions." He repeats the news to his sister, before turning back to me:

"But, what are sanctions? They don't stop you making chips at home."

Thankfully, it's a long walk to the supermarket, so I can explain. UN sanctions have cut Serbia off from the world economy as a punishment for the war in Bosnia. Now exports and imports have to be considered by a sanctions committee in New York, so trade is at a virtual standstill. The staff at McDonald's told me the chips are imported from Germany although they told Tim that the problem was that there was no diesel to get the chips, or the potatoes, to the restaurant. The extraordinary thing is that there is a working McDonald's in a country at war. It seems out of place. Ben however is more interested in talking about the Kingdom of Heaven again and changes the subject back to Lazar:

"Why did Serbs choose the Kingdom of Heaven?"

"Do they have chips there?" asks Esti.

War or no war, life definitely goes on. I'm now three months pregnant. It has come as a big shock. It was exactly the same with Ben. One surprise was okay but twice? Tim is delighted but my first reaction is total panic. I have just found Maja and, as the war just drags on and on, I'm getting used to it. It's a backdrop to everyday life and I have been thinking about getting some work. After a week of feeling that this pregnancy is a terrible idea, I'm suddenly overwhelmed by a desperate desire to have another baby. It's time to call an obstetrician. I get a number from a friend. When I tell the doctor why I'm calling and that it's my third pregnancy, he just laughs loudly and says:

"You don't need an obstetrician. You need a housekeeper. While you get one fixed come to my clinic all the same. Friday at 10am. The hospital is at the end of Knez Miloša, you know it, don't you?"

He's still laughing when I turn up for the ultrasound. Serbs have one or two children at the most. Three is clearly a big event. He isn't the only person who has found our growing family amusing.

Six months later, at the end of May 1993, Rachel is born in Cornwall. Yet again it's safer to come home for the birth but this time I leave it as late as possible and the whole event is rather like an early summer holiday. She arrives bang on her due date, which is very amenable of her, as Tim has timed it to arrive home the night before. Yet again the excitement has sent me into labour.

"One day he won't make it on time," says my mother.

Rachel is born just after six in the evening. This time I managed to get some drugs to dull the pain and as I lie in the ward recovering, Tim says:

"Right, when shall I book the flights?"

I'm too weak to answer. I look at him in astonishment. I wonder if the war has taken him over.

Ben is delighted with the new baby as, to my surprise, he wanted another sister. He gives her the nickname Rainbow, which is soon corrupted to Ray, and even though my mother thinks it is terrible and sound like a boy's name, it sticks. Ray is an easy-going baby. She is lively, rarely cries and has beautifully defined features across which flickers a cheeky expression. She is even happy to be called Ray and for a week she thinks she comes from a windy, peaceful corner of Europe. She lies happily in her pram in my mother's house. Then she has a rude awakening, as she's flown to Budapest and in the boiling heat of early June, she's bundled into the back of a car for the six-hour drive home to Belgrade. Because of sanctions, we can't just fly there directly. No international flights are allowed into Serbia. The whole journey takes two days.

"Grandma flew straight to Belgrade once," Ben tells Esti as we board the plane. Esti looks at him in amazement:

"Wow!"

I'm not sure if she thinks my mother has magical powers or she thinks Ben is fibbing.

Unfortunately, Ray doesn't think much of Belgrade when we finally get there. She cries endlessly for the first 24 hours. Balkan summers are unbearably hot and this one is no exception. The thermometer is hitting 37°C. Eventually I decide that it's better not to bother to warm up her milk. She has it straight from the fridge. She calms down as we stretch out in front of the fan that I keep at the end of the bed.

"Why doesn't Ray like it here?" asks Esti bewildered. "I'm glad to be home. It was all right at Grandma's but I prefer it here. Why doesn't Ray? It's much better at home. England is odd you know. They don't sell *Smoki Flips.*"

Two days after we get back, Tim leaves for a six-week stint in besieged Sarajevo. He is beaming from ear to ear as he packs his case. We wave him "goodbye" from the little, wrought iron balcony that looks over the Yugoslav parliament building. Esti holds my hand tight:

"Will he be okay?" she asks quietly.

"What about snipers?" asks Ben.

Unfortunately they know just how dangerous Sarajevo is now.

They've seen the pictures on the TV news in England of people being shot in the streets, journalists among them. They don't show these images on Serbian television. I can't hide things from them anymore. I try to sound definite:

"Of course, he will."

I feel a shiver run through me. I know I am actually, really frightened but I don't want to show it. I must wave Tim off happily. Tiny Ray is in my arms and the other two gaze in the direction that Tim has just driven off in. A lot of journalists in Bosnia have armoured cars but Tim has the red, family saloon car, which is covered in biscuit crumbs and the stains from leaking milk bottles. I don't want to let the three of them out of my sight for a moment. I want to pick them all up and hold them as tight as possible.

"Cheer up Mummy!" says Ben. "Well look after you won't we Esti?"

He pats my arm. I think I'm going to cry as a wave of motherly slush rushes through me.

Summer in Belgrade is wonderful. Life erupts out on to the street – and so do we. We spend weeks digging in the sandpit in the park, opposite the flat. When we aren't in the local playground, we are eating pizza in the square by the fountain. I think about Tim all the time. There is always a worrying thought, somewhere at the back of my mind, that something terrible might happen. It's a bond that keeps us tied together. Then one afternoon, we are having such fun in the park, I forget all about him. When we get in, the phone rings. It's Tim. He says shakily:

"I'm just calling to say that I'm not dead."

I stand with the receiver in my hand, without moving. My mouth is wide open. He tells me he has been in a car crash but is all right. I always thought I would know the moment something went wrong. Just like people in the movies. It makes me more nervous than ever. I decide that I'm not getting used to this war after all.

"Daddy's had a car crash but he's not dead. He just called to tell us he's fine," I tell Ben.

"Poor Dads. Glad he's not dead." He looks quite chirpy and asks: "What's for dinner?"

Most Sunday afternoons we go to Kalemegdan. It's a large park, which is built in the grounds of an old, rambling Ottoman fortress that stands on top of a rocky crag above the point where the Danube and Sava rivers meet. It's not often that you can actually see political fault lines, but here you can. The rivers were once the border between the Ottoman and Habsburg empires. Ben gazes out over the plain below.

"The Turks were here and the Austrians were there," I explain. "That's why Croats are Catholic and use the same alphabet as us and Serbs are Orthodox and write in Cyrillic."

It's no surprise that he will grow up to be fascinated by empire building. It's extraordinary to watch his personality being put together. It's like building a Lego castle and adding a brick at a time, slowly, over the years. I wonder what he will be like when it's finished?

The highlight of a visit to Kalemegdan is the zoo. You can pick up a lot about a place on a trip to the zoo. Belgrade's menagerie is chaotic. It's built into a corner of the huge, ramshackle castle. There's a smell of popcorn in the air as we buy our tickets. Esti loves the salty variety that they sell here and clutches her bag carefully as we walk past the elephants.

"Hey Esti!" calls Ben. "Do you remember when we went to the zoo with Grandma and that elephant leant over the rail and ate all your popcorn? You almost had a heart attack."

Most people buy the popcorn to feed to the animals.

"Ray, you missed the giraffe," says Esti sticking her head in the push-chair. "Someone gave it a bag of crisps and it died. It ate the whole thing. It didn't open the packet first. It gobbled it all up!"

We move on past the howling wolves. Ben is waving at them through the bars. My heart leaps and I yell at the top of my voice:

"Come away Ben!"

He turns round and makes a rude face. Why? More fool him. After we leave Belgrade, one of these wolves will bite the finger off another correspondent's little boy. Round the corner, there's a baby monkey in a nappy that is the star of the show this summer, but Esti rushes past him and on to the lions. The enormous lion is the only thing she wants to see. He lives in a tiny enclosure, built into the walls of the fort. He's clearly gone mad and he stands on a rock all day roaring. Esti is less than a metre tall, but she stands in front of the cage staring at him. She seems fearless. She is like her brother and her father, defiant in the face of danger. Ben pulls the strap of her sundress:

"Come on! Let's get a move on Esti. We want to see Arkan's tiger."

"I don't. I like this one," she says firmly. He can't boss her around.

Serbia's most notorious and brutal gangster-militiaman keeps his pet tiger in a cage, not far from where the giraffe used to live. The murderous paramilitary band that he runs is called the Tigers. They are the shock troops of ethnic cleansing and operate under the control of Serbia's Ministry of Interior. The most exciting moment of a trip to the zoo for Ben is gawping at his favourite big cat. I don't mind, as he has a fairly clear idea of what Arkan gets up to and can see what is wrong with it. There's another little boy standing next to him in khaki trousers. I wonder what is going through his mind. There is no escaping the war, not even here. Ben turns with a cheeky look on his face:

"Can we go to his bakery, Mummy?"

Arkan has a bakery near his headquarters, in a smart suburb of town. It gives his business a legitimate front. Ben's winding me up. It works. I fall for it and start to rant:

"No, I'm not buying bread off him and you know it. I'm not giving him any money."

He laughs and leaves me feeling that I am the fool for taking the moral high ground.

10 - A Festive Confusion

After Lazar, Ben's biggest hero is Tintin. French schooling, I have learnt, is all about creating little Frenchmen, not just learning another language. We may be in Serbia, but Gallic culture is coming a close second to Serbian epics. The school has a small video library and we borrow copies of *Tintin et l'étoile mystérieuse* and *L'oreille cassée*, to while away the autumn weekends. I don't understand a word.

At school, the main theme of the term is *Spot va à l'école*. That's more my style. The homework is to glue little pieces of paper with the words, "*Spot aime sa maîtresse*", which means, "Spot loves his teacher" in his exercise book. Both Ben's teachers are lovely, so he is happy to do this. They are French, married to Yugoslavs. The eldest son of one of them was at university in Sarajevo when the war broke out and left his university records book behind when he fled. They think Tim is wonderful because, on his last trip, he managed to track it down and bring it back. As a result they lavish affection on the kids. There's nothing unusual in that though, as French kindergarten teachers are big on kisses anyway, even if they are strict. They give a formal peck on both cheeks to every child when they arrive and again, when they leave. The homework is actually a piece of propaganda. You are supposed to "*aime ta maîtresse*" and do exactly what she says.

This term, Esti has started school. She loves it and is happy to kiss teachers and tidy up, probably because Ben is still a reluctant recruit. He just can't understand why he has to go to school every day, let alone get there on time. There's no flexibility about obeying the rules in a French school. It's something that will always be a problem for him. It brings out his laddish qualities. Although he may kick and squirm against teachers telling him what do, on the whole, he gets away with it because he enjoys the work and he's determined to speak better French. It's years before he realises that not everyone goes to school in another language from their mother tongue. It's amazing what children don't realise if you don't bother to point it out.

The Lycée itself, is tiny. Since the international community has all but disappeared in Belgrade, there are hardly any pupils. Esti is in a class of two. In fact, Esti and Ben are the only children in the infants' school, who are even technically French.

"So we are French and they are not," Ben announces to Esti.

No wonder they have a reputation, as a nation, for being superior. To my amazement I realise that slowly, part of him is turning French or maybe it always was. Perhaps he was born with this sense of superiority running through his veins.

One morning, walking to the market, I try to encourage him to read. I see a sign that isn't in Cyrillic (Serbs use both alphabets). He reads it in a thick French accent:

"'ot Duug."

I look at him in disbelief. He sounds like a foreigner. The notice, actually, says: "Hot Dog."

As the weeks slip by, I get increasingly lost when it comes to trying to talk to the teachers and help with the homework, so I resolve that, in order to keep up, I had better take French lessons as I can't rely on Tim to do their homework. They'd hand it in weeks, maybe even months, late. The crunch comes when Ben decides to invite some friends for lunch. They are two, immaculately turned out little girls, in smart dresses. One, Charlotte is Belgian; the other, Isidora is Yugoslav. They gossip and joke with Ben and Esti in French and I can't keep up. I have nightmare visions of my children marrying people who only speak French and having Gallic grandchildren with whom I can't communicate. I live in Serbia but I have to learn French to get to know my kids. Indeed, one day Esti will bring home her first boyfriend and he will not speak a word of English.

Soon it's the end of November and icy cold, but at least Tim should be home later tonight. It's a ten-hour drive from Zagreb to Belgrade these days. The motorway has been closed for years, so he'll have to take the back roads through Hungary. Last year we had a terrible crash on the very same route. He called me when he left at lunchtime but now it's long after midnight. I'm worried and have no way of contacting him. Even though it's freezing cold I hang out of the window looking for the car. He's nowhere to be seen. There is just an icy, empty road.

When dawn breaks he's still not back. I watch the door waiting for the sound of a key sliding into the lock. Eventually around nine an exhausted and dirty Tim walks in. He has spent the night convincing the Croatian police that he was not a black marketeer. He's been Christmas shopping. It was the enormous, white Barbie car that he had bought as a present for Esti that had aroused their suspicions. He flops down on the bed next to me, puts his head on my chest and falls asleep.

Christmas is coming – there's no stopping it and Ben, who is now almost six, has already decided that he wants me to make "some proper stuff this year", as he so kindly puts it. "Proper stuff" is, I'm informed, a *galette du roi* at Epiphany. This is a special marzipan cake, with a bean or little trinket cooked into it. The person who gets the prize, the *fève*, gets to become king and choose a queen - or vice versa. Ben explains all this, slowly:

"And we must have a *bûche de noël*, too."

I'm stunned:

"There's more?"

"The teacher says it isn't Christmas, without a *bûche de noël*," he announces with a flourish of his hand, as if he is addressing an audience. I, a mere English person, have missed the significance of this and, clearly, have failed to celebrate properly all these years. I fight back:

"That's a chocolate log isn't it Ben?"

He slaps down his school bag on the table:

"Ugh! It's a *bûche de noël*, that's its proper name."

He has both the recipes stuck in his exercise book. The French are big on teaching baking. It's his homework to read them through. He translates, while I take notes on what we need to make a "proper" Christmas. It could take weeks to get all the ingredients together.

"I guess, I'll have to blanche the almonds and grind them. I wonder how difficult that will be?" I muse.

"Come on Mummy! It's Christmas!"

I think, I am coming on but obviously I am not.

"If I'm French, I should eat proper stuff."

I feel like his housekeeper. Only later, do I discover that, if we lived in France, I could buy all this "proper stuff" ready-made in the frozen food cabinet. Why don't they teach them that?

Then it's on to the carols. He launches into *Mon beau sapin*, "My beautiful fir tree"

I recognise the tune:

"Hey Ben! Isn't that the Red Flag? You must be singing a French version of that German carol, whatever it's called."

I get a withering look.

He carries on singing. He has to learn it off by heart for tomorrow. I get my revenge in moments, when he asks me what it all means. Dictionary in hand, I dissect the song.

"Ah! I've got it. This bit Ben, "*quand par l'hiver, bois et guérets sont dépoilés de leurs attraits. Mon beau sapin, roi des forêts. Tu gardes ta parure,*" means when all the trees in the forest and fields have lost their leaves, that's *dépoilés*, you keep your finery. You stay green."

He's crestfallen. What have I done wrong now?

"I thought it meant all the trees in the forest were decorated with *poulets*, chickens you know, *du poulet.*"

After that comment I decide that, that's enough French culture for one day. I'm glad to get back to life in Serbia.

But the next thing on the agenda isn't Serbian at all. It's the first night of Hanukkah. I busy about making a party tea and wrapping the kids' presents. They are Christmas colouring books. It was the best thing I could find. It's not very Jewish but will have to do. Tim is back in Bosnia. I want to make an effort for his sake. Tonight we are lighting the first candle. The festival goes on for eight nights and each night you light one more candle. That much I have worked out. I have bought some tall thin tapers, the kind they use in church here. They are all I could find. I decide that if we are going to do it we should try to do it properly and I launch into the blessing. "*baruch ata adonai elohainu melech haolam asher kiddyshanu…*" and forget the next bit. I opt for a lecture and explain that Hanukkah commemorates a siege of Jerusalem hundreds of years ago but what it was about I haven't the faintest idea so I tell them we should think about the people in Sarajevo:

"Daddy isn't here lighting these candles properly because he is trying to make sure that the world knows what is happening to them. Be grateful you have a party tea."

I sound like a vicar. We have pizza and yet more *Smoki Flips*. I have no idea that we should be eating traditional things like doughnuts, which are fried. I feel it's a cock up but I blunder on. We will always eat pizza and crisps at Hanukkah. I am glad I am miles from London and can sort out how I want to do this without anyone interfering. Exactly how I am sorting it out and what I am doing I have no idea but I think I'll get there in the end.

The next day we head off down the city's main shopping street, Terazije. We are off to the supermarket, to see if there are any almonds to make marzipan for the "proper stuff" that I'm supposed to be cooking. As it's a few weeks before Christmas, the whole place has taken on a jovial, festive air. There are Christmas lights all along the street. People bustle in and out of the half empty stores. You wouldn't guess this was a country at war. A few hours drive away however it's a different story; one of mass rape, ethnic cleansing and murder. That's Tim's world. Esti pulls my coat:

"Mummy, look at those decorations! Look! Are you listening?"

She never thinks I'm listening.

"Will they light up, Mummy?"

Esti has very low expectations of life and me, unlike her brother.

"Wow! Of course, they'll turn them on. It'll be magical."

Ben waxes lyrical on the other side of Ray's buggy about Christmas. Jewish, Christian, Serbian or French, he is equally enthusiastic about all festivities. What will emerge out of this confusion? Ray ignores them both.

Esti doesn't listen to his Christmas lecture and is more interested in finding out how much the chocolate cars in the sweet shop cost:

"Can we can afford one for Daddy?"

The truth is that we could buy the whole shop thanks to hyperinflation, but I'm not going to tell her that. It's the same with the ice creams. There's a nice, elderly lady who sells lollies at the corner of the park, by the traffic lights. Once or twice a week, I let them have a strawberry *Rumenko* lolly. The Cornetto-style cornets are only for special occasions, like birthdays. I don't let them know that they cost less than 1p each, in case they become spoilt. Ben is twelve when he realizes that I pulled off this deception, and is still furious. Perhaps they would never have noticed the war if, in a similar fashion, I just hadn't mentioned it.

Before the shopping, we have an obligatory window shop at the toyshop, just before the supermarket. Esti presses her nose against the window:

"Look Mummy! It's Dr Barbie!"

"She wants it! Let's get it now before it goes," pleads Ben.

"It costs 120 marks!" I exclaim. That's about £40. This shop has abandoned the pretence of pricing in Dinars. Ben is determined:

"But Esti wants it!"

I think Esti must be hearing everything but she says nothing. Evidently, she's leaving the negotiations up to Ben. "See it. Buy it," is his philosophy. You never know when you might find it again. In the end, he twists my arm and he buys her Dr Barbie for Christmas. Toys like this are brought in by sanctions-busting black marketeers who can charge what they want. I'm caught. My money does, in the end, line the pockets of men like Arkan.

It's dusk by the time we have finished the shopping. On the way back from the supermarket, Esti wants to stop to see if the decorations will really be turned on when it gets dark. She's never seen Christmas lights before. Ben, however, is in a hurry, as he wants to watch his favourite cartoon, *Jonny Quest*, who is a dated rather stilted action hero, on the new satellite service that we've just had installed. He's making up for lost time and has become a TV addict. We can't reason with him.

As I open the front door he sprints over to the TV but before he can sit on the floor cushions in front of the TV, the electricity goes off. His wails echo up the stone stairwell:

"Joneeeeeee Queeeeest! I want Joneeeee Queeeeest!"

The Christmas lights have gone on in Terazije and, as a consequence, the system is overloaded. Our electricity only comes on again when the Christmas lights are turned off at midnight. It's cold turkey for Ben. He's furious:

"Why does Milošević have to have Christmas lights now?"

The question isn't as stupid as it sounds. The first year we were in Belgrade, Ben and Esti made Christmas trees out of coloured paper and stuck them on the window. That year there were no Christmas decorations around. Orthodox Serbia was keen to differentiate itself from Roman Catholic Croatia. A few days after we had pinned up our decorations, we went to play in the park opposite. Our Christmas trees stood out like a sore thumb. One look and I called the kids:

"Get off the swing Ben! I think we should go straight home and move those trees."

"No! What's wrong with them?"

"It's mid-December. Serbs are Orthodox. They don't celebrate Christmas until January and then it's a low-key religious affair. People might get the wrong idea and think we are Croats."

"But we're Jewish," says Ben, looking mystified as if that means he can do what he wants with his Christmas trees.

Two years later, *Jonny Quest*, or the lack of him, is still a personal battle in Ben's eyes between him and Mr Milošević. Why shouldn't the appalling wiring of the lights be anything else than Milošević's personal responsibility if he is the one who runs the show here? It gets really serious, as far as Ben is concerned however, when he finds out that the necessary approval from the UN sanctions committee in New York to import Santa's toys for the French Embassy Christmas party and the school Santa visit are seriously delayed. Santa can't come until January, when he gets clearance from the UN. Ben growls:

"How can Milošević do this? How can he interfere with Santa?"

He's frozen to the floor in anger and holds his fists firm in front of him.

"It's the least of his crimes, I think Ben, don't you? What about poor old Mr Parking?"

We celebrate Christmas, but in Serbia it's a normal working day. New Year's Eve is the biggest night of the year. Between the two Tim is off to eastern Bosnia where the fighting is escalating. The Bosnian Serbs are busy driving the Bosnian Muslims out of territory they want but, at this stage, they are fighting back hard. It's a bloodbath. Many of the Muslims have fled to the enclave of Srebrenica which the UN has pledged to protect. It under siege and conditions are appalling – food and medicine are in short supply; even water is scarce. I want to look after Tim when he gets home and make him a special meal to see in 1994. So, in my parallel universe, it's off to the shops again. The market in Belgrade is packed with people stocking up for the festivities and the streets that lead up to it are blocked with dented, beaten up and mostly cream coloured cars. Peasant farmers with weather-beaten, nut brown faces have come to sell their produce.

"Wait! I want to see!"

Esti pulls on the buggy sharply, so it grinds to a halt with a jolt. Ray gets a dose of g-force. Esti is eye level with the open boot. Ben stretches to grab her sleeve, trying to yank her away:

"That's disgusting! Esti don't look! Mummy they are *porcs!* It's full of *porcs!* Dead ones."

The boot is, as he says, full of small, dead piglets. He's getting on so much better at school that, now he can't speak English! Esti is busy inspecting them:

"How many do you think there are, Mummy?"

I don't believe this can be my daughter. She's a clone of Tim.

"What? I'm not counting them! I'm a vegetarian, Esti!"

She ignores me and carries on:

"How do they kill *porcs?*"

I'm horrified.

"I'm not inspecting them to see if they have slit throats. Come on! Let's go!"

The owner of the pigs pops up and asks how many I want. The last thing I want is a dead pig. I'm a vegetarian, married to a Jew.

I take Esti firmly by the hand and turn around to see where Ben has got to. He's gazing at the roof of another pale cream car, which has an enormous, skinned sheep strapped to the top. A glassy eye looks down at him accusingly.

"Why are its legs sticking up so straight?" he asks. He doesn't seem to have noticed that it has no fleece and demands:

"Who eats this stuff?"

I'm wondering if these two have anything to do with me. Some days I feel like I have just bumped into them for the first time.

"Who do you think? Serbs? They think it's 'proper stuff', you know, Ben"

He doesn't get the joke.

It takes ages to get round the market. We buy a cucumber for the unearthly sum of ten marks off a trader with a picnic table covered in luxuries, some Christmas tree chocolates from a man, who's just driven back from Austria and a wooden Christmas tree-style candleholder that's come from Ikea in Budapest. Thanks to hyperinflation it costs more than Maja's father, who is paid in Dinars, earns in a year. By the time we leave, the market is winding up. Quite a few of the peasants, who've sold their cheeses and vegetables for a good price, are already drunk and sleeping it off on top of their metal stalls. Like the *porcs* they are eye level with Ben and Esti, who inspect them as carefully as they have done the carcasses. We walk out past the man with the pigs. Esti darts off to stick her head in the boot:

"How many *porcs* has he got left? Can we see?"

Years later a teacher asks Ben what peasants do, while they are discussing feudal, medieval society in class. Ben answers that they go to market sell their stuff and get drunk. He is sent out of the class for being cheeky.

Ben at the grave of the Romanian dictator, Nicolae Ceauşescu. Bucharest, June 1990.

Ben and Mihai fill up the car with petrol stored in the boot of his father's Trabant. Bucharest, June 1990.

Ben and Esti with Elena.
Bucharest, 1991.

Ben sketches while Esti sleeps through the last moments of peace in the Bosnian capital.
Sarajevo, February 1992.

The only tourist in town.
Ben in the Croatian city of Split
as the country cascades into war.
May 1991.

Watching events unfold live on TV in the Holiday Inn during the first day of the
conflict in Bosnia. Sarajevo, March 1992.

Ben tries out his Dad's new
bulletproof jacket. Rosie's mother
is seated in the background.
Belgrade, May 1992.

Where's Mr Parking? Rosie, Esti and Ben with the family car in front of
the Yugoslav Federal Parliament just outside their flat. Belgrade, 1992.

Tim waits to board a flight out of Sarajevo, 1993.

Chris plays soldiers with Ben. The Battle of Waterloo is under his arm. Belgrade, December 1993.

Esti looks after Evie and Jacob as the family get ready to go to the Rambouillet Conference. February 1999.

Ben tries out the podium for size at the ill-fated peace talks at Rambouillet outside Paris just before NATO goes to war. February 1999.

Ben outside a burned out restaurant. Bosnia, August 2001.

Tim (right) and Chris (left) visit a photographer's studio with their translator just after the fall of the Taliban. Kabul, November 2001.

Ben and Jacob set off for some sun, sand and anti-Semitism in the South of France. April 2002.

A meeting with Santa. When the picture is e-mailed to Tim in Iraqi Kurdistan he is unable to open it. Rovaniemi, August 2002.

11 - Hungary: Duck Bread and Circuses

We are cuddled up in bed reading *Topsy and Tim go to the Park*. The park could be in any British town. In the picture Topsy and Tim are standing by a small, round pond, scattering bits of bread to the happy, quacking flock of ducks. In Serbia, the heavy metal shutters of the flat are locked tight. Outside I can hear the rumble of the engine of a bus as it pulls away at the traffic lights. There's a cold draught coming from the window. There is no sign of spring yet. I pull Esti close. She looks up at me plaintively:

"I've never fed any ducks. Why aren't there any ducks here?"

I've never thought of it before but it's true. I haven't seen a single duck pond in the entire Balkans.

"I guess, they've all been eaten up," I say and then tell them a story I've heard about some Romanian gypsies, who went to Vienna and were arrested for barbecuing the swans. Ben laughs and claps his hands. Esti, who will grow up to love roast duck is however appalled and studies the picture of Topsy and Tim and their feathered friends, tenderly running her finger over the page. Cosy suburban England seems far away. Momentarily, I miss it.

"I really want to feed them, Mummy. Can't you find some?"

The gentle, vulnerable tone of her voice is so entirely out of character that Ben strokes her shoulder, in an unexpected show of brotherly love, and says:

"Don't worry Esti! Mummy and I will find some. We really will."

I wish he hadn't said this, as Esti is not the kind of child who forgets promises made in haste and neither I, nor Maja, have any idea how we are supposed to conjure up some ducks.

Within days NATO comes to my rescue. It's 1994, almost two years since the siege of Sarajevo began and, at last, the Western powers have threatened that they will bomb the Bosnian Serb artillery on the hills around the city unless the shelling stops. It comes in the wake of a devastating attack on the city's Markale market which has left 64 people dead and 144 wounded. Tim is sitting in the Bosnian Serb gun positions waiting for the bombs to start falling on them. Everyone in Belgrade has always been friendly to us but I have begun to wonder what would happen if they do actually start bombing. I push the question of what would happen to Tim to the back of my mind and worry about what might happen here.

All the non-essential staff, at both the British and French embassies, have been evacuated. The night after the duck-feeding incident an official calls from the French embassy to ask me if we are going to leave. I have no intention of going anywhere but the call sows a seed of doubt in my mind. The last thing I want to happen is for the situation to turn nasty in Belgrade and for angry crowds to start attacking NATO members' embassies. Tim might then try to make some dangerous dash through the night, to make sure we are all right. It's time for a serious discussion. He agrees that perhaps we should leave until the situation resolves itself and *The Economist* and the *Times* agree to pay to evacuate us to Budapest the day before NATO's deadline falls.

Ben darts out of the room looking for his sisters the moment he hears the news:

"Esti! Did you hear that we're going to Hungary? Wow! What shall we buy? Last time, you got a Barbie wardrobe. We'll have to get Mummy to give us some jobs. We need some real money, if we're going there."

Esti is sitting next to Ray playing with her Barbies on the rug. She has a head of brown curls. Ray is still alarmingly bald. It gives her an elfish air that adds to her cheeky manner.

"Ray, it's amazing in Budapest, you can buy all sorts of lovely things. There's loads to eat. I'm sure there'll be some choccy pud for you," says

Esti gleefully.

I'm grateful that I have a suitcase to pack as the activity will stop me thinking about the impending bombardment that could rain down on Tim's head.

The next day we clamber on board a wonderfully old fashioned train, with separate compartments and acres of brown, wood panelling. Serbs love wooden panelling. It's everywhere. We settle down for the six-hour ride in our own cabin. Outside the window, the snow goes on and on. It's February. The train goes at a steady, slow pace. Just before we cross the border, a white hare runs along beside the window.

The brakes screech and the train lurches to a halt at the frontier, where Serbian policeman board and begin searching every nook and cranny of the train.

We get up to stand in the corridor to watch what's going on. Two young men are taken off the train and led away.

"Why are they taking those men off the train?" asks Ben staring at them intently.

The station is silent. People waiting on the platform watch but they don't say a thing. I explain to Ben that the two men are probably trying to avoid being called up to fight. Thousands of young men have fled the country to avoid the draft. He turns to me, eyes gleaming:

"Maja's boyfriend Milan has to do that, Mummy. She says he sleeps in a different house every night. Imagine how many people he must know!"

Esti lets out an impressed gush of air. From the boyish tone in his voice I can see he doesn't really understand what is going on. For him it is an adventure.

"He doesn't sleep in a completely different house every night, Ben," I explain. "He goes around a handful of addresses, I expect."

He deflates visibly losing an inch in height. He looks out of the window again quietly studying the scene and then turns to me and asks:

"What will they do to those men?"

"I don't know," I answer. I genuinely don't know what will become of them.

He looks sharply at me:

"Why not?"

I shrug my shoulders and he wiggles his mouth and blows out his cheeks sullenly.

Next, it's the turn of the Hungarian police, who come into every compartment to look under the seats - everyone's but ours that is. It's a mess. There are toys and biscuits all over the place. I can see that they can't face it. Perhaps they assume draft dodgers and refugees wouldn't put up with this chaos either. Esti is put out and demands to know why the police didn't look under her seat.

We are booked in at the Hyatt, which is another atrium-style hotel. I've gone off this type of accommodation after Sarajevo. In the lobby there's an old plane hanging precariously from the ceiling. The next morning, at breakfast, we bump into a gaggle of British embassy wives, who evacuated from Belgrade some time ago. One of them I recognise from a cocktail party. She is a tall, elegant woman in late middle age, and is married to the defence attaché. She has a clipped Home Counties voice:

"I'm so pleased to see you," she says as if we have just arrived at a coffee morning. "It's great to have some new faces around here. We are getting a bit bored."

After she has wandered off to peruse the buffet for a second time, Ben turns to me:

"How can she possible get bored here? Hasn't she been to the military museum?"

"What about the shops?" says Esti breathlessly.

I think about our nearly empty suitcases upstairs in the room and my huge shopping list. Sanctions and hyperinflation mean that things are short in Belgrade. Esti's main aim is to stuff as many packets of Coco Pops in the suitcase as possible. That's only after she has ganneted some crucial Barbie accessories.

"We should eat up quickly and do some shopping straight away," I tell them. "What if nothing happens tonight and we have to go home? We should have it all ready just in case."

No bombing would mean we would have to go back the day after tomorrow. Esti hasn't thought about this. A worried look passes over her face, as she munches on a mini Danish pastry. I know she's thinking about the shopping, not her father.

A wave of panic, about what will happen to Tim, floods over me. When I called my mother last night she took a sharp intake of breath when I told her what was going on. I haven't dared call Tim's father. Fretting about breakfast cereal seems like madness. One part of me would like to run upstairs and hide until it is all over but the other half knows that worrying about buying Coco Pops is the best way of ensuring that everything will be fine. I think, irrationally, that Tim is more likely to get home safely to a house stocked to the brim with cereals.

Another embassy wife pops up before I can get my thoughts under control. She is chubby and clearly enjoying the drama of the evacuation. She has a reassuringly motherly and practical air about her. She is the sort of person who, if she lived in England, would run the local Women's Institute. She's dressed in a pale, baby blue jumper and tight, dark blue trousers that do nothing for her rounded figure. She is bubbling over with the news her husband has just passed on, by phone, from Belgrade. He is a non-descript character, who does something boring at the embassy. We've met before but I can't remember her name, let alone his.

"I have been so worried about him staying there. He's coming tonight, so we are all safe, in case the bombing happens. When is your hubby coming dear?"

I am thrown:

"Hubby?" I mutter.

I have visions of Tim in tweeds, smoking a pipe. Tim could never be a "hubby". These sort of men stay at home and read the paper.

Esti is confused too. She leans forward anxiously:

"Dads isn't coming is he?"

"No! He's with the Bosnian Serbs," pipes up Ben proudly. "He's sleeping with the soldiers in the hills above Sarajevo, waiting for the bombs."

Esti nods sagely. The embassy wife looks a bit lost.

"No. He's not coming. He is in Pale," I explain.

Pale is the Bosnian Serb headquarters.

"Pale!" she shrieks and calls across to the embassy wives' breakfast table, where they are relaxing over coffee.

"Rosie's husband is in Pale!"

At the sound of her voice Ray drops her bowl of cereal all over the floor. I can feel everyone looking at us. Mrs Defence Attaché, to my surprise, comes over and starts picking up the mess. She looks up sternly with a hand full of Rice Krispies. We are obviously lowering the tone.

"It's not safe. I think he should leave," she says. "He must keep his head down. Where is he staying?"

She sounds like a headmistress. It makes me feel that I will act as if the situation is totally normal, which in fact in many ways it is, only the heat has been turned up.

"Well, he's going to spend tonight in the Serbian gun positions, actually," I say casually.

She stands up quickly with an indignant look on her face.

"He says, they won't bomb them anyway," I continue.

She pulls her chin in. I guess she's thinking that I shouldn't know something she doesn't. On the other hand maybe she does know that this is the gossip. She is someone who might. I hope Tim isn't wrong and she isn't, actually, privy to some information that Tim hasn't heard. The report on *Sky News* I just watched gave me the distinct impression that they would indeed bomb. I feel that he is in considerable danger.

"Let me know if you need anything," she says abruptly, putting the Rice Krispies on my plate and wanders off. I feel dismissed.

I once had a puncture outside the British Embassy in Belgrade after a Bonfire Night party. All the guests filed out after the fireworks laughing and joking, while I struggled to undo the wheel nuts put on by a spindly Romanian teenager. No one offered to help. In the end we had to drive home on the flat tyre. Belgrade is considered a tough posting but all the diplomats I've met live in enormous houses stocked to the brim with luxury imports. I wonder how much they actually notice of what is going on around them. I think I would rather not ask her for help.

The baby blue jumper is still standing next to the table. She looks genuinely concerned and glances around the table at the children:

"You should take them to the circus dear. It's wonderful. Take their mind off things. They'll get you tickets at the reception."

Esti almost chokes on the pastry she is stuffing into her mouth and splutters:

"Really! Can we go, please?"

"Don't talk with your mouth full!" advises the baby blue jumper patting her on the back.

Esti moves defiantly on to yet another cake. They forget all about the imminent bombing in the excitement. I long to do the same.

I really have no desire to see or do anything so I let Ben decide what we will do. First stop is a funicular ride up Castle Hill to the Military History Museum. I'm becoming quite an expert on military museums, as he is addicted to them. Here there is no escaping conflict and bloodshed. This is our third visit to this particular one, which has some of the best miniature battlefields on the continent. Castle Hill is a plateau, one mile long, that's laden with churches, old mansions and a huge palace. It towers over the majestic Danube. Budapest is a grand city, full of dramatic, highly decorated art nouveau buildings, elegant coffee houses and large department stores. Coming from Belgrade it makes me feel like a hillbilly peasant. Esti is marching alongside me with her hands in her pink pockets and her fake fur hat pulled firmly over her eyes. Her mouth is curved down in a theatrical frown. Her boots are stomping on the pavement. It looks like snow. The sky is a dark grey. She is furious that Ben has been asked what he wants to do first.

Once inside, I am taken aback as the museum is very busy. Esti looks around bewildered:

"Who are all these people? Why are they here?"

"People come here for their holidays, Esti," I explain. This is the other Europe.

"Here?"

She scans the room.

"No not 'here' specifically. To Budapest. This is one of the things to see."

"This?" she says in disbelief.

I try not to smile. I understand why she is confused. There's a wonderful military museum in Belgrade's Kalemegdan fortress but it is always deserted. The place makes my skin crawl. Visiting it is like walking through a park at dusk, when you really know that you are doing a stupid thing, wandering alone in such a lonely place. There aren't even any attendants, just a soldier, who occasionally marches round. On average, we go there twice a month. I think we are the only visitors.

We move along the busy galleries to an exhibition about the 1956 uprising. Ray has fallen asleep in the buggy in her tartan snowsuit. I point at the grainy black and white pictures of Russian tanks and I try to explain, why the Hungarians rose up against the Soviet-backed government:

"Things were terrible here then. Communism was a horrible thing. Look, these men are being shot."

I jab my finger at the photograph. They gaze at it.

"Everyone here had a very bad time. They hated the communists."

The two of them look at me, sceptically. They regard Hungary as a shopper's paradise where, as Esti has just discovered, people come on holiday. They can't make the transition back in time, to the Cold War.

We have lunch in a trendy American-style bar, with wooden booths and Tiffany lights. It's Esti's choice. The Coke comes in mega-size glasses. I order guacamole, while Ben and Esti stare at the video screen, where the latest hits are playing. I wonder what Tim is doing.

The waiter puts down the plate and Esti starts sniffing my lunch:

"What's that green stuff?"

I flap at her nose, that's hovering over my plate:

"Avocado. Get off my food."

Ben admires the small pile of pale green mush:

"Wow!"

There's a tone of awe in his voice:

"Mummy ordered an avocado once in the Sheraton in Sofia. The waiter brought it to the room on a silver plate. Then he asked her what it tasted like, didn't he Mummy? Avocados are a luxury, Esti. Ordinary people can't eat them."

I am not sure whether I should be delighted that I am not part of the riffraff or to be concerned that he has a superiority complex because he has seen me eat an avocado twice in his life.

After lunch, we cross the road and start the first of our big shopping sprees at the Austrian supermarket chain, Julius Meinl. First on the list are ten packets of Disney soup. Ben and Esti think this minestrone with pasta shaped like Goofy and Donald Duck is the height of chic. There is a pile of avocados on sale, so I get one to try out on Ray for supper. Esti is shocked:

"How come she gets that? It's too expensive for her." Esti is keeping accounts and adds quickly:

"What do we get?"

At a stall outside Ben picks up a nationalist postcard, showing a map of Greater Hungary. At first glance, it looks like one of those cards they sell at seaside resorts with castles, beaches and villages marked on them, designed so you can write "We are here" with a big arrow pointing to your holiday cottage. This one, however, is far more sinister. You see postcards like this all over the Balkans. It's for people who want to write; "I want to be here" or: "This is really mine. Give it back or I'll shoot." Everyone is coveting his neighbour's land and flaunting it unashamedly. The map shows Hungary owning everything to the south of its present border as far as Dubrovnik and, of course, Transylvania in Romania. Until the collapse of the Austro-Hungarian Empire in 1918, it was part of Hungary. Many Hungarians want it back.

"Don't send that to Mihai, Ben," I say as a joke.

"No. I'm starting a collection," he says stuffing it in the pocket of his khaki green coat.

I glance down at my watch. It is still only 3.30pm. This day seems to be going on forever. I am not sure if I want the deadline for the bombing to arrive faster or not. At least we have the tickets for the circus. It is all the kids can think about. I am grateful to the baby blue jumper for that.

Standing on the street corner outside the supermarket my cheeks feel tight with tension as it wafts over me once more. Budapest is busy and noisy, too busy and noisy for me at the moment. The restaurants are packed and people are bustling in and out of the shops. The stress is like a low hum inside my head. I don't think anyone here could care less what is happening in Pale, they are all too preoccupied with their own lives, just as I am with mine. I don't care about them either and I am not interested in Budapest at all – only Pale, bombs and Tim. I would like to loose myself in the hum inside my head. Maybe it will take me closer to Tim. But I put the kids' hands firmly on the buggy and decide to walk up to the circus. It will help kill the time. I pull the city map, which the man at the hotel reception has given me, out of my pocket and see the circus is next to a park.

We get there with plenty of time to spare. It's twilight, icy and cold. I think perhaps a walk wasn't such a good idea after all. Ben is grumpy. I dislike him when he is like this.

"Can't we go somewhere indoors?" he moans.

I am wondering where when suddenly, he shouts:

"Hey! What's that noise?"

Ray is straining forward, over the padded arm of her buggy. She's heard it too.

"Ducks! Mummy there's ducks! See Esti! I told you we'd fix it. Great! It's great. Ducks!"

He's jumping up and down and the earflaps of his snow hat are flapping like wings. He looks as if he is about to take off. It's so funny I start laughing. Then he turns to me with a worried expression:

"Where's the bread? Oh No! I don't believe it! We've come all this way and you don't have any bread. You stupid woman!"

Bread? I feel like shouting that bread is the least of our priorities but bite my tongue.

"Don't talk to me like that," I mutter lamely. "I didn't know there were any ducks here, did I?"

I rummage around in the heap of carrier bags on the back of the buggy, searching for the supply of cakes and buns, which I wrapped up in white paper napkins at breakfast and slipped into my handbag for emergencies.

"What's this place called? We need to remember its name for Esti," says Ben beaming as I hand him a Danish pastry. I glance at the map that is still in my left hand:

"Városliget," I read slowly.

"Wow! Varo..what? Cor Esti! There's even a funfair. I can hear something over the trees."

I think the ducks are good omen and relax a little.

Budapest Circus is a permanent affair, but inside, it's laid out as if it was a real big top, with a proper sawdust arena. When we arrive I discover it's the Chinese National Circus that's performing.

"Will there be animals?" asks Esti, wide-eyed.

In fact, the show is an endless succession of miniature stick insect women who lie down and twirl bigger and bigger pots on their feet. Ray sits on my lap with her eyes fixed on the gyrating pink and blue ladies, waving long chiffon scarves, who are dotted around the arena. They are hypnotic and I forget all about Pale and bombs. The show ends with the acrobats making a human tower. Esti has forgotten the animals and is cheering with the rest of the crowd. The acrobats disappear behind the screens while the cheering continues. Then the whole troop marches back in a long procession, waving enormous Chinese red flags. The house falls silent. Ben and Esti look worried. I signal to them to be quiet. They ignore me.

"Red flags mean communism Esti," Ben says in a loud voice.

Her eyes open wide:

"Are they so stupid? You mustn't do that? Not here!"

Ben was right; the military museum was the best place to start the tour of Budapest. They had listened to my lecture on the 1956 uprising after all.

"The Chinese are communists, Esti," I whisper.

She looks astounded. This little incident will keep the conversation going over dinner and stop me thinking about Tim and bombs.

Back at the Hyatt, they fall asleep the moment they get into bed. They have forgotten about Tim. I tuck Ray into the makeshift cot that I've concocted by pushing two armchairs together. The embassy wives have already bagged all the hotel cots. I turn off the light. The bombing is due to begin in the early hours.

Tim calls at midnight. He is insistent that it won't actually happen.

He sounds so definite that I begin to wonder what I have been worrying about. I hope he is right and that makes me feel terrible. What about all those people in Sarajevo who are desperate for some help and are longing for the bombs to rain down on the Serbian gun positions around the city? I doze with the TV remote next to the pillow. Bang on cue, I wake up and watch the coverage live on television. There is to be no bombing. I am so tired I roll over and fall into a deep sleep.

Yesterday's breakfast was such an embarrassment, that I decide that we'll have it in the room today. When the waiter arrives, Ben wakes up:

"What happened? Have they bombed Dads?"

As if I would order a full breakfast, if his father had just been bombed. He can be a very strange child. It is probably my fault.

"No, nothing happened. He was right," I say pulling back his sheets.

He doesn't move.

"But, they said they were going to do it."

"Well, I guess, they didn't mean it."

"If you say you'll do it, shouldn't you do it?" he asks standing up slowly.

"On the one hand yes, but on the other, I'm glad they didn't bomb your father."

I take his hand and guide him to the breakfast tray.

The modern, utilitarian hotel bedroom and the off-white winter sky outside the window seem to reinforce the anti-climactic atmosphere. Nothing has changed. My sense of relief is marred by the depressing thought that the fighting looks as if it is just going to drag on and on. Ben gobbles down his fried eggs. I wake Esti in case he tries to eat her plateful. Between gulps, he is trying to fathom out how NATO can say one thing and do another. I'm boiling up water in the kettle I've brought from Belgrade to make Ray a bottle. I tell them to hurry up and get dressed. We are going back home tomorrow and we must stock up. That's the end of worrying about a bombing that didn't happen.

At Julius Meinl we buy six packets of Coco Pops and ten boxes of formula for Ray. We "um" and "ah" at the vegetable section. What will keep and what we can feasibly carry home? We settle on a big box of nectarines for Ray who, if she had her way, would only eat fruit. She'll grow up to be a vegetarian. I take some avocados for her as well. Ben and Esti opt for cucumbers. Clearly one way to get kids to eat vegetables is to make them a luxury. Esti wants tomatoes too, but I'm sure they will get squashed. This puts her in a bad mood, especially since Ray has some avocados. She won't keep her baby sister entertained at the checkout.

At lunchtime we straggle back in through the hotel doors. I'm carrying Ray, while Esti pushes the laden buggy. Ben dawdles in behind dragging the bags of Coco Pops behind him. We look totally out of place in the smart lobby full of tourists.

"Been shopping?" calls a voice from across a trolley, laden with suitcases.

It's the pale blue jumper, only today she is in pale lemon. Not a great colour for a snowy day. She sounds as if she is a neighbour watching me unload my car in a suburban driveway.

"We need to get supplies," says Ben authoritatively, as if he is the harvest mouse talking to the grasshopper.

"It must be so difficult in winter for you dear," she says bustling over. "A van brings my shopping from Hungary once a week."

I boggle at the thought of home delivery, embassy-style. Before I can say anything she reaches for the shopping:

"My hubby came in the van with a driver. Just give me all the bags. We'll drive back whatever you need. Go and get everything else you couldn't buy and bring it to my room, dear. We're leaving first thing tomorrow. Perhaps we'll see you at the pool later."

I could kiss her but there isn't time. We rush back to Julius Meinl cheering as we go. This is an excuse for another big shop. Tomatoes are top of the list. We love Budapest.

The next morning, we ask the taxi to stop outside the Julius Meinl near the station, as there are still a few gaps in the suitcase where we can stuff some packets and more cucumbers. I've decided that we can give a few to the old lady next door. The station is a seedy place even though, architecturally, it's a piece of faded grandeur from a bygone era. It doesn't tempt me to linger. The entrance hall is full of begging gypsies in brightly coloured skirts and babies in shawls. We shake them off when we walk down to the very end of the platform where we wait patiently, watching the engines shunting about. The Yugoslav train however, pulls in at the next platform, not the one indicated on the board. We are too far down the one that it was supposed to arrive at to run back to the top, so we have to scrabble across the tracks at a small point where it's been made safe to cross. The wheel of Ray's buggy gets stuck in the rails and I think we are about to meet our end until the waiter from the restaurant car jumps out of the train and wrenches the wheel free.

He installs me in a compartment. I feel guilty as he loads the carrier bags of groceries on to the luggage rack. I know he would probably shop here if he could afford it.

"Lunch in half an hour," he announces with a big smile and, although it appears the train is virtually empty he adds: "I'll save you a table."

There's grilled cheese. It's already ready when we arrive in the buffet. It feels cosy. The waiter laughs and ruffles Ben's hair. I like Serbs despite their faults. I'm sorry they have ended up in such a mess. We rattle back home across the snowy landscape to Europe's top pariah state.

12 - Goodbye Gangsters

"My friend Isidora watched a gangster being shot in the flats next to her house last night."

Ben drops his school bag to the floor. He starts struggling out of his coat. Isidora's mother, who has picked him up from school for me, has just dropped him off. Esti has flu. I am busy serving the lunch.

"Oh, how terrible! Poor her."

I put the bowl of pasta on the table.

"Pwah! No! She said it was great. She got to watch them carry the body out. It was in a grey bag."

Isidora's mother is a Serb and her father is a Bosnian Muslim. Her grandma is trapped in Sarajevo. She is a pretty, frail-looking little girl who is always immaculately dressed. It's a façade though, as under this veneer of femininity, she is a gutsy number. I can imagine her watching this with fascination.

Tim is writing a big feature on gangsters. Belgrade is rapidly becoming like 1920s Chicago. The opportunities for looting and pillaging in Bosnia and Croatia combined with the money that can be made in sanctions-busting, have drawn Yugoslav gangsters back home from abroad in droves. They have teamed up with the paramilitaries. It's a deadly mix. Deadly enough to make it a big story and keep Tim at home for once. We live like a normal, married couple. I make breakfast. He drives the kids to school and in the evening we read in bed next to each other. It seems too cosy to last long.

As I serve the pasta, Tim calls Isidora's mother to get the low-down. She tells him a man was gunned down on the stairs of the adjoining block. As I thought, Isidora didn't see the actual murder, but she did insist on seeing the corpse, which was zipped up in a body bag, being carried out. Her mother decided to let her. She thought it was the best thing to do. No wonder she is Ben's friend. She is perfect for him; frilly but with a ghoulish side. Ben thinks the whole thing is an enormous laugh and takes the phone so he can discuss it with Isidora all over again. I worry about the affect Serbia is having on him.

One morning a few weeks later, I'm making the beds in Ben and Esti's room. In domestic bliss Ray is toddling around the plastic cooker making me an imaginary coffee, when there is an enormous explosion on the other side of the park. The windows rattle ominously. Ray screams and bursts into floods of tears as shaking, she clutches the small plastic teacup in terror. A car bomb has gone off in front of the casino.

When we get to school, I discover that the driver of the car, who was apparently a well-known gangster, was the father of one of the pupils. The school used to be a sedate, middle class enclave, where the families of the once enormous diplomatic community sent their children in the heyday of Tito's Non-Aligned Yugoslavia. Since the war began however large numbers of embassies have closed or Belgrade has been deemed a "non-family" posting so there aren't enough children to keep the school going properly. As a result they have bent the rules a bit, about who is let in. The Lycée population has been boosted by an influx of gangsters' offspring. They are virtually the only people who can afford the fees. It isn't that they are astronomical but they have to be paid in hard currency. The average Yugoslav takes home about £3 a month.

While I am waiting for the bell to ring, Isidora's mother knocks on the car window. She is as smartly turned out as her daughter. Elegant and multilingual she watches the disintegration of her country with a mixture of anguish and aloofness. She says that she is going to insist that the school should tighten the rules and expel the gangsters' children. She asks if I will support her. I nod in agreement but really I don't think anything will change. I'm sure they won't dare tell the gangsters that their children are to be expelled and I have no intention of getting involved in this. No one asks about the family of the man, who's just been blown to pieces. There are a couple of rich, young Serbian mothers wearing skin-tight leather trousers, collecting their kids in their enormous jeeps. I decide that I won't park too close to them in future.

As I put the kids in the car, an outraged Dutch mother runs up to tell me that, at a children's party the weekend before, another gangster father had pulled out his pistol and passed it around, so the seven-year old guests could inspect it.

"Oh No! Esti we missed it!" says Ben, who didn't get an invite, even though the boy is in his class.

The boy's mother is a snotty Frenchwoman, who helps out in the video library. She always gives me a disdainful look when we go in as, my French being so bad, I stammer as I attempt to ask for the kids' favourites. She is a perfectly dressed gangster's moll. I am the unkempt, scruffy wife of a frontline reporter. She makes me feel like an idiot.

A few days later spring has finally arrived. The weather is wonderful. It's one of those mornings that you feel glad to be alive and happy that you are miles away from the atrocious British climate. The sky is a deep, Mediterranean blue.

"We're just going to the playground for half an hour," I call to Tim from the front door.

Ray always wants to go out. As soon as we get back in, she always stands by the front door wailing plaintively:

"Out! More out!"

She is clearly Tim's daughter. She is already at the front door waiting.

As I put my hand on the lock, there is an explosion and the sound of shooting outside. We both run to the window. Tim runs downstairs to find out what is going on. A policeman has been killed by a hand grenade and is lying dead at the edge of the sandpit. He was chasing another young man, a suspected criminal, who has tried to shoot himself in the head - but failed. I decide that there's no park outing for Ray today. We watch *Barney* on the satellite TV instead.

Within hours, there is a small shrine for the policeman by the bus stop, with candles, photos and letters. It's there for weeks and inspecting it becomes an integral part of an afternoon trip to the swings, after we have gawped at the edge of the sandpit.

"Why are there biscuits?" asks Esti.

"Yes, it's not like the policeman can eat them is it?" Ben adds.

There's a large box of uninviting Yugoslav biscuits, in their 1970s-style wrapping, tied to the lamppost and a packet of marshmallows by the candles. They have been left as an offering. They are Ray's favourites.

"Do you think he liked marshmallows or was that all they could get?" asks Esti.

Ray looks down at them from the buggy with a cheeky, lively expression on her face. She would eat one if I gave it to her. The packet is dusty and slightly soggy after last night's rain.

Our latest craze is going to the swimming pool at Belgrade's luxurious Hyatt Hotel. It is our big treat of the week. When we arrive at the front door, there's a small queue. The man in front is checking in his gun. There is nothing unusual in that. Most cafés and restaurants ask their clientele to leave their weapons at the door these days. Ben is inspecting the box.

"Don't touch!" I shout. They are probably loaded.

"Can we go up to the first floor?" asks Ben.

A famous gangster was recently gunned down in his bedroom. He is desperate to snoop about. It must be the journalist in him.

"Do you think they tell guests what happened in there?" he muses.

I look horrified. I don't tell him that I find it all rather exciting too.

"Ben! Most people would rather not know. These guys are foul. They're not heroes."

He snorts. We take the lift down to the pool in silence. Unfortunately, it's full of the thugs whose guns were at the reception. They are weighed down by the gold chains round their necks and have stick insect girlfriends draped around them. One pair is virtually coupling at the end of the pool. There are no lifeguards, so they are free to do as they please. Not that a mere attendant would dare tell them what to do. You don't mess with these guys. They are killers, not just gangsters but paramilitaries who have probably been busy massacring people in Bosnia. They weren't here when we first started frequenting the pool. Now even this simple pleasure has been ruined. I probably won't bring the kids here again.

A suntanned young man with an enormous gold watch and bulging muscles is in the shallower part of the pool. His girlfriend is heavily made up and he is fondling her under the water. When we get in, they move to the sun loungers by the Jacuzzi. I'm disgusted. I don't want to hang out with people like this. We have a quick swim but don't linger. As a result, the kids are still bursting with energy as I get them out of the pool. I take their waterwings off and, as I am strapping Ray in the buggy, Ben starts chasing Esti towards the Jacuzzi. She can't swim. I shout after them:

"Stop it! Come here…"

I am about to say, "or you'll fall in," but before I can finish, she slips. Out of the corner of my eye, I see her plop in the pool. I jump straight in after her but she's on the other side and has already sunk like a stone to the bottom. I am sure she is going to drown. I am completely panicked. I am a terrible mother. I have let my daughter go to a watery grave. I can't swim quickly enough to get to her. Try as I can, I can't dive deep enough to reach her.

Then suddenly, there's an enormous splash. It's the young gangster with the gold watch. He plunges down to the bottom and scoops her up. Seconds later he brings her up tenderly in his arms. She is spluttering. I scurry after him as he carries her out and lays her on the sunbed next to the buggy. He gently covers her in a towel.

"Thank you! Thank you! Thank you very much," I gasp in awe.

"No problem! Anytime," he says casually.

Then he wipes his hands on a towel and saunters off to the bar, before I can say anything else. I don't believe it. I am, forever, indebted to a gangster. I could kiss him – perhaps more. I wonder how many people he has killed and if any of them were children. I will never forget him. He saved Esti's life.

A few weeks later, we are playing football under the trees in our park, just by the sandpit, when we come across the biggest criminal of them all. Ray is parked in the shade having a bottle of milk in her pushchair. It's only a small park and just across the grass is Slobodan Milošević's office in the presidency building. In four years of digging, swinging and climbing, I've never seen him walk in or out. We can confirm that he has a reputation for being elusive. Then, just as Ben kicks the ball into a bush, I look up and there he is.

"I don't believe it! Guys look! It's Milošević!" I shriek.

Ben freezes and we stare at him. He is dressed in a smart grey suit. He looks as if he has been polished and lacquered. As he steps out of his big, black limousine, he adjusts his cuffs. He looks around confidently and right through us. He has had so much influence on my life and yet he doesn't even notice me. I feel an irrational, irresistible urge to wave and cheer, as if I know him. He is so well turned out that he has a celebrity air about him. He turns and disappears inside followed quickly by his bodyguards.

"Are you sure that was Milošević?" asks Ben.

He has come and gone so rapidly I can understand why Ben has his doubts. I assure him that it was. Esti is busy retrieving the football from underneath the bush and doesn't see him. Ben sprints off shouting at the top of his voice:

"Esti! What are you doing you idiot? You missed it all! We just saw Milošević. Mummy's gone mad. She wanted to cheer him."

"I don't care," she says dumping the football at his feet.

I'm not sure if this refers to seeing Milošević or me going mad. I have had enough of Belgrade.

It isn't just the gangsters that have made me long to move on. Maths is my other big problem. Ben is locked in a running battle with his teacher. He is now in the junior school and the teacher doesn't kiss, but snaps and growls. There are no textbooks because of some problem with sanctions and getting them sent from Paris. In maths, this causes a serious crisis, as Ben can't make out what he is supposed to do on the grainy photocopies. He always manages to get the wrong number of nuts, apples or whatever he is supposed to be sorting out into the right boxes. Order and organisation isn't his thing. He gets more and more depressed while the teacher shouts louder and louder. Most days he comes home in tears. The headmaster sides with the teacher and there is nothing I can do to alleviate the situation. There are so few children in the school now that I think it may well close down. Tim and I begin to think we should take the kids somewhere where there is a better school. I have begun to think too that if we don't leave soon we run the danger of never leaving. I definitely don't want to grow old here. I feel as if I am stuck in a festering rut and I want a new life.

Tim flies back to London to renegotiate his deal with the *Times* and raise the question of moving elsewhere. To our surprise, the foreign editor announces that he is closing down the Belgrade office and that Tim is out of a job. The foreign editor has decided that nothing is going on in the Balkans anymore and that's that. Luckily Tim is simultaneously offered a contract to write a book on the Serbs and we agree that the best place for him to do this is in London. As Belgrade remains a big story for another six years this is good news for Tim and his book. The less than perspicacious foreign editor is soon shunted aside.

Ben is delighted to be going home to Britain. He has no qualms about packing his bags and moving on. Esti however is mortified and doesn't want to go. She sulks for weeks. Even though I explain to her that we have no choice, I can tell she doesn't believe me. She is much more inclined than Ben to make attachments.

"But this is my home," she says plaintively.

"Don't worry Esti, we'll make a new home," says Ben optimistically.

He is just like Tim. The two of them always believe everything will be fine. I am more like Esti. She expects the worst.

Moving out of Serbia however, is a lot more complicated than moving in. We are foreign residents but not diplomats and so the sanctions rules apply to us, as much as to anyone else. If we want to get a removal firm, we have to apply to the sanctions committee in New York. That could take six months and would result in costing us a small fortune to move a plastic cooker and a couple of boxes of Lego. So the simplest thing to do is to sell everything that we can replace. Fortunately, Belgrade is one of the best places to do this kind of thing and an endless line of friends and acquaintances troop through the flat buying whatever they fancy.

One evening I even sell the can opener. In the excitement, I forget that I still have some tins sitting in the kitchen cupboard.

"It's the revenge of the vacuum cleaner lady," Ben says sagely. He hasn't forgiven me for that after all these years.

At the traffic lights at the top of Knez Miloša, near the old lady who sells the ice creams, we have a daily encounter with out local car cleaners; a motley crew of scruffy children armed with rags and buckets. Ben and Esti have a rather superior attitude to them, as they sit in the car waiting for the lights to change. I'm never sure whether to give them something or not. It depends on my mood. Now we are leaving, I am ruthlessly chucking things out. Last night, I left some old clothes by the front door. I knew that someone needy would pick them up. Out went Ray's favourite *Spot the Dog* vest, which had two big holes in it. The youngest child, who is about three-years old, approaches the windscreen.

"Mummy, look he has a vest just like me" says Ray innocently. Esti sniggers.

Ben looks at me astounded:

"How could you do that to Ray? What will you say when she wants her shirt?"

Later that evening, outside the window, there's a strange, strangulated cry.

"Quick it's the bear!" shouts Esti as the three of them scrabble up onto the white plastic chair by the desk and start waving. "Mummy, look! It's the dancing bear. The car cleaners have brought the bear."

The animal is led by a man with a gnarled face that looks like a walnut. He has a dirty blue shirt on and a black hat. I guess he is their father because they are running around him happily as he sings. They are gypsies. His voice is strange and twisted. There is the hint of the Orient in it. I wonder what language he is singing in. The bear has a metal collar, chain and a large muzzle. He walks on his hind legs and dances lethargically in the sultry heat. The woman next door throws a packet of biscuits onto the grass verge opposite. The child in the Spot vest runs to pick them up. Esti dashes to get a packet of Jaffa Cakes and we throw them out too. They are so at home here I wonder what they will make of London.

Now everything is sold, or been thrown in the dustbin, there is the question of how to get back. I hate flying and my phobia has only been made worse by living in a country that has no international flights. I'm not going in a plane - I'm going in my car. To put the children in a plane and ferry them rapidly from one world to another doesn't seem a very good idea anyway. I want them to see the crazy, zany Balkans give way to the more controlled Mitteleuropa of Hungary and to drive them across the Austrian border and into the West. Tim thinks this is a great idea. He has a real sense of adventure. That's one reason I love him.

At last it's time to leave. It's a hot, sunny, July morning. It's so hot it's almost difficult to breathe. The kids are sitting in the car, which is loaded with everything we still own. We have borrowed a huge roof box. The children are sitting on their duvet covers and blankets. The boot is full of boxes of photos and books. By Ray's feet is Ben's most treasured procession; his enormous white, wooden fort. He won it in a raffle in Cornwall. He had this idea that if he bought a ticket it would automatically be his. He obviously thinks life is simpler than it is. But perhaps it's my attitude that is wrong. Weeks after we had flown back to Romania, my mother called to say that he had in fact won it. She then struggled all the way here with it on one of the last flights from London to Belgrade before the war really got started in Bosnia. How could we possibly part with it? She'd be furious.

While Tim straps the kids in, I go upstairs, alone, for one last check to make sure we haven't forgotten anything. The flat is completely empty apart from the furniture. It's as if we had never lived here. There's a pillow left on the bed. I pick it up and shut the door. The old lady next door pops out. I give her the cushion. She starts crying:

"You'll need it, in London, it's expensive," she says trying to push it back into my arms.

She's never been there. How can I say no one in England would care about this battered old pillow? So I explain we have no more room in the car. She is delighted with it and she gives me a hug. I can feel where she broke the top part of her arm in a fall last winter. The bone still has a distinctive kink in it. I wave one last farewell "*dovidjenja*", as I press the button in the cranky old elevator and disappear out of her life.

13 - The Drive

After crossing the border into Hungary we stop at a small outdoor restaurant. We have salad and *pohovani sir*. It's called something different here, but it's the same old grilled cheese. We eat in the garden, in the shade of a tree. The restaurant is attached to a tower that was once a prison and has commanding views across the plain. Inside one of the cells, prisoners have drawn pictures, in their own blood, on the walls. I can't read the Hungarian notice to find out when this happened. Once I would have assumed it was long ago but now I am not so sure. Ben sticks his nose up against the plaster and sniffs the dried blood.

"It doesn't smell of anything," he says looking rather disappointed.

Tim ignores him and moves towards the door:

"We should get a move on. I want to get as far as possible tonight - to somewhere new."

I couldn't agree more. We speed around the rest of the tower and jump into the car.

As we cross the border into Austria, Ben has his nose shoved up against the window. He's leaning over Ray, who is asleep. There are rows of parked lorries and prostitutes. He opens the window to get a better look:

"What are all those women doing standing around?"

I don't answer. Some things he can find out about later.

After twelve hours cooped up in the car, we arrive in St Pölten, a small town west of Vienna. The hotel is chrome and white, with black veneer furniture. There's not a single piece of Balkan brown wood or a splash of beige paint anywhere. There's an extensive menu in the restaurant and prices to match. Ben is impressed and tucks in to what is, naturally, one of the most expensive dishes on offer. He has a talent for picking them.

In the morning, we set off to explore but don't get much further than the toyshop on the corner. Ben grabs Esti's arm and yanks her over to the window:

"Look at that Barbie, Esti!"

They stare at a Barbie in a red, flowery bikini until Esti asks how much it costs.

"Roughly the equivalent of ten marks," I tell her.

She's outraged:

"That's less than Alice!"

Alice was a cheap or, obviously, not so cheap Chinese imitation Barbie, that we bought in the market in Belgrade. Her legs fell off constantly and she was relegated to being the Barbies' cleaner. She didn't make it out of Serbia. Esti looks furious:

"How can it be just ten marks, Mummy?"

"Things like that are cheaper here, that's all."

Ben looks exasperated:

"You don't have to pay gangsters to bring them in for you, twit!"

But, in her mind, it's clearly not as simple as that. This is a personal insult to her Barbie collection. She considers the dolls are worth at least a hundred marks each. Her beloved Dr Barbie has just been devalued. She is happy to leave St Pölten, where they don't know what toys should really cost.

We whizz along the motorway again. It's one of those terrible two lane ones, where you get stuck between the lorries as the Mercedes shoot past, in the fast lane. There's a wail from the backseat:

"I want to go to the loo!"

It's Esti. Tim, who's driving is craning trying to listen to the latest news from Srebrenica on the car radio. He turns up the volume. Not long before we left the Muslim enclave in eastern Bosnia fell to the Serbs.

"Do you want me to pull off," he snaps. "Decide now! There's an exit coming up. It says there's a palace called Stift Melk or something. I think it said that. Do you want to stop Rosie? Say yes or no now!"

The reporter on the radio says that thousands of men and boys fleeing the town have been murdered in scenes reminiscent of the Second World War. I don't feel very decisive:

"I don't know. What is it? What's Stiff Melk?"

Tim looks exasperated:

"I don't care. Decide. I'm trying to listen."

I wish he would just keep his eye on the road for once.

"Stiff Milk, Ray, it's for you," says Ben poking Ray, who is gazing out of the window from her car seat and doesn't get the joke. There isn't much to laugh about.

"I want to go to the loo!" Esti wails from the back seat.

"I'm hungry," growls Ben.

"Pull off," I order Tim.

"Yes! Sure?" One quick check and Tim turns the car sharply.

Stift Melk turns out to be one of Europe's most famous Baroque abbeys.

Inside the monastery, which is really more like a palace, things are less surprising. Ben marches up and down the enormous library, with his hands behind his back muttering:

"I would love a room like this."

Esti giggles:

"Who does he think he is?"

Ben strides out onto the huge, sunny terrace. There's a panoramic view of the Danube and he announces:

"No wonder Napoleon liked it here!"

That's the answer to her question. He fancies himself as conqueror of Europe. After a close inspection of some bones in a gruesome reliquary, it's back in the car for an explanation of why people put bits of the deceased in boxes and put them on display. On the radio, the reports begin to detail the bloodbath in Bosnia. Some dead bodies are worth more than others.

Next stop Linz. On first impression it does well. It's an industrial town but it's surprisingly pretty. There's a network of narrow lanes nestled underneath the castle and splendid town residences with pretty inner courtyards hidden discretely behind arched gates. The beautiful baroque main square is full of cafés and there's a relaxed atmosphere. Ben is sitting in the middle of the back seat as we drive around looking for a hotel. He turns to Esti with a serious, slightly malicious look on his face:

"Do you know who went to school here, Esti?"

He's reiterating, what I told him, while Esti was dozing a few minutes earlier. She looks blank.

"Adolf Hitler. That's who."

Esti still looks blank.

"He wanted to take over the whole of Europe and kill all the Jews. He'd have killed you if he had had a chance. Jews like us would all be dead if he'd won the war."

Esti looks put out and closes her mouth firmly. She turns it down at the corners in an exaggerated grimace.

I tell him to be quiet. Why did he wait until now to start discussing Adolf Hitler in a loud voice? I don't tell him that the remains of the notorious Nazi concentration camp Mauthausen are just a few miles away. Tim turns up the car radio. Then a correspondent says that General Ratko Mladić, the Bosnian Serb army chief, after having assured the inhabitants of Srebrenica that no one would harm them, ordered that all men be separated from their families and executed. Ben forgets Hitler and starts listening to the news:

"What's he saying Dads? What's happened?"

"Just listen!"

"What about Mr Parking?"

Tim ignores him. He turns to me anxiously.

"I don't know. It doesn't look good," I whisper.

The weather is gloriously hot. The hotter the weather, the worse the war gets. We walk over the bridge to catch the Pöstlingbergbahn, Europe's steepest mountain railway. Romantic old carriages grind up the small mountain, on the other side of the river from Linz's elegant town centre. At the top of the mountain, there is not only a wonderful view, but also a grotto full of model gnomes. A mini-train with an ornate green dragon prow takes us into a kitsch, turn-of-the-century collection of fairytale scenes.

As we pass Little Red Riding Hood, Esti takes a sharp intake of breath. French school children learn a lot about wolves. It starts with the Three Pigs and goes on to stories about man-eating beasts in the Alps gobbling up lost children. They even study how wolves live and breed. It's an odd obsession since there are hardly any of them left in France. Esti has obviously been paying attention in class and leans into my skirt in fear. I forget all about Srebrenica. At the exit, we buy three plastic gnomes to put in the garden of our new house in Shepherd's Bush. Ben is delighted with his new purchase.

"I wonder if Hitler liked it here?" he asks jauntily.

I look down at the brown paper bag he's clutching. I will never feel quite the same about these chaps. They remind me of what terrible things men are capable of doing to each other.

We spend the next night in Salzburg. The hotel bedroom is decked out in blue chintz and teetering side tables decorated with lace. We haven't been in the room five minutes before Ray brings a lamp crashing to the ground. Tim looks tense. Ray grins. We decide to take the kids out to the nearest park. It's an elegant, baroque garden with fountains and immaculate lawns. Suddenly Ben leaps up:

"A rat! A rat!"

He's shrieking, deliberately loud, so everyone can hear. Watching the rats run around in the street from the safety of the balcony was his favourite evening activity back in Bucharest. The sleek, shiny black creature runs across the road and down towards the river.

"A rat here! I don't believe I saw a rat! I thought Austria was supposed to be clean. That's what you said."

I'm not sure if Salzburg has gone up, or down, in his estimation.

The next morning we do some sightseeing. Mozart has ruined Salzburg. The main streets are full of tacky souvenirs and chocolate shops. They seem cheap but alluring and are jammed with tourists. I don't like classical music but am still determined to see Mozart's birthplace. We follow the tourist trail and tramp around the composer's uninspiring home.

"Mozart wrote music. He went to Vienna and wrote some wonderful tunes. He fell for an Austrian princess, who later married the King of France. She was Marie-Antoinette. She had her head chopped off."

I try to generate a bit of interest, although I am not really sure of any of the details of the composer's life.

"What happened to Mozart?" asks Esti sullenly.

She clearly thinks he should have had a sticky end. As far as they are concerned most people do. Not to disappoint, Mozart probably did too.

"He died very young - some people say he was poisoned. He died in agony whatever was the cause," I add.

The house is full of endless pieces of highly polished furniture and musical instruments. Neither his life history, his death, nor his home does anything for them. Or me, for that matter. We leave.

The souvenir brand of Mozart does better out in the main street. It's a narrow road with cute little wrought iron shop signs and rack upon rack of postcards. Ben searches in vain for a map of Greater Austria.

"You won't find that here," I explain.

He looks dubious. Tim adds:

"Well, not anymore."

Do countries expand and then contract as part of a preordained feature of their existence?

Every shop on the street sells chocolates emblazoned with a mug shot of the town's most famous son.

"Can I have one, please?" Ben puts on an ingratiating look. It's a Mihai look.

"He won't like it," says Esti.

They cost a small fortune but Tim is in a good mood and agrees to buy him one in a red wrapper. He takes a bite of the round, sickly smelling chocolate and lets out a loud spluttering noise, as the runny liqueur hits his tongue. He spits it on the ground. It's the only dirty mess in Salzburg.

"Told you," says Esti.

As we drive out of Salzburg, Tim has the car radio on at full volume as the true horror of events in Bosnia is related again and again, on the hour, every hour. I know he wishes he were there. I'm glad I am not.

Pewter coloured clouds hang over the mountains. Ben leans forward:

"Dads why can't we drive up there? Mummy told me Hitler had a mountain hideaway. I want to see it."

"No! We don't have time. We're going to show Esti the Alps," says Tim determinedly.

A potted version of Heidi is one of Esti's favourite books at the moment. Tim has clearly decided that Esti should see the real thing. He likes to read fairytales to the children not discuss politics. The girls cheer. Heidi beats Hitler hands down. Maybe there is hope for Europe after all. We have an uneventful drive through the Alps where we picnic in an Alpine meadow. *Spot the Dog* and reports from Srebrenica alternate on the car stereo.

We cross the border into France from Switzerland at Basel. After a long drive past mile upon mile of cornfields, we see a sign pointing to a small *chambre d'hôte*, a bed and breakfast. It turns out to be a gourmet restaurant with two rooms for rent. The tables are in a small courtyard. The waitress hands out the menus and asks what Ray would like. Ray wants an omelette. Esti can't take her eyes off the young girl, who must be about nineteen. I wonder why. She is very plain and wears a dark dress. When she goes to get Ray's food, Esti peeps over her menu at me and whispers:

"She speaks French!"

"Oh course she does! This is France! Everyone speaks French," says Tim, putting his arm around her protectively.

"Everyone?"

Her eyes are completely round.

"Yes, everyone," he says softly, giving her a hug.

The only people she has ever heard speaking French are the pupils and the teachers at school and Granny Marion, of course.

As she is no longer a Balkan babe, Ray needs to be re-styled. So we spend the morning in Mulhouse, buying some elegant French fashion for two-year olds. Unfortunately, her wispy tufts of brown hair give her a scruffy look whatever we do to smarten her up. Esti is still amazed that everyone speaks French. She goes into a bakery with Tim to test it out and emerges with a bag of *pains au chocolat*:

"Look! Just like they used to sell at school."

Every Friday, the snooty French gangster's moll helped out selling *pains au chocolat* after class. In London, earnest mothers sell them on a Thursday afternoon. The money goes to the parents' association. Well, at least in London it does. She holds them up triumphantly.

Then it's all back in the car and off we go. We stop in a small forest on a hillside, to have a picnic. There is a cemetery from the First World War on one side. After lunch, we take a walk to look at the graves. Esti sighs deeply:

"Oh No! There's not a war here in France is there?"

I wish she had more innocence. We stole it away. It's too late to give it back to her. I hope it doesn't matter.

"No. Not anymore. This one is over," I say taking her hand and giving it a squeeze. All the same, she eyes the endless cemeteries that Ben insists on stopping at in the Somme, with suspicion. I can see she doesn't trust me that this one is really finished.

As we drive up towards Calais the road empties out.

"Where's everyone gone?" asks Ben. "Are we the only people going to England?"

He's right. The motorway has a deserted look about it, like no one has bothered to tell us that England has floated off and is now moored elsewhere. The news on the radio gets no better. The death toll from Srebrenica just goes on rising. How nice it would be to sail off to another part of the world.

Eventually we drive into London through the suburbs of Lewisham and Peckham, past gloomy looking barbers' shops and newsagents, all with grilles on their windows. It looks urban and menacing. It's filthy.

"Where are we?" asks Esti.

Ray looks up at her from her car seat, with a worried expression that is quite out of character.

"London. This is London. We're here!" says Tim, triumphant.

"Is it?" says Esti.

She's looking around wildly, with a desperate look on her face:

"I don't remember Granny Marion and Pa living here. Where is Holland Park?"

14 - Housework and Ethnic Cleansing

Upstairs, in his room in our new house in London, Ben is rearranging his soldiers in his wooden fort. He's almost eight-years old. It has stickers adorned with the Bosnian Muslim crest stuck on the keep. From the turret, there's a Macedonian flag flying and parked outside is his old white plastic truck with UN written on the side. He's painted half the plastic soldiers' helmets blue. They are peacekeeping troops and have been escorting an aid convoy. They've been attacked and their truck is on fire. I know this because flames, orange bits of paper, have been shoved in the windows. Scattered among the brightly coloured Lego bricks on the carpet in the corner, are his endless doodles of knights and sieges. Ben is humming away, happily.

"How was school?" I ask him.

"Boring. I got into trouble, again, because I spelt everything wrong."

Ben and Esti have moved seamlessly from their school in Belgrade to the French Lycée in South Kensington, where they follow exactly the same curriculum. He tosses his school bag at me:

"There's a note from the teacher. Here. Read it."

"Oh no! What now?"

Last night Ben and I spent an hour and a half, trying to learn how to spell the word *brebis*, or "ewe", for today's test. I can't believe it hasn't gone well. Why *brebis* is always in French spelling lists is a great mystery to me. How often do French children write the word *brebis* in their lives? The teacher wants Ben to see the school speech therapist. I'm not sure how that will help with spelling, particularly as he is one of the most articulate people I know.

Two weeks later, she's assessed Ben and asks me to come to meet her in her office. At last, some help is at hand. Perhaps, we can finally learn how to spell *brebis*, and move on to more important things. *Cendrier*, or "ashtray", is another favourite.

We troop into her office. I'm carrying Ray, who sits down on my lap. Esti, who can't wait to find out what this lady has got to say about her brother, has managed to wangle a day off. She says she's ill, but in fact, she doesn't like this new school much. She wants to go back to Belgrade and it doesn't help that Tim is back in Serbia. The Serbian-held parts of Croatia were retaken by the Croats days after we moved in and Tim left immediately. I was left to unpack the suitcases and paint the house all on my own. I'm beginning to think that, if we had spent more time together, we would have been divorced years ago. Most people say "Poor you!" or "can't you tell him to come home?" The truth is I like the freedom it gives me to do exactly what I like for a few weeks. I can chuck out all his rubbish while he isn't looking and sort out the house exactly the way I want it to be. Anyway, if I clipped Tim's wings and told him to stay home, he wouldn't be the man I fell in love with. One of the reasons I love him is that he has the guts to flit off to places other people would never dare to go.

Esti is parked at a miniature desk next to me and told to draw a picture. The therapist slips another drawing across the table:

"Have you seen this?" she asks, with a worried look on her face.

Peeping round Ray, who is bundled up in a big fluffy coat and hat, I recognise one of Ben's siege scenes. It's actually a rather good one. A man is shooting out of the top of the castle as a canonball explodes nearby. Red flames leap around the walls. I feel very proud of him. I say innocently:

"Yes, it must be Ben's. He draws loads of pictures like that."

She moves closer across the desk, adjusting her glasses:

"Does it worry you?"

"No why should it? I think it's great. It's very realistic, isn't it?"

I have no idea what a stupid thing I have just said.

"Precisely, it's very realistic. You've just arrived back from Yugoslavia, haven't you? Don't you think it should worry you?"

I still don't get it:

"No! He's always drawn these pictures. He loves playing with toy soldiers, too."

She lowers the tone of her voice:

"But, look at the scene, it's very violent."

"Well, it's a battle isn't it?" I can't understand what this is all about.

"Does Ben worry about war?"

"No. Not especially, no more than anyone else."

I suddenly begin to realise that, perhaps, I have to watch my words.

"But, this is a picture of a medieval siege, not a real war," I say desperately.

"Does he draw modern battles?"

"Yes, of course, sometimes. He's always doodling."

I look down at Esti and can't believe that she is drawing a castle and some knights. She has never done this before. I panic. How can she do this to me now?

The speech therapist, who clearly fancies herself as a psychiatrist, fixes her eyes on me:

"How was life in Belgrade?"

There's really no neat answer to this question. I hear myself say:

"Very nice. We had a very nice time, thank you," I start muttering about trips to the zoo.

"But, the war?"

She drags out the word, elongating the 'a'. It sounds like "roar".

"Yes, but, there wasn't a real shooting, firing war in Belgrade. We had a very nice time, most of the time. Esti is furious that we've left."

Fortunately, she doesn't look at Esti, who is colouring in some blood on one of her injured knights. She usually draws pretty flowers and houses. She's quick and has worked out that battle scenes get more attention.

"Did Ben draw pictures like this in school while he was in Belgrade?"

"Yes! Loads. I remember a rather good one he drew during the siege of Dubrovnik, which had a row of aid trucks pulling up outside the city. He drew his father in the siege, holding a little boy's hand. The teacher was impressed and showed it to me. She thought is was rather tender."

She pulls her glasses down her nose:

"These pictures are a sign of severe stress, I think."

I cannot believe what I'm hearing. His father is a war correspondent so he's interested in war. What's so odd about that? My father was an obstetrician so I spent all the time pretending my Cindy dolls were having sex and giving birth. When we first came back to England, when the war had just broken out in Yugoslavia, I felt then that people didn't really know what was going on. This is confirmation of it. This woman thinks my highly intelligent, astute son is suffering from some kind of war trauma. She doesn't know anything. She has no idea. How can she? She just met him this week. He likes drawing, that's all, and playing with soldiers just like every other boy on the planet. I think about all the poor children who have had their lives destroyed by the war and wonder why she is wasting my time. So, I say matter-of-factly:

"But, Ben didn't have any stress, not really, not compared to everyone else. He lived a happy, cosseted life. He just likes drawing battle scenes. He's interested in wars. So he should be."

I am really angry:

"He's never seen real fighting. The teacher was very pleased with the aid trucks in his picture; all the other kids had drawn these sorts of pictures too. She liked the way he saw what his father was doing - something to protect the people who lived there. I'm sorry but this is just silly. Knowing about war isn't necessarily being traumatised by it, that much I have learned."

I begin to wonder if she's about to refer me for counselling too. What would she do with Tim and Chris? I think about all the light-hearted, relaxed war reporters I know. What would she make of them cracking jokes and laughing? Maybe they are all in denial. She leans forward, again:

"But, the life, the war..."

It's clear that this woman does not know my child. I'm getting even crosser now:

"He went to school, came home, had lunch, and went to the park. Sometimes a friend came over and if he was lucky he watched cartoons and went to bed." What does this woman know about his life? "We didn't live in Sarajevo. It was miles away. We went once but he didn't live there. The war was in Bosnia not in Belgrade. It's in a different country. Do you know your geography of the Balkans?"

She looks surprised.

"It's been much more stressful coming back to England," I add. She has to get to grips with herself. She needs to live in the real world not one she has seen on TV and read about in the papers. I hit back some more:

"You can't imagine what it's like, suddenly, living in a place full of cars, luxuries and everything you could want. Taking Ben for a walk around Harrods is much more stressful for him than anything he ever experienced in Yugoslavia. It's very difficult realising that people here are so rich and that they can have everything and anything at the drop of a hat. They're the ones who are in denial. Just seeing rows of packets of Frosties, in the supermarket is a shock. Belgrade was normal for the kids, rows upon rows of Frosties are not."

She, clearly, thinks I'm mad. She has no idea what I am talking about, as she takes her cosy world for granted. I think she should get on with the job she is supposed to be doing.

"He's anxious," she says. "It must be the war."

"Listen, he's anxious because the teacher is shouting at him because he is finding spelling a bit difficult. The war is an everyday boring activity as far as he is concerned."

"Yes, perhaps, I have made a mistake," she says ushering me to the door.

We never get round to talking about why Ben can't spell *brebis*, which is the only real problem in his life. After an hour and a half of idiotic discussion, we are free to go. I come downstairs and discover a parking fine on the windscreen of my car. London is extremely stressful. I can't stand this risk-averse culture. It was far more relaxing in Belgrade. I hope Mr Parking got away.

Then, it's on to Sainsbury's. I wish I had that speech therapist here with me now. That would be a laugh. I am still fuming about this morning's conversation. Ray toddles after Esti, as she inspects every packet on the biscuit aisle. As usual Ray is dressed in a strange combination of trousers and dress. Not my choice but hers.

"What's that one got in it, Mummy?" asks Esti, who is naturally suspicious about anything on sale in England.

It doesn't help that I like to read the labels, as I don't want them eating gelatine because, I think they might catch mad cow disease. Britain's herds are infected with it. This seems much more dangerous to me than living in Serbia. The main problem is that there's a misunderstanding and the kids think gelatine and jam are the same thing. She pokes a packet of biscuits with little red hearts on:

"Those are called Jammie Dodgers, Ray."

She pulls back and pushes Ray, protectively with her hand:

"No Ray! No, good! They could kill you!"

Ray waddles on behind Esti, who doesn't pick anything up, but runs her fingers along the packets cautiously. They disappear around the corner. I hear them giggling. What can possibly be so funny about the household cleaners? Esti is dancing around with a feather duster:

"Wow, Ray! Look at all these things you can put in the loo!"

She turns to me:

"Who needs all this stuff, Mummy?"

It's a good question – one that I have been trying to get to grips with.

People work all hours to pay for "this stuff" but the fact is they simply don't need any of it. They would be better off coming home earlier from work and spending time with their family. Living in Romania and Serbia has taught me you don't need these things to be happy. I hope I'm right. I seem to be swimming against the tide.

"Come on girls! I need some milk."

"Oh Mummy! Can't you get some normal milk? That one tastes horrid, doesn't it Ray?" says Esti, as I pick up a litre of organic, semi-skimmed.

She is still addicted to long-life Serbian milk. Ray nods in agreement:

"Can't we go back to Belgrade? I don't like it here. I want some real milk."

The two of them, who have never lived in England, don't think of this as a homecoming but a move to a foreign country. It makes me look at the place more critically as I introduce them to my home.

It's only the beginning of October, but the Christmas sweets are already on sale. The three of us pick up and finger the chocolate coins and lollies in the shape of Christmas trees. The girls don't ask for anything but put each one back. They move on slowly down the aisle, stroking and inspecting the confectionary. This is their favourite pastime.

"It's not Christmas! I haven't had *my* birthday yet! What's wrong with these people?" says Esti.

"What's wrong with her?" screeches Ben incensed when I tell him about what the speech therapist said that morning. "It's hardly like I was in Srebrenica is it?"

I have trouble adjusting too as England seems to have changed beyond all recognition. The shops stay open all hours. It seems so modern and bright, as well as full of useless things you don't really need. But I settle back into the pace of things eventually. I start freelancing and pick up where I left off, although now I write articles about childcare instead of making programmes about foreign affairs. I can do this at home. I may not make as much money but it is enough. One thing I have learned by now is that if I have a choice I won't hand my children over to someone else to look after them. They are far too precious.

The big excitement is that we have another new baby on the way! Now, it is Tim's turn to give birth. His baby is a book about Serbia. It's an intense six-month pregnancy. He spends most of it locked in the upstairs sitting room. When I pass the door I can hear the clatter of his keyboard. Periodically he emerges with a draft for me to read. When the book is published to critical acclaim it is dedicated to me and "my slash and burn tactics". I ravaged the first draft mercilessly. It was a very intimate moment but when I had finished Tim staggered up the stairs in an odd fashion as if he was about to have a heart attack.

On the whole, things seem pretty sorted until, when Ray is four, I discover I'm having twins. I wanted one more baby - now I'm going have two! How come they keep sneaking up on me like this? Tim is delighted. In the consulting room he couldn't stop giggling when he heard the news. I felt numb. But, again I'm shocked by what people have to say about my latest pregnancy. I can't believe how many friends tell me how sorry they are, as if I am some sort of downtrodden wife. They should ask Tim – he'll tell them I never do anything I don't want to.

Two new people are about to arrive and so has another war. The conflict in Bosnia came to an end in November 1995 when, exhausted, and bullied by the outside powers and especially the Americans, the Bosnians of all stripes had finally agreed to a peace deal while virtually locked up together in an American airbase in Dayton, Ohio. Now the action is in Kosovo, Serbia's southern province. Serbs say it is the cradle of their civilisation but the problem is that now, of its two million people some 90% of them are ethnic Albanians who have always chafed at Serbian rule. They want independence. Horrified by the ethnic cleansing that has taken place in Croatia and Bosnia they have followed a line of passive resistance until now. But has it got them anywhere? No, it has not argue hardliners, who think it is time to take up arms.

As my stomach grows so big that I think I will explode, fierce fighting breaks out between the Serbian police and the ethnic Albanian, Kosovo Liberation Army (KLA). Tim spends the summer with the KLA watching a guerrilla war unfold while I spend most of it in bed unable to fathom what is going on. It's bad enough trying to concentrate with one baby but with two it is impossible. I feel as if the family has gone into suspended animation. All I can manage, and all we can afford for a holiday, is a week in Norfolk. Ben hates it and is furious with me for not making more money. I hope he'll see it differently when he gets older.

Finally, Jacob and Evie are born in October as the armed unrest escalates and the Serbs launch a brutal crackdown. They look stunningly like Ben and Esti. Within weeks Tim is back in Kosovo. He's built a very successful freelance career. Now he has written a book he's an "expert" and much in demand. I am left to change Jacob and Evie's nappies and fill their milk bottles while he gets on with the gruesome side of life. I learn to type with one hand and hold two babies in the other as the pressure is on to earn more money to pay for all the milk they drink. Tim may put his life on the line but the pay cheques don't reflect the effort we all put in.

Something however has really revolutionised our lives. Tim has bought a mobile phone. Now I can rant, wail or whisper sweet nothings to him whenever I feel like. When the car breaks down I can ring him up and ask him what to do. He can keep tabs on what time the kids got to school. I'm not very good at getting up in the morning.

One afternoon when I'm collecting the kids from school he calls to tell me about the looting of a Serbian Church by Albanians that happened moments ago and how the situation had turned very nasty. He got away just in time:

"I just had to tell you. I wish you had been there. Is everything alright with you?"

I can feel the adrenalin pumping down the phone. It lights up the playground.

As the conflict escalates out of control I book a holiday in the French countryside. It's supposed to be a rural idyll. The war has been profitable. En route to the romantic looking stone watermill in the heart of the Berry however, we are forced to divert to the Château of Rambouillet just south of Paris, where the British, the French and the Americans are trying to broker a peace settlement. In effect the Serbs have been given an ultimatum: Sign or we'll bomb you.

The moment I pull the ticket out of the machine at the tollbooth just south of Calais, the phone rings and Tim agrees to appear live on *Channel 4 News* outside the château to analyse events. As I hit the rush hour on the Périphérique, the ring road around Paris, we immediately grind to a halt in slow moving traffic. Tim is on his mobile phone calling contacts in the hills in the Balkans and KLA men in Switzerland for the latest. We sit silently while he does a live interview for the *BBC*. Esti pops the babies' dummies into their mouths and we pray they won't make a sound as the car edges forward in the traffic jam. The four of us get a crash course on what as been going on in Kosovo while we were battling with the twins.

We learn that the KLA, finding little resistance took control of a large part of the province. Then the Serbs struck back hard and some 200,000 ethnic Albanians were driven from their homes. Attempts to end the fighting have got nowhere. Now, in response to an ambush by the KLA in which three Serbian policemen were killed the Serbs have hit the nearby village of Racak apparently murdering 45 Albanian civilians in cold blood. They deny it, but it is the trigger for action. That's why the big guys have called a conference at Rambouillet. They are terrified of Srebrenica happening all over again and being accused of having learned nothing and done nothing.

As soon as the interview is over, Ben, who has a terrible cold, throws up in the back seat but there is no time to stop. Esti helps clean him up, as I drive through Versailles at 50 miles an hour. Then she shovels spoonfuls of tomato rice into Jacob and Evie who are in their car seats on either side of her – it's their dinner time. What would I do without her? I lurch to the left and pull into Rambouillet town centre two minutes before Tim is due on air. We screech to a halt at the police barricade in front of the château. Tim leaps out and runs off. Evie wails. Her nappy reeks. A policeman walks up and explains politely that we can't park here. I pretend I don't understand. He takes one look inside the car and decides we aren't a security risk and walks off.

The next day we amuse ourselves in the shops on Rambouillet high street, as there's a last ditch attempt to broker the deal. On the way out of the Monoprix supermarket, where we have stocked up on nappies and jars of baby food, I bump into Bridget Kendall, the *BBC* Diplomatic Correspondent. She's a former colleague of mine. In fact, she used to terrify me because she always got everything right and I was usually the producer who had booked the inarticulate speaker. She is as immaculately dressed as ever and as she clucks over the kids, she tells me not to worry, as she is sure that there will be no bombing.

"It'll happen this time," I say. "I can feel it in the air."

I am not sure that I feel so definite about this simply because I can't bear the thought of Milošević getting away with it again or that, when it comes to the Balkans, I have learned that if you expect the worst you are probably going to be right.

Soon after we get back to London, Tim leaves for Albania. The Serbs won't give him a visa. They don't want him snooping about. A veneer of business as usual masks the chaos of life in Shepherd's Bush. Ben and Esti watch TV while they cuddle the babies and I cook the dinner. They have to help or nothing would get done. The house is noisy, chaotic and dirty. I have given up on vacuuming years ago. A lot of people think we are barmy to have such a big family. There are days when I agree. This evening, the kids are glued to a children's programme about Newcastle. I can't make out what they can possible understand:

"Do you know what that girl has just said? She wants to buy a new 'cozzie'. Do you know what a 'cozzie' is guys?" I shout from the kitchen.

The three of them look blank.

"A swimsuit, guys!"

They look amazed. I chuckle to myself and stir the pasta.

The news just gets worse and worse. NATO's bombing campaign of Serbia is now well underway. It will only stop when Serbian forces withdraw and peacekeepers are allowed in. Hundreds of thousands of Albanian refugees are flooding out of Kosovo. One night Tim calls to tell me he has just interviewed people on a convoy as they crossed the border into Albania. They are almost all women who tell him that the men and boys of fighting age have been forcibly taken away. They are desperate to discover what has happened to their loved ones. What they don't know yet is that the refugees behind them have seen the bodies. I have never heard Tim sound so flat. He's with Chris, who comes on the phone and asks me to call his editor. He sounds exactly the same. It's as if someone had picked them both up and wrung all the spirit out of them. He passes the phone back to Tim who says he has to go. So do I: Evie has woken up. She wakes Jacob. I wish I was there to look after Tim. At this point Ben and Esti appear at the bedroom door. I tell them what has happened and how tired their father sounded. Esti takes Evie and gives her some milk. We sit there gloomily. I wish I could say something light-hearted but nothing comes to mind. The inhumanity of what is going on at the end of the phone line is too much. I think that their experiences are so different from the majority of the kids who are getting into their beds across the country that it is no surprise that they seem unable to make any really deep connections with Britain. I feel guilty that they have ended up with parents like us. Perhaps they would be happier if we were more like everyone else.

Eventually, my mother makes a rare visit to London to lend a hand. She's sitting on the sofa looking at Esti curiously, as she gets ready for school:

"Mummy, where's my *trousse*? It's not in my *sac*. Ben, can I borrow a *stylo plume* and an *effaceur*? Oh God! Don't tell me you haven't got one, you idiot!"

She's rifling through Ben's satchel and doesn't even wait for Ben to answer. I'm not even sure that her brother is in the room. What Esti wants are her pencil case, a fountain pen and an eraser pen.

"Can't you speak English? What do you want?" asks my mother in exasperation.

Esti, who is growing up to be a stylish, sophisticated girl, drags her brown curls out of her eyes. I panic. I think she is going to be rude. She has a quick temper but to my relief, she smiles and says:

"I don't know what they're called in English, Grandma."

Ray appears:

"Mummy can I have a *goûter*?"

"She wants a snack, that's a *goûter*. Can you get her one?" I ask my mother, who goes off with Ray to inspect the cupboard.

"What's acceptable for a *goûter*?" she asks.

"Anything without jam in is alright, Grandma."

"What's wrong with jam?" asks my mother mystified. "I don't know about you lot. I really don't"

One day, she asks Ben:

"Where are you from? I just don't understand what you are. I've never been sure about this." He doesn't say anything, which is unusual for him to miss a chance to be provocative. Perhaps, he doesn't know.

"Guess that depends where I am," interrupts Esti.

I'm surprised that she is taking the question so seriously.

"Once, I thought I was from Serbia. Now I'm from London."

"I remember when you only spoke Romanian, Esti," adds Ben. "Pa was like that, you know, he understood some Indian language, as a little boy."

Grandma looks confused. Tim's father was born in Calcutta, I remind her, but that's another story, altogether.

"Give me a call when you have worked it all out," says my mother. "I think it might be an idea."

Ben turns on the TV. It's 6pm. The news is just beginning. Esti watches in horror as cruise missiles smash through Belgrade city centre. The Ministry of Defence on Knez Miloša is hit. All I can think is:

"At last! Whoopee!"

"What about the old lady? What about Maja?" asks Esti. "Who is looking after them?"

I feel numb. Tim's aunt rings to complain that I have forgotten her birthday.

"But they are bombing Belgrade," I stammer.

15 - Beans, Madmen and English Ladies

The years slip by but the kids seem no more at home outside the M25 than when we first arrived back in Britain. They talk about the English, as though they were a race about which they know little. They pick up the array of cakes that my mother serves up when we visit her in Yorkshire with a nervous fascination. She has abandoned Cornwall to be closer to my sister. There are a host of strange things to discover up north, like *fat rascals* and *parkins* and all kinds of other buns and biscuits with funny sounding names.

After a morning tour of the cake shops, we end up in the playground with my sister, Jane, and two of the kids' cousins, Kate and Jo. It's almost lunchtime and Jane suggests we eat at the small outdoor café by the river:

"You can try one of Kate's favourite chip butties, Ben. I'll get some for everyone."

She walks over to the kiosk, before he has time to answer. He leans across the wooden table:

"What? A what?"

"It's a classic English sandwich, Ben. It's made with chips," I hiss.

Esti and Ray, who looked downcast at the sound of a sandwich, have perked up at the magic word "chips". My sister arrives back smiling with the sandwiches wrapped in paper napkins. Esti and Ray miss the point altogether and pick the chips out of the white bun, as if it's some sort of padded container. Ben looks at his lunch with disbelief, as he unpeels the white paper. When my sister gets up and goes with her daughters to buy a coffee, Ben leans across the table, wide-eyed:

"Whatever was that? You can't seriously tell me that people eat that sort of thing here?"

"Was I supposed to eat the chips *in* the bun?" asks Esti in disbelief.

It isn't just chip butties. We spend the night in a farmhouse bed and breakfast. The next morning, the farmer's wife cooks a full English breakfast, complete with baked beans. She puts the plate down in front of Esti. Luckily, she goes back into the kitchen to get the toast.

"What's this?" says Esti, poking her fork at the orangey red pile next to her fried egg.

"Baked beans. It's beans in tomato sauce," I reply under my breath, "just eat up."

Tim is sniggering into his coffee:

"How can they never have seen baked beans, Rosie? They must be the only people in Britain who've never seen a baked bean."

I can't believe it. Now, I've failed because I've never served up beans on toast. He seems to have forgotten that this would have been a bit tricky in the Balkans, where there simply aren't any baked beans, or rather any that would pass as such for a discerning British palate. What is even odder is that I have never seen him eat them in his life. I can't imagine Granny Marion ever bought such a thing. It's time to hit back. I put the ball firmly in his court:

"Well, they don't serve them at school do they? Can you imagine a French canteen serving baked beans?"

The farmer's wife appears with the toast and immediately shoots off to get some jam.

I growl under my breath at them while Tim is still spurting and giggling into his coffee cup:

"Just eat them up fast before she comes back!"

Amazingly, for once they do what I say. In seconds, they've gobbled them all up. When the farmer's wife comes back, Esti asks for more. Their British genes have scored a point, even if chip butties were an own goal.

Not long after this we embark on a tour of England. I've recently found myself a niche writing and updating travel guides for families. It's great. It is a job we can all do together. I'm lucky. It's been a hard journey but I think I've got the balance right at last. We're in Scarborough updating a guidebook. Evie, Jacob and Ray are riding up and down on donkeys along the long sandy beach. I say to Esti that I think Scarborough looks just like the sort of seaside town that a child would draw – it looks like the kind of place that *Topsy and Tim* might go on holiday. There's a huge Victorian hotel or two, a castle on the headland and a long sweep of sand. People are sitting, eating chips behind windbreaks and drinking tea. There's a funfair and, of course, the donkey rides.

"Err..., I suppose so," says Esti.

I forget it was Ben who really liked the *Topsy and Tim* books. Esti always found them rather alien. She preferred to read *Juliette*. The star of these stories is a little French babe, who skips around on the beach in a red polka dot bikini and dreams of going windsurfing. She gets the boys to make her a sandcastle, while she looks slinky. Esti gazes about her, taking the whole scene in with one enormous roll of her big eyes:

"I don't know. I've never been anywhere like this before."

"Oh, Esti! Come on." I say. "You must have seen the holiday specials on *Blue Peter* and Saturday morning TV. They always come from resorts like this."

She hasn't. The great British seaside experience obviously is in the black hole, where once tins of baked beans lurked.

When we get back to the hotel, Ben phones. He's in Paris with Granny Marion. He recounts his day and impersonates the people he has met. He always gives French women a high pitched squeal and men a deep growl. He speaks so quickly that the jokes are lost on me as I haven't the faintest idea of who has said what. Then, as ever, he's changed the subject before I can ask for a translation.

"What's it like there?" he asks.

"Pretty much like you'd expect but nicer than you would have thought," I answer.

"What's that supposed to mean? You're supposed to be a writer but you can't describe a thing! Let me speak to Esti. I want to find out what it's really like. She'll tell me."

I'm dismissed. I can't believe how grown up he sounds. Esti takes the phone:

"Oh Ben! You should see this, you'd never believe it…"

Her voice trails off as she takes the phone out onto the balcony. I lurk by the door to hear what she has to say. She describes the day in Scarborough just as I've heard her recount traveller's tales down the phone to my mother while we have been abroad. She concludes:

"It's one of those places English people like."

A lot of things are mystifying about Britain really. Our attitude to children is one of them. The week Tony Blair's youngest son Leo was born, I was asked by *Channel 4 News* to make a short film about how un-child-friendly Britain was. Gleeful at the chance to rant about family friendly restaurants or hotels where you end up trapped in a ghetto of overpriced chicken nuggets and bad service, I accepted without hesitation. But what happened when we started filming was a revelation. I tried to get on a traditional London bus in Kensington High Street with the twins in their double buggy. While I was trying to hold the two babies and fold the pushchair, I heard the bus conductor's feet clattering down the stairs. I assumed he was rushing to help.

"Get off lady! You're holding us up," he screamed viciously.

A voice further down the bus growled:

"Yeah! Get off, you!"

There was a chorus of abuse. What was the rush? Where were they all going? I was face to face with British yobs and the majority of them, in this case, were pensioners! Was this the last bus out of London and no one had told me? Come to think of it when I was evacuated from Sarajevo the bus had waited for me. I had no choice but to retreat back to the pavement. Not a single person helped me or even appeared to notice that they were being filmed. Or what is worse maybe they were happy they were being filmed. Getting me off the bus was more important than anything else. I was clearly doing something that the English don't like.

Just what *is* important to people baffles me. The country is full of toyshops, the supermarkets are stuffed with kid's snacks and there are endless designer baby boutiques but, if you ask a child what their parents do, the majority of them will look blank. Parents work long hours to pay for it all and the majority of them define themselves by their careers but don't bother to take the time to explain to their children what they actually do. It's also extraordinary how many parents never seem to be at home out of office hours. The other night Ben came back grumpily after being ordered home before the last tube.

"What have you been doing?" I asked anxiously.

He spun a garbled tale of drugs and drinking. Tim and I asked in chorus:

"Where were the parents?"

He shrugged:

"They're never there."

Panic! I must be more stay-at-home than ever. Oh my God – just imagine what could happen while I'm at Sainsbury's! But where *were* the parents while their children were getting stoned? At the cinema? Late night shopping?

Or perhaps they were too busy talking about the Royal Family? On the way back from Scarborough, we stop at Althorp Park, where Princess Diana is buried. It seems you can't be British, without having an enduring fascination with the "dead princess", as Evie calls her. We have the luck of living close to the luxury children's playground in Kensington Gardens, built as a memorial to her with money donated by people from all over the country. I thank them wholeheartedly for being so generous, so we can enjoy ourselves. That's how Evie and Jacob know who she was. There's a photo of her in the rain shelter, where the benches are made of wood from Bosnia, from somewhere near Tuzla. If Mr Parking survived, maybe he cut down the trees, as most of the survivors from Srebrenica ended up there. I speed down the motorway still trying to grapple with the thought that some 8,000 men and boys were murdered and decide England isn't so bad after all. Esti isn't convinced. I wonder if she has any roots, if it is my fault, and if it really matters anyway.

There's torrential rain as we pull off the motorway at Northampton, where we promptly get lost in the town centre.

"Ugh! What's she doing living here?" says Ray, as we whizz past a B&Q.

"What is it with the English? Why do they love home improvements?" says Esti who never even hangs up her clothes.

"We love those TV shows don't we Mummy?" says Ray who is currently addicted to the decorating show *Changing Rooms*.

"I bet the Queen watches it, Ray, what d'ya think?"

Esti has a point. There was recently a big story in the tabloids about how Her Majesty watches *EastEnders*.

During the summer of 1997, at the end of which Diana was killed in a car crash, we were in Paris. It may sound exotic but it wasn't. We went because my mother-in-law has a flat there and this was a budget option. One afternoon, I took the kids to the hairdresser. While they were being dolled up, I read *Paris Match*. There were pictures of Diana, on a luxury yacht in the Med, looking a million dollars. I was really jealous. After she died, I vowed I'd never feel envious of anyone again, in case I cast an evil spell on them. Esti recounts this story to Ray as we are ushered into a spot that couldn't be further from the main gate, by a parking attendant.

It costs a whacking £28.50 to get in. We are escorted along an avenue where the guide tells us that the Earl, Diana's brother, who owns the place, has planted one tree for every year of her life. Esti makes a face at Ray. The tour starts in the stable block, where you can see a collection of Diana memorabilia, from her first ballet shoes to her wedding dress and watch cinefilms of her childhood. Some of her most famous outfits are on display. The girls think they are hilarious.

"Don't tell us you ever wore anything so terrible, Mummy! Look at that! It's foul."

"Yuk!" says Evie.

I try to explain, that when Diana was dancing with John Travolta, I was in Belgrade, where there wasn't much call for sparkly evening dresses, unless you were a gangster's moll, but they have shot on to gawp at the books of condolence and miss this.

"Where's the book that was in Tesco?" asks Esti, debasing what is supposed to be one of those moments where you stand hanky in hand.

We trail round the house, which is about as boring as stately homes can get. For Esti the highlight of the tour is checking out the Earl's CD collection.

"Oldies' taste, Ray," is the verdict.

Then it's on to his drinks' trolley:

"Wow! There's Coke! Do you think his kids get to just help themselves? Maybe not, it's a bit flat."

She scans his book collection:

"Bet he's never read them all. What do you think Ray?"

They look so dusty. I wonder if he has any new ones.

Now we've trailed past the family portraits, we can get to the main purpose of the visit: The grave. Diana is buried on a small island, in the middle of a lake. It's a disappointment. It's tiny, more like a pond. Evie and Jacob sit in the double buggy looking at the depressing, wet, scene. Evie's sandy blond curls have been matted onto her forehead by the rain.

"I wanted to go to a Diana park. Where are the swings?"

Jacob looks crestfallen and glances anxiously at his twin sister.

The guide tells us that beside the family, the only person who has ever been on the island is Nelson Mandela.

"How come he gets everywhere?" asks Esti.

We stand in the rain contemplating the scene. It's dismal and if you remember the funeral, an anti-climax. I feel a need to bring it alive:

"You know, when your Dad went to cover Diana's funeral and he was standing outside Westminster Abbey all night, he stood next to the man who shot Jill Dando? They got talking and the next thing, Dads recognised him on TV being arrested."

"Who's that Dando person?" asks Ray.

Esti leaps in to explain:

"Oh you know Ray! The newsreader - that one who was gunned down on her doorstep during the war in Kosovo. She had done some appeal for refugees and Mummy thought it had something to do with the war, of course. Then she decided that because Dads was reporting the war in Kosovo, telling everyone what a terrible time Albanians were having, some mad Serb might assassinate her on the doorstep."

"What's that got to do with Diana, Esti?"

"Ray! She looked just like her. Don't you get it? He was mad. She was one of those English-looking ladies. He had a thing about them."

I glance at Esti; she is a curvaceous, eleven-year old with long, wavy brown hair, dark eyes and slight tan. I'm glad she has no resemblance whatsoever to Diana, just in case a crazy man is lurking in the bushes.

"Just imagine if Ben had buried me in the middle of a lake like this. What would his wife think?" she muses.

I just can't imagine Ben doing this, so I decide not to fret too much about it. According to the tabloids Charles Spencer, who has so far had two wives and a large number of girlfriends didn't care what they thought about anything either.

"We want to buy a postcard." Evie has her priorities in order.

Jacob is indignant. This time he glares at her. He mutters:

"I don't want a postcard Evie, I want a pen."

So, it's off to find the souvenirs.

Unfortunately, this is the only gift shop in the country that doesn't sell key rings, rubbers and badges. All that is on sale are expensive copies of Diana's jewellery and perfume bottles. Her brother is standing at the counter ready to sign his latest book. I wonder if he's in need of psychiatric help or is just cashing in. In the café, there's no hot food, so we buy some sandwiches to eat in the car. Esti opens hers in the front seat, while I pull out of the car park. It's duck - her favourite:

"Just look at this!"

She's indignantly picking at the limp lettuce:

"He's ruined it by putting some horrible soy sauce on it! There are even some cranberries. Why does everything in this country have to be a crazy mixture of practically every other place on earth? Can't they just sell something English? You know the English teacher told us they invented sandwiches here, not half way across the world."

While Esti is ranting I have visions of Diana's brother buttering sliced bread in the café kitchen.

"Should have chosen egg mayonnaise like us," pipes up Ray from the back seat.

Jacob brandishes his salt 'n' vinegar crisps. What would she have said if Diana's brother had stocked the café with chip butties?

16 - Germany: Tinsel and Total War

"Do you think we should take this one with the reindeers and the sleigh, or the other one that has Santa with his sack and a fir tree?"

Ray is selecting a Christmas candleholder in a room festooned with tinsel. Across an array of baubles, I can see the now thirteen-year old Ben eying a stylish, young Japanese girl in a tartan mini-skirt, who's standing next to him fingering a music box seductively. Everyone in the shop, apart from us, is either Japanese or American. This isn't just any old store. It's the Käthe Wohlfahrt Christmas market in Rothenburg ob der Tauber in southern Germany. Outside, in the main square, it's a boiling 34°C. It's late July 2001. I'm here to write a festive feature. Christmas travel articles need to be sold to magazines in the summer. In the centre of the shop floor is an enormous, revolving Christmas tree. The blurb in the leaflets at the desk says it is decked out with over a thousand balls and more than 7,000 lights.

"God! It's plastic! They could at least have got a real one don't you think?" says Esti flicking a silvery cherub, which I have just put in the shopping basket, back into the pile. "Too kitsch, that one!"

She extracts a delicate wooden train with a trail of cotton wool smoke from underneath a small, green wreath:

"We're having this one, aren't we, Jakie?"

"Woo-woo!" is the answer.

Jacob is mad about trains. Tim eggs him on. They spend hours watching *Thomas the Tank Engine* videos together. Esti pops it in the shopping basket with a flourish. She loves spending other people's money. Jacob gazes at her in admiration. He's almost three. He has pale brown hair and fine features. His eyes are blue grey - the colour of the North Sea. They are my father's eyes. Sometimes he looks at me with a knowing expression that unnerves me and makes me feel I should own up to not having done my homework.

The Christmas market is big business in Rothenburg. The tills are clocking up the Deutschemarks, and the staff are busy organising for box loads of sparkly tat to be shipped back to Tokyo and the States.

"Don't they have any Christmas decorations there?" asks Esti.

We head upstairs to find out more. On the first floor of the shop there is a small museum, which is goes by the amazingly unpronounceable name of the Deutsches Weihnachtsmuseum. We pay a few marks to get in and discover that we are the only visitors. The other tourists are happy to part with their money but clearly aren't interested in what they are buying.

"Don't show Ray this! It's not suitable," whispers Ben, taking my arm and guiding me past an exhibition of the history of the "gift giver" or *weihnachtsmann*.

"It's about Santa. What are you talking about? How can it not be suitable? I want to read what it says!"

"No! Be sensible, you can't. I don't want her to see anything about him. She might be upset. You know, it might say Santa doesn't exist or something that might make her cry."

He has odd expectations of what Ray is supposed and not supposed to know.

Outside, we meet a guide from the tourist board. She's a short, elegant, late middle-aged woman with blond curls, rather like Evie's. The street is swarming with visitors. She leads us through the crowds and up onto the ramparts, where she outlines the history of Rothenburg. The city is a perfect medieval walled town built on a rocky crag above the river Tauber. We are told it's the most stunning of a string of towns that lie along what the tourist brochures call the "Romantic Road".

"Why's it called that?" whispers Ray.

"It's pretty, makes you think of princessy stuff, I guess," mutters Esti.

We are the only people on the ramparts and we are getting an extremely thorough tour that has started in the Stone Age.

By the time we arrive at the park, which is built just outside the city walls, we have reached the Thirty Years War. The guide looks right at Ray, but doesn't draw breath:

"Do you know how terrible it was for the people?"

Ray has no time to answer. What follows is a graphic description of total war, death, disease and destitution that left the locals too broke to do any rebuilding work. Not much princessy in that. Ray is anxiously watching the guide's lips and biting her fingernail. She is looking like she's glad she missed that war, when Ben butts in:

"You know your ancestors lived through all that, Ray? Granny Marion's family came from Germany and Austria-Hungary, don't you know that? They were in this one."

Ray does in fact know this. She mutters something vicious under her breath at him. The Thirty Years War has always fascinated me, but to my surprise Ben, and now Ray too, don't just see this conflict as something you read about in a book but a part of their personal history. It suddenly seems more real. The guide moves on to show us a war memorial. Ben sticks close to Ray:

"You know Granny Marion's father fought in the First World War and won an Iron Cross?"

"Yes!" She hisses through her teeth. "I know that! I'm the one, who found it at the bottom of the toy box in the spare room. Remember, Jakie had hidden it and Granny Marion was mad at us?"

I find the fact that they have grandfathers that fought on both sides amazing. I'm the only person in the family who finds this a surprise. I was brought up in a world where it was a black and white conflict, "us against them" not "us against us". They have a worldview I've not encountered before. The guide leans over to interrupt. Perhaps, she is about to tick them off for talking on her tour:

"When did your family leave Germany?"

"1933," says Ben.

Her face lights up:

"I was about to finish, but for you, I have something special that I want you to see."

We head to the end of town, where there are no tourists. The tour continues:

"This is the Judengasse. The old ghetto," she announces.

It turns out that she is half Jewish. Standing in the narrow street, she now busily paints a picture of medieval Rothenburg. I get the feeling that Ray doesn't fancy this any more than the Thirty Years War. We learn that this was an important centre for Jewish scholarship but there were a succession of bloody pogroms until, in 1520, the Jews were forced out. In the nineteenth century, a small community re-established itself in Rothenburg but, in 1938, the last remaining 17 were finally evicted. Today, the street is home to trendy, young couples and is tastefully restored. One man is sitting at a small table outside his front door having a coffee and reading the paper. I think it's extraordinary how things move on so quickly and wars are forgotten.

Later, on the guide's advice, we go to the Reichsstadtmuseum. A woman in a tweed suit and squeaky shoes follows us around, checking up on us. It's just the way things are in some German museums. Uncharacteristically, our stalker gives up and leaves us to ourselves when we finally find the small back room, where there are a few bits of Jewish memorabilia and a couple of old Jewish headstones surrounded by gravel.

We stand about. Ben picks up a little stone and in the Jewish tradition places it on top of one of them. Esti sits down on the floor:

"I'm not sure all those Christmas decorations make it better or worse. On the one hand I'm glad everyone is having fun but... no; I don't know what to think really."

"Sorry," I say limply.

I hadn't bargained for this. In fact the truth is I hadn't thought about it at all and if I hadn't come with them I would never have stumbled over this side of the town's history. As I muse, I realise that I'm not really sure that I am part of this conversation either.

"Granny Marion had Christmas decorations, Esti," says Ben. "They were completely assimilated. She didn't even know she was Jewish until after the Nazis came to power."

"Oh no!" explodes Esti. "Not more about them! I am just so fed up with you and the Nazis. It's finished. Move on! Is there nothing you like about Germany, Ben?"

Ben looms over Esti, looking incensed. This I see is not my argument.

"You should have come to Hamburg with us," he says. "Hamburg is different. You get a different take on things there. It was flattened by British bombers in the war."

"It's got a great model railway hasn't it, Jakie?" grins Ray, as her eyes twinkle roguishly.

"Whoo! Whoo! Douglas!" says Jakie who grins back at her.

Douglas is his favourite character in *Thomas the Tank Engine*. Esti looks at the three of them in disbelief.

"It's true. Hamburg does have an enormous model railway. It was very nice there," I add, ineffectually.

No one is listening to me. They are indeed sorting out their identity in their own way, just as I told my mother they would. She was right - it matters and it's fascinating just watching them work out who they think they are. I never imagined that I would find out things about my children in the way you find out about a new friend's thoughts and experiences. There are some things about them that I know absolutely nothing about.

"Some of Granny Marion's family came from Hamburg," says Ben, as if this explains everything.

I look at them in a slightly different light as we walk back to find Tim, who is working in the hotel. He is writing a feature about the trade in bushmeat in Africa. He's just back from Gabon. He has moved back to old pastures now peace, albeit an uneasy one, has descended on the Balkans. Milosevic has been arrested and while he spends the summer in a prison cell in the Hague awaiting trial, Tim has booked a holiday house in Croatia.

Next stop, the Alps. We row and squabble our way down the motorway. I'm worse than all of them. When Tim has been away for weeks, I usually end up picking rows with him when he gets back. I don't know why, but it always happens. All those little squabbles that you would normally have mount up inside me and have to explode out somewhere. Out of me that is, not him, because silly day to day squabbles are about who puts the washing machine on and cleans the bath and he hasn't been part of everyday life. I threaten to abandon ship and catch a plane home as we near Munich airport. I shout at the entire family for 40 kilometres and begin to feel better. Then, as the car winds its way up into the mountains, the family mood lifts.

Eventually, we find a bed and breakfast in a 1970s-style chalet. In the corner of the sitting room is a strange electric fountain, that lets off steam when the water falls on the small pile of heated stones, which are lit a luminous pink. The place is immaculately clean, as is the town of Berchtesgaden, which is just across the valley. It's all oddly suburban. The owner is a beautician, who wears a nurse's uniform, and runs her practice from home which also doubles up as a B&B. The whole place has an unnervingly clinical air about it. The owner says to Esti what beautiful eyes she has. Ben whispers in her ear:

"Cor, Esti! Careful! Or she'll have them out and sell them to her clients."

Although they both find this joke hilarious, I am disgusted by their racist attitude and we don't linger after breakfast because I'm in a hurry as I have promised Ben something.

As we drive to Obersalzberg, Esti turns on her brother:

"You are obsessed - I think you should see a doctor. Why do you want to see this? Can't you just let it rest?"

He looks exasperated and replies angrily:

"Hitler had his mountain hideaway here. It was right on this spot that he entertained Chamberlain during the Munich Crisis. It's interesting, more interesting than Heidi. Last time we were in this part of the Alps, I couldn't come here because you wanted to pretend to be a goatherder and we had to run around Alpine pastures. Those fields aren't as sweet as they look Esti. You have to hunt out history and learn from it. You'll find it interesting."

She frowns and crosses her arms. They are both right. Outside the window is a meadow full of wild flowers. The main buildings that made up Hitler's country residence were destroyed at the end of the Second World War but his mountain teahouse, the *Kehlsteinhaus* or Eagle's Nest, survived.

After a terrifying bus ride up the mountain, we walk along a long tunnel to catch a lift to the summit. Ben is in his element looking around wildly:

"It's got a thirties air, don't you think?"

It's a period classic, everything down to the lighting, but standing in the crush of tourists, the place is robbed of its impact.

"God! Who are all these people? You mean there are more people like you, Ben?" Esti remarks acidly.

From the lift we emerge into the lobby of a small building and are guided by the force of surging tourists out on to the top of the mountain.

"Look at the view!" gasps Ray. "It's like being on top of the world."

The mountain peaks are so magnificent that I forget why we are here. The only problem is that I don't like being on top of the world. I don't have a head for heights but I only ever remember this when I get to the top of mountains. I push Jacob and Evie around in their buggy, a safe distance from the edge. Jakie is eating pretzel sticks and calmly enjoying the view. Evie, who can be rather bossy, is counting them out. She's in charge. I'm surplus to requirements, so I gaze at the gift shop window. On display are a mouse mat, a set of schnapps glasses and a wall plaque all inscribed, "I've been to the famous Berchtesgaden." I wonder if, in the translation, they forgot the "in" before the "famous". Out of the corner of my eye, I see Ben climbing up a rocky outcrop. There's a sheer drop. I bellow:

"Get down, you idiot!"

Everyone looks at me, as if I am the idiot.

He comes back in a sulk and it doesn't enter his head to say: "Thanks for saving my life, Mum." All I get is a grimace:

"Where are the others?"

"They've gone up to the viewing point," I reply tersely.

Silence. Then Ben says:

"Why do you come up mountains if you don't like them? I will never understand you. This is the Eagle's Nest. It's obviously on a precipitous summit."

Ben has his head in the guidebook that he's taken out of my bag. There's a pause and then:

"Look! It says here that Hitler couldn't stand heights either and didn't like it up here. He hardly used the place. He was a vegetarian too Mummy, like you, you know that?"

"What are you implying?"

"Nothing." he says with a wicked grin. "I'd love someone to build me a place like this. Hitler was given it for his birthday."

For once, I feel sorry for Hitler. This is last kind of present I would want. I bet someone cooked a huge roast to celebrate; obviously it wasn't his lucky day.

Inside the building there are two rooms stuffed with people eating hearty lunches. It smells meaty. Ben sticks his head round the door and comes back to report:

"It's incredible. There are videos of Hitler visiting the teahouse running in there. They are eating and watching!"

Although most of the visitors are German, there are plenty of British and American tourists tucking in.

"What have they come to do? Gloat?" he says waving his arms wildly. "I feel sorry for anyone who's German and my age having to deal with this."

That's enough Hitler tourism. The ladies' room is opposite the lift. Esti and I pop in before we leave. Inside, she whispers:

"What a spooky toilet. Makes you wonder who came in here. Glad I don't have to go to the men's."

Next stop Slovenia. As we emerge out of the long Karawanken tunnel under the mountains that mark the border with Austria, the standard of housing drops a notch. Ben and Esti give a huge cheer. The countryside is suddenly wonderfully old-fashioned. It's dotted with haystacks and unkempt hedges. It's a far cry from the suburban Alps at the other end. It's refreshing. Tim reminisces about the war as we have lunch by the glacial, emerald-green Lake Bled. This is almost the Balkans, although no Slovene would be publicly glad to be lumped in with their southern neighbours. Ever since their ten-day war with the Yugoslav Army in 1991 the Slovenes have never looked back. In 2004 they will join the EU. In the meantime they are keen to play their old Yugoslav connections to the hilt, especially by buying up businesses in Serbia and Bosnia.

There's no menu in the restaurant, so we order *pohovani sir* and chips. It's called something different in Slovene but it's the same thing. Tim is outraged that grilled cheese for seven with Coke costs the equivalent of an un-Balkan, £30.

I decide he needs to cool off on the beach. It's an enchanting spot. The Julian Alps soar up around us. In the distance, I can just make out a medieval fortress clinging precipitously onto a rocky cliff. I haven't had time to blow up Jacob and Evie's waterwings before Ben disappears. In the middle of the lake is a picture-postcard island. A fairytale looking church spire rises above the trees. As I gaze at the magical setting I realise Ben is swimming frantically towards it. I panic! It's at least a mile a way.

"Oh my God, Tim he is going to drown! Go after him!" I shriek.

Fortunately, Tim is a strong swimmer and catches him up. When Ben is finally back, safe and sound and has been told off by me - not by Tim, he doesn't seem to think the whole thing is a big issue, I ask him:

"Why did you do it?"

"It's there, that's why," he answers grinning.

He has a daredevil streak, which is alluring, so is the island.

I opt to get there the easy way, in a gondola-style boat. Esti is the first out at the landing stage. She runs up the huge flight of steps that lead up to the church. There is evidently something irresistible about this place:

"Look Dads! *Smoki Flips!*"

She is jumping up and down excitedly by a kiosk. The red packets are stacked high in the corner behind the glass.

"I've got to have some! Please!"

They are the first bags of Serbian peanut puffs that she has seen in five years. In her opinion, it is the most exciting thing about Slovenia.

A packet of *Smokis* costs ten times what it would in Serbia, but as far as Esti is concerned it's money well spent and she scoffs the lot.

17 - Bosnia & Croatia: Sea, Sun and Shell Shock

It's about 6pm, when we arrive in Karlovac in northern Croatia. It's a nondescript town between Zagreb and the coast. It was built by the Austrians to beef up their southern defences against encroachments from the Ottoman Turks. Today it's full of run down, shabby nineteenth century buildings and scruffy, modern apartment blocks. A lot of buildings are still damaged from the shelling and there are craters in the roads from the explosives lobbed into the town by Serbian artillery. Karlovac it seems is doomed to always be on the frontline. The war here has been over for more than five years and much of this damage was done as far back as 1991. Even though that is now ten years ago new plaster and paint have yet to consign it to history.

"Do you remember Esti, when we stopped here to have a Coke in 95? Mummy was terrified we'd get hit by a shell," says Ben.

I do. It was another attempt to get a family holiday while Tim did some work. We were on the way back from Dubrovnik, where our bucket and spade adventure had ended up as another frontline weekend break when the Bosnian Serbs resumed shelling the city airport. Ben thought the whole thing was a hilarious adventure and I was petrified.

"Things were bad then," I mutter in my defence, but I'm actually far more worried about finding a shop, before it gets too late, to discuss it further. I need to buy some food to make a picnic supper, when we find a room for the night. We want to drive into the countryside for some peace and quiet.

We pull up outside an uninspiring supermarket, at the bottom of a crumbling apartment block. I push the heavy, unpainted metal door open. Esti is quick on my heels:

"Do they have *Smoki Flips*?" She's hunting along the half empty aisles.

"I doubt it Esti. They make them in Serbia."

"What about *Cipiripi*?"

"I don't think so. That's Serbian too."

I move along the half empty shelf to the cold cabinet:

"Wow, Esti! Look! They have that cream cheese that I used to like."

"How come they have that?"

It's a good question. So I explain:

"The cream cheese is made in what was the Serb controlled bit of Croatia when we lived in Belgrade so I could buy it. Now, the factory is back under Croatian control again, so it's here and not there."

A Balkan war encapsulated in a small, white, plastic box of soft cheese. All that sorrow and distress, for what? There are about twenty of them in the fridge. They are the highlight of the shop. Otherwise it's a depressing supermarket, even by Balkan standards.

Among some bags of dried pasta, we find some cans of sweetcorn. Esti chucks them in the basket:

"Here. These are compulsory on holiday."

She's right. Canned sweetcorn is a holiday staple, as I can rarely afford to take them all to a restaurant. A can of corn is the one thing that you can always find, wherever you are in Europe, or at least in every corner that I have ever visited. The happy, jolly green giant has conquered the continent. He has succeeded where Napoleon and Hitler failed. Then, just when I'm about to get dispirited, I spy a large, yellow plastic box. It's just what I need to keep the picnic supplies in, even if they are in short supply tonight. I'm ecstatic. Esti gives me a strange look:

"It's only a box, Mummy."

"Yes, but at least we have found something."

"I can't eat that! What about dinner?"

I love this kind of shopping. Ferreting about. I'm back in the Balkans. It's wonderful! That said the evening meal still looks like being a problem. The vegetables are sold out. There are only a few onions, a couple of carrots and two bitter, stumpy cucumbers left. They go straight in the basket. I'll have anything. I head over to the bakery counter and decide to stock up on bread. There's only one type of loaf on sale. They are stacked behind the counter. A woman in a white coat asks me what I want. I speak to her in Croatian, which is virtually the same as Serbian, even though most Serbs and Croats hate to admit it. In their defence the word for bread in the two languages is completely different. Esti looks at me oddly:

"How did you know what to ask for?"

"How do you think I did the shopping when we lived here?"

"I just never knew you could do that, that's all."

"Why not?"

Proof at last that I'm taken for granted.

We jump back in the car and head out of town but immediately run straight into a solid line of traffic that stretches all the way from Karlovac to Split. We edge bumper to bumper through what was, during the war, the Krajina, the Serbian controlled part of Croatia. The Serbs were driven out in 1995 when the Croats recaptured the region, days after we moved back to London. There are miles and miles of untended fields and overgrown gardens. The road is jammed with Czech, Slovak and Polish cars. It's an extraordinary contrast from the way it was when we drove this way on the eve of war in 1991 when it was completely deserted apart from the tanks outside the Plitvice National Park.

"What happened to the Serbs?" asks Ray.

Ben leaps in to answer:

"They were forced out at gunpoint, Ray. They got on their tractors and fled. Some of them didn't make it. They were murdered. Dads saw an old couple hanging from a tree, dead. They killed themselves instead of giving up their land. They chose the Empire of Heaven, like Prince Lazar."

He's about start on a rendition of the epic poem of the Battle of Kosovo but she ignores the cue for embellishment:

"Who are all these people living here now then?"

"Many of them are Croats driven from their homes in Bosnia."

Tim answers Ray's question without Ben's tabloid spin. In fact, most of the Serbs, some 200,000 of them fled before the Croats got to them and he never saw a dead couple hanging from a tree - that's how myths are made - but it is true that many of the elderly who did not flee were indeed murdered.

We have some supplies for dinner but finding a room to eat them in proves a problem. It's almost 9.30pm and the hotels are all full. It's getting dark and it's exceptionally cold. The temperature gauge on the dashboard reads an incredible 10°C even though it's mid-July. Esti is huddled in her jacket:

"It's supposed to be hot in the Balkans in summer! I can't bear it. It's like England."

The roadside is lined with little old ladies, selling cheese. They have long black dresses and headscarves. Ben recognises them instantly:

"Hey Ray, I remember them! They were selling that stuff last time we were here."

Then he shouts loudly:

"It's disgusting! Perhaps it's the same stuff. Do you think they ever go home?"

"Who'd buy that stuff?" mumbles Esti through her collar.

Her father, that's who.

"Let's stop! We could have some for dinner," says Tim. "I'll ask them, if they know where a B&B is. Maybe, they'll let us stay with them."

"God! What! I don't want to say with them," shrieks Esti, as he gets out of the car.

He sticks his head through her window:

"Got a better idea, then?"

She pulls her coat around her and settles back in a sulk. As Tim starts talking to one of the old ladies, the other smiles a horrible toothy grin. Both have dark, lined, suntanned faces and point excitedly further down the road. To my relief I see there's a small white notice that has *Zimmer* scrawled on it in black paint. I don't fancy staying with them either.

"What's a *Zimmer*?" asks Ray.

Ben answers:

"A room, dork! It's German."

"Why's it in German here? This isn't Germany."

The car bumps down a dirt track. It's pitch black. Ben forgets to answer Ray's question, so she never finds out why the word is written in German.

We pull up outside a typical Yugoslav house. It's a large, half-finished, four-storey building with a big garage in the basement. A couple of unfriendly dogs run around the car barking. A young woman of about twenty comes out of the house and walks leisurely down the stone staircase at the side. The shuttered door bangs closed behind her. She's wearing a sloppy, black sweatshirt and bedroom slippers that are far too big for her. It is as if she is dressed in someone else's clothes. She takes Tim upstairs to show him the room. We sit quietly in the car. I hope it will be all right. There is nowhere else. He comes back in minutes and strides back jauntily to the car:

"It's great! She said my Croatian was so good that she thought I must be a Croat from England. I'm really flattered. When I said I was a journalist she asked me if I was the reporter in the film, who saved a girl from Sarajevo and took her to live with his family in London. She thinks Esti is the girl in the film, *Welcome to Sarajevo!*"

Esti is delighted and preens herself. Ben nudges her:

"It's all those *Smoki Flips*; they've turned you native, Esti."

Tim opens the car door and ushers them indoors, quickly:

"Go straight up to the room! Don't go running around, until I ask if it is safe. There could be landmines."

Ray's eyes are as big as saucers. Ben looks delighted. I don't like the way he likes danger for danger's sake. I must watch for that telltale glint in his eye.

The room is clean. There's a beige wardrobe, a tan coloured bedspread and a bare bulb hanging from the ceiling. Tim arrives with the bags:

"The family are Croats who have just moved back. Their house was burned down, so they have moved in here."

"What happened to the people who lived here?" asks Ray.

"I don't know, maybe they're in Serbia."

187

"Maybe, they're dead Ray," says Ben with a wicked grin. "Do you think they killed them?"

"No, they weren't here at the time; most of the Serbs fled. I said they only came back a few weeks ago," says Tim definitely. He sounds like a lawyer.

"I think it's creepy," says Esti.

The house is huge. The room opposite is unlocked. Inside there are six unmade beds and a multitude of overflowing ashtrays. It doesn't look as if it's rented out. I wonder who sleeps here. Maybe no one has slept here for some time and the last occupants smoked all those cigarettes. Upstairs there are more rooms with unmade beds. I agree with Esti; the house has a sinister atmosphere. She pulls her jacket round her tightly:

"What do you think went on here?"

I dread to think. We go back into our room and shut the door. Inside it's warm and cosy. The world is shut outside. I open up the large, yellow plastic box that I bought in the supermarket in Karlovac, and spread out what I managed to find. The tin of sweetcorn, the two carrots, a couple of onions, the two cucumbers, the cream cheese and two loaves of bread. There are biscuits for afters, as well as the cheese Tim bought off the old ladies, a bottle of wine and some water. I'm quite pleased with myself. Ben is not:

"What! Is that it? Is this some kind of slimming holiday?"

Esti laughs:

"Yeah! It's the weekly shopping. No more food until Dubrovnik!"

There's a beautiful moon. Later we make love on the balcony because the bed is full of sleeping children. There's something in the air that makes you feel more alive.

The next day the rain is pelting down. This time I had wanted to see the famous lakes at Plitvice but this isn't the weather. No way am I getting out of the car in this. Now, I'll have to come back for a third time. In fact, it takes two hours to inch along the road to the main entrance as the route is still blocked with a solid line of traffic as if the whole of eastern Europe is migrating south.

"Forget this," says Tim. "I'm going to drive through Bosnia. It'll be quicker."

No one else turns off. Our brand new car isn't insured to drive in Bosnia but he doesn't seem at all bothered about that, even though we pass two bad accidents minutes after we cross the border. It's rather sexy.

"Esti first ate lamb in Bosnia, didn't she? We should get her some more, don't you think?" he says grinning.

There are plenty of lambs roasting on spits outside the restaurants in and around Bihac, which is an almost solidly Bosnian Muslim town, but it's only just 11am so we stop for a Coke and decide to eat later. Bihac is doing better than Karlovac. The market is full of vegetables but I don't buy any as we have promised the kids a roast for lunch.

After Bihac the road is completely empty, the countryside eerily quiet and now that we have agreed to splash out on lunch, there isn't a single lamb spit anywhere to be seen. There are huge stretches of uncultivated fields and then, outside the odd destroyed house, there is the occasional caravan and the land immediately around it is clean and ready for planting. In some areas people are returning slowly; tentatively edging their way back. The Dayton peace agreement succeeded in ending the war in 1995 but it has left the country divided. There is a Serb-run part of the country and a Muslim-Croat federation, although here whoever dominates in terms of numbers rules the roost.

Ben wants to have his photo taken by almost every burnt-out building along the side of the road. Tim is happy to oblige. It's poor Evie who is suffering as she is really hungry now. As we pull off the road for yet one more photo, she takes one look at the shell of the house that once stood here and says:

"Oh no! The restaurant's bombed!"

It is indeed an old café. They learn fast. She isn't yet three. As she bursts into tears, Jacob shoots her an anxious glance and then looks at me steadily. I feel guilty. Esti sinks deeper and deeper into her jacket. Ben is enjoying rubbing her up the wrong way:

"What's wrong with you?" he asks provocatively as he clambers back into the car.

"Who's ever going to look at all these pictures?" she groans. "This war has been going on all my life. I want to forget about it."

Undaunted he poses by a notice alongside a cornfield, warning of landmines and then in front of Tito's name spelled out in trees on a hillside. I remember it from before the war and it's amazing that it is so well preserved. But there's still nowhere to eat.

We drive into a town around three in the afternoon.

"There must be somewhere to buy something here," says Ben hopefully.

"It doesn't look too promising," warns Esti.

Tim drives up and down the main high street that is festooned with Croatian flags and lined with empty burnt-out shops. The atmosphere is threatening. While the Serbs carved out their section of Bosnia, the Bosnian Croats were no better and proclaimed their Croatian statelet of Herceg-Bosna. Everyone here is clearly in full support of its continuation, even though it has long been officially abolished. But these people don't look like they feel too secure either. They're Croatian refugees who have been settled in a town, which was once mostly Serb. I wonder how long they will stay? We drive past the Hotel Sarajevo. The front of the building has been completely blown off and the rooms are open to the elements.

"My God! They had better change the name if they ever want to get anyone to stay there," says Esti.

That seems to be the least of its problems. On the terrace, there is a policeman with a gun drinking with a man in a militia-style outfit. The stereo in the bar is blasting out a fascist song from World War Two.

"We could ask here if they have some food," suggests Tim.

Esti looks horrified, and stammers:

"I'm not eating with them!"

We drive on. Tim is hungry and clearly thinks we are far too fussy. A few minutes later, we pull into an alleyway to turn the car. At the end of it, a spit roast is in full swing.

"Wow! At last!" shouts Ben triumphantly.

We drive up closer and he explodes in horror:

"I don't believe it! He's roasting a pig! Why is he cooking the one thing we can't eat?"

Tim reverses the car and we drive on. We give up on lunch and buy a loaf of bread.

The road takes us back into Croatia and into Knin, which was once the Serbian Krajina capital. We spent the weekend here in 1991 when the Serbs voted to stay part of Yugoslavia and thus played their part in plunging the country into war. We stop to replenish the picnic box with supplies. This time it's the Serbian shops that are boarded up and looted.

We spend the night in a small house, unnervingly close to the flames of a large forest fire. The owners are extremely friendly and pour glasses of wine and juice, while we sit at their kitchen table. Our host says that someone started the fire on purpose, so they can build on the land. The kids are full of questions, so Tim acts as translator and filters out the things it's best not asked. As I tuck Evie and Jacob into bed in between the old yellowy sheets, I can hear Ben and Esti chatting outside the window with some other kids their own age in a mixture of English and Slavic gobbledygook that Ben has invented. As the twins suck on their milk bottles, I realise that the conversation is in fact a heated debate, about the latest episode of the television series *ER*. The argument centres on the crucial question of whether one of the main characters is a Serb being played by a Croat or a Croat playing a Serb. No one seems to know. That he comes from Vukovar is all they can agree upon. One of the fiercest battles of the recent war was fought there. Both Serbs and Croats claimed the town for their own.

In Split, we have to make a pit stop at a doctor, as Ray has an ear infection brought on by listening to too many story cassettes on her Walkman. She can't plug in for two days. Ben is delighted that he has enlarged his audience. He shouts at top volume from the back seat:

"How can you enjoy this drivel? It'll do you good to join in the conversation. Anyway, cheer up Ray. This is your road!"

She shoots him a glare. He ignores it:

"Ray, you were sick so many times the last time we came here that, in the end, we didn't bother to stop. We just slowed down and emptied out the sick bucket and drove on."

Poor Ray has been born into the wrong family. She suffers from chronic car sickness.

"I'd like to go back to Bosnia. It was the most interesting thing I've seen," she says ignoring her brother's jibes.

Tim can't resist. We pull off the coast road and head for Mostar.

There's silence as we drive into town.

"It looks like Warsaw in 1945," says Ben, as we edge along a street of gutted buildings riddled with bullet holes.

"Look at the park on the left," says Tim, like a tour guide.

He was here during both wartime sieges, although oddly I remember very little about them. Parts of the war have faded into one large blur. Serbia was so cut off from the rest of the world that Mostar had seemed a million miles away. Jakie and Evie look hopeful at the word "*park*" but unfortunately this one is a graveyard. During the sieges there was nowhere else to bury the dead. I can see from Evie's face that she isn't too keen on Bosnia.

Tim explains how at first, Serbs attacking the city were repelled by the Muslims and Croats. Then when the Bosnian Croats decided to make Mostar the capital of their newly proclaimed state within Bosnia, the Muslims were chased into the eastern part of the city across the river Neretva. He recounts how many men were separated from their families and taken to their deaths as the children stare silently out of the window. In the months that followed, thousands of shells were lobbed at the Muslim part of the town, while in the Croatian section people sat outside in cafés drinking coffee. That bit I remember clearly as Tim was shocked by how they could just ignore what was happening five minutes walk away. He could never do that.

We park the car not far from the place where the famous, arched Ottoman bridge once stood. It was blown up by the Bosnian Croats during what was an orgy of destruction in 1993. As we get out, a man comes up to us. He's shaking and twitching and mutters like a bee:

"Crazy Mostar! Crazy Mostar!"

Then he wanders off aimlessly.

"What's the matter with him?" Ray whispers.

"I think he must have shell shock," I answer.

Her eyes follow him. I have the feeling that she would like him to come back so she can study him more carefully.

At the riverbank, Tim explains what it was like here in the war.

"I can imagine that. It still seems real," says Ben.

We are the only people admiring the view across the deep, blue, freezing waters of the Neretva. There's a tense atmosphere, as it's clear that this war isn't settled yet, even though some of the old Ottoman buildings have been beautifully restored. This crack has yet to be papered over. There are no tourists in Mostar yet. We pile back into the car.

"I think I want to be a journalist," announces Ray.

I'm surprised as I wasn't expecting her to say that at all but there was something in the way she looked at Mr Crazy Mostar that makes me think she means it.

Before we leave we stop off to buy more food. The children are hungry regardless of where they are and, war or peace, they still want to be fed. The shop is surprisingly well stocked and has *Smoki Flips*. Everyone is jubilant, even Jacob and Evie, who didn't get any in Slovenia. Tim suggests Esti sets up a business importing them into England.

A few hours down the coast and back in Croatia, the main street in Dubrovnik is again seething with tourists. The city got off relatively lightly compared to some other towns in the former Yugoslavia. The city walls were so thick that a lot of the shells just bounced off them. The main damage was done outside the historic centre. Now, it's business as usual. A huge ocean liner is anchored in the bay. The sea is sparkling and it's scorching hot. The old city is bustling with tour groups and there is a swift trade in postcards of the siege and books of photographs showing shell damage to the tiled roofs. Months of blood and tears have been cleaned up and repackaged as souvenirs. I wonder why I bothered to feel so anxious about Tim while he was here. Now the war seems so tacky laid out alongside the rows of plastic tat.

The last time we were here, in 1995, we were the only foreigners and the place was empty. A woman came up to me and asked me where I was from. Luckily Tim interrupted and said London, before I could say Belgrade.

"I remember that. She looked so pleased. Everyone thought we were tourists and that things were going to get better," reminisces Ben with a mischievous laugh, at the forced deception. "Then there were mortar attacks somewhere nearby and Dads thought there might be another siege. He was terrified, we'd get trapped and he'd have to pay our siege hotel bill. Ah! Those were the days, Ray."

He pats her condescendingly on the head. She wriggles away. A large tour group surges past. In 1995 we had the place to ourselves. The local tourist board want to keep tourist numbers down. It is currently at fifty percent the level it was in 1989.

"It must have been horrible," says Esti with a look of disgust. "How could you breathe?"

"Have no fear Esti," says Ben. "They won't come back. Not if they end up in a place like ours."

We have rented a disappointing apartment in nearby Cavtat. It was supposed to have a sea view, which it does in a way, only the sea is across a main road and past an electricity pylon, some way off, in the distance. It's a major let down, especially as Tim's parents have come to join us. The balcony is the size of a postage stamp, there's no oven or washing machine and it costs the same as fully equipped villa in a lovely part of France. Granny Marion and Pa don't appear to notice.

We take a personal tour of the siege hot spots with Tim as our guide. Ben is hopping with excitement:

"Show me where the Serbs were Dad."

Tim points calmly up to the crown of the hill.

"Can we drive up? I want to see what they could see."

At the top, there is a magnificent view across to the Old Town. Ben and Pa stand gazing out across the bay.

"It's as lovely as it was when I came after the war," says Tim's father. "You were just here, Pa?" asks Ben amazed.

"No! I haven't been here since 1947."

"Ah! Wrong war, Pa."

We hire a small boat and take a trip along the coast.

"Look at all those destroyed hotels!" Ray points at yet another gutted shell. "It looks much worse from the sea."

"Forget that Ray!" calls Ben, from the front of the boat, where he is lounging in the sun, on the roof of the cabin like a playboy. "It's beautiful here. Look around you. Bring her up here, Mummy. She is obsessed with war."

Poor Ray. Now, she is condemned for being too interested. He has the arrogance of the first-born and, at times, an exaggerated sense of self-worth. Tim, Pa and Granny Marion are busy stopping Jacob and Evie jumping overboard, as the captain of our little boat swigs watered down wine. I decide that this is my moment to pretend to be Princess Diana. Despite my earlier resolution not to be jealous of her now she is dead, I'm still aggrieved that she spent the summer of 1997 on a yacht and I didn't. Ray and I have a ten-minute sunbathe on the front of the boat in the late August sun.

As we return to the harbour, an evening sea mist rises up from the water. Everything looks mysterious, beautiful and peaceful. It is almost too perfect.

"I feel like Ulysses," says Ben.

18 - Stalking the Frontline in Shepherd's Bush

It's an overcast September afternoon in London and I've just parked the car in a small mews in Knightsbridge. I'm about to collect the twins from their first afternoon at nursery school. They are almost three-years old. The new academic year seems to have got off to a good start for all of us, especially me, as I have been asked to write a guidebook to the South of France. My summer suntan is still glowing nicely and my mind is awash with olive groves, tumbled down farmhouses and Van Gogh pictures. The car is still full of sand and collections of pebbles. As I wander up to the front door of the small white house where the school is based, one of the other mothers, who is already waiting outside, runs across the road towards me waving her arms excitedly. She has a slightly crazed expression, rather like a madwoman, as she tells me that a plane has crashed into the Twin Towers in New York.

She can't get the news out quick enough and the words tumble into one another, while visions of a small biplane, puttering into one of the skyscrapers, passes through my mind. In moments, I learn that she's a New Yorker and her brother works in Wall Street. She has two children and has just moved here. She sees that, while I have been concentrating on her life story, I have totally failed to take in the intensity of the moment. She repeats herself slowly, as if she is talking to a person of very low intelligence:

"It's a jet! A huge jet! It was full of people. Don't you see? It's war! It's war! It's got to be war!"

I feel like someone has just woken me up:

"Ah! What? War?"

"It's a declaration of war!"

"By whom?" I ask confused.

I don't get an answer, as she dives away into the crowd of anxious parents waiting for the teacher to open the front door. I hear her telling them the news:

"It's war! It's got to be war!"

By this point, everyone is excitedly discussing what's happened and the upcoming conflict. I can't imagine a war in America. I don't join in. I'm bewildered by what's going on. Even though the New Yorker is utterly convinced that a war has started, I'm left wondering how she can be so sure. Does she know anything about war? A war in New York? As I wait for the teacher to open the door of the school there is a slight ripple of panic creeping up through my legs. I can't stand still all of a sudden. If it's war, it's bound to have something to do with us. I need to get home.

I bundle Jacob and Evie into the car, forgetting to ask them what they did at nursery, and drive to collect the others, as quick as I can. The first tower collapses just before Ray walks out of school. When we get home, I am relieved to find that Tim is just standing in the kitchen watching the news on TV, having a cup of tea. A week later, he's on a flight to Tajikistan and about to drive into northern Afghanistan. The war isn't in New York; it's miles away on the other side of the world and the woman at school has, by now, forgotten all about the conflict that's just broken out and is busy discussing more mundane things. It doesn't come up in the conversation at the school gate for weeks until, one day when we are chatting she asks me what we both do for a living. She's not interested in me but lets out a deep:

"Wow!" when I tell her what Tim does.

Then she cranes forward, eyes wide open:

"What's it like having a husband on the frontline?"

I feel like I'm some kind of freak with an extraordinary impediment. I mutter:

"It's alright, thanks," although it doesn't feel very alright at the moment.

In fact, I hate this kind of question because people expect you to say that it's terrible and traumatic, when it isn't. It's great fun. She wants me to say:

"I'll divorce him if he doesn't become a chess correspondent."

What she doesn't expect me to say is:

"Actually, I've always wanted to go to Afghanistan. I'm rather jealous."

But she doesn't listen to my answer. She's shot off to talk to the other parents, and is busy telling all the other mothers and fathers, as if she knows him intimately, that Tim is in Afghanistan. They all look at me and whisper at each other. I give Jacob and Evie an extra big cuddle when they come out.

Life goes on as normal most of the time. I get them up, make breakfast and drive them to school. I pick them up, make dinner and tuck them into bed. They laugh, lark about and fight and argue their way through the day. I read up on the South of France. We are no different from any other family except that there is always an edge of tension to everything we do. It's like a little twisted ball at the back of my brain that I can't get rid of. I know it is the same for the children. Pages of Provençal lavender, honeybees and olive trees can't budge it. Neither can hours of the *Tweenies* on TV, trips to Sainsbury's or mindless computer games. The Balkans seems like a tea party; a sideshow in comparison to this major international conflict.

One evening I'm tucking Jacob into bed. He stares at me steadily over the covers:

"Where's Dads?" he asks quietly.

Evie pipes up from across the room:

"Gone to the war, Jakie!"

As I walk over to settle her in, she looks worried. There's a heavy pause while I wait for her to say something. I'm not sure if what she has to say will be momentous or ridiculous. I try to untangle a knotted curl above her left ear.

"Why, Mummy?" she pauses again, "when I tell my friends, that my Daddy has gone to the war, do they think I'm telling them, my Daddy has gone to the *wall*?" She pauses, "What would he be doing in a wall?"

There's a silence, while I work out what to say. What is going on in their little friends' minds? Fortunately, Ray is helping me get them into bed:

"They always think that, Evie," she says with a grin as if war is a big joke. An image of Tim smashing cartoon-style into a brick wall springs to mind.

The older kids' friends aren't much more use. One boy says to Ben: "Your Dad must be stupid to go there."

Another asks if he's joined the Taliban. Esti complains that most of her friends don't know where Afghanistan is, or what is going on there. As a result, they've nothing to say to her about the war and move the conversation onto something else. I watch the two of them rely on each other for reassurance and even companionship. They watch more TV together and argue less. There is an uneasy truce between them that's drawn up immediately the fighting starts in Afghanistan. Ben is thirteen and Esti is about to turn eleven – they are old hands when it comes to wars. We concentrate our efforts on taking Ray's mind off things. They seem older than their peers, wiser and more able to understand what is going on. They don't care what their contemporaries say to them and shrug off their idiotic comments with a laugh. I'm proud of the way they deal with the situation. But there's another factor that I haven't considered, now that they go to and from school on their own - what they may read in the newspapers left lying around on the Tube.

One Wednesday morning Ben, who's broken his toe falling down the stairs, hobbles off to school. He has a project on the Russian space programme tucked under his arm. He's been up late working on it. He's decided to take a GCSE in Russian, since he wants to be an astronaut and calculates that this might help him get into space. I'm sure he has decided on this as a career option, just because he wants to travel further than his father. Today however, his sights are set on impressing the Russian teacher. He has a late start, so when he gets out of the Tube, the *Evening Standard* billboards are already up flashing the latest. Today's mid-morning extra is: "Journalists Killed in Afghanistan." With this in the back of his mind, he begins his presentation in class. He has to stand up at the front. His toe starts to throb; the heat of the room gets to him. He passes out and wakes up with a black eye. Back at home, I am clearing up the breakfast and haven't heard the latest news when the school nurse calls. Ben has concussion and we spend the next five hours in casualty. It's all right for Tim. He doesn't have to deal with this.

When we get back from the hospital Tim calls. He phones home every evening. Tonight, he's camping in a garage, close to the Kabul frontline, with his old friend Chris. It's the only accommodation they can find. The children think this is hilarious. They are quick to see the joke in most things. Not surprisingly, he has gone down with a very bad stomach bug but still issues a long list of instructions about how I should renew the car insurance and the suchlike. How come he knows how to do this and I don't? Despite what the lady at the school front door might think, there is nothing very glamorous about his job. It's so expensive on the satellite phone that we try not to talk too long. (It's one month into the war and the bill is already pushing £800 and in two days the phone company will cut me off. It will take days to get reconnected because they need to speak to Tim as his name is on the bill and that isn't as simple as it sounds.)

I hang up and think:

"Well, if he's ill, he can't go out to the front, so I can relax a bit."

It's a busy evening doing the homework and settling the twins. It's late and I'm still exhausted from dealing with Ben when I go to tuck in Ray, who looks out over the duvet with big, worried eyes. She's eight and a half. A muffled voice comes from under the covers:

"Why is Daddy ill? Has Daddy got anthrax?"

I wasn't expecting this.

"What!"

I have to get her to repeat the question to make sure I have heard right and I feel terrible that it has taken me so long to get upstairs to kiss her "goodnight". She must have been worrying in the dark for at least an hour. It's all over the news that terrorists are plotting to kill people with biological weapons.

"He has a stomach bug, Ray. I'll explain about anthrax tomorrow but Daddy doesn't have anthrax, ok?"

She nods quickly but clearly isn't convinced.

Down in the kitchen, Ben and Esti are eating biscuits and watching the news. I tell them about the anthrax problem and after a good laugh at their sister's expense, Esti is the first to regain her composure:

"Oh no! We can't let that happen again! Poor Ray!"

"Keeping her mind off things is no good. I'm always telling you that you should keep her better informed, Mummy," adds Ben, sternly.

I feel as if the whole chaos is my fault but I know that he's right. From now on it's a crash course in making sure everyone is fully aware of the facts, not just Ray. I get down a map of Afghanistan and trace exactly what is going on, who is who, and where they all are. I try to reassure the children by reminding them that at least their father has a garage roof over his head.

Tim has been heading for Kabul but could, according to one scenario, end up stuck where he is now unable to retrace his steps if the city doesn't fall. He could be away for months. I miss him most at odd moments. I make a tomato sandwich for lunch and think I'd rather eat the sandwich he would make for me if he was here. He'd add onions and the whole thing would taste so much better. One thing I hate to do is look in his wardrobe. I cope with these long absences by keeping him compartmentalised and slightly at a distance. If I open the cupboard door he leaps out and I feel overcome by all kinds of emotions.

"What about Christmas?" says Ray anxiously.

That seems the least of my problems. It's only October.

At half term we go to Scotland, as I have been commissioned by a magazine to write a feature on Edinburgh for kids. I can't wait to get away. One day, after a whirl of sightseeing, we are sitting in the ultra tidy kitchen of the rented flat, when Tim calls from Bagram airbase. He and Chris are watching the place being carpet bombed by American B-52s from the control tower. The Taliban are about to be driven away from the other side of the runway. It's a crucial moment in the war. Bagram is just a few miles from Kabul. I can hear the sound of explosions in the background, but Tim wants to speak to the kids, to find out how they are. Jacob tells him about the aquarium that we have just visited and Evie about her new, pink, fairy dress. After this surreal round of conversations, we all sit down at the kitchen table of this Edinburgh mansion flat and think about what is going on. Esti breaks the silence:

"Does he always sound like that when it's all happening?"

"Like what?" I ask.

"Excited but calm."

"Just think how you would sound, fool!" retorts Ben.

The words "boy's own adventure" flash into my mind.

"Scared, I think," says Esti. "I'm not sure I'd call home either. Would you?"

I think I might choose a better moment, I agree. But I'm glad Tim has such an inclusive job. It feels like a family business.

"No time to waste, Esti!" says Ben leaping up from his chair in excitement. "He's seeing history being made. He wanted Mummy to be there too."

Inspired by his rhetoric, I phone Tim back. I want to know what is going on. He sounded too excitable on the phone for my liking. Maybe he has that dreaded glint in his eye. I don't want him to do anything dangerous and I think I need to try and take control of what my husband is up to.

Although we are physically in Edinburgh, we are in fact in Bagram, with him. As the news filters in via my mobile we get just as excited as Tim. It looks as if the Taliban lines could crumble. Perhaps we are all going a little mad. I open a bottle of wine and a packet of crisps as we celebrate seeing the light at the end of the tunnel. This is a joyous moment of family togetherness. Five faces of differing sizes beam up at me as I propose a toast:

"Maybe Dads will be back for Christmas."

He's got just over six weeks. This war had better be over by then. He's never missed Christmas.

One pitch black November night, Ben can't sleep. Since Jacob and Evie spend every night in my bed, I have a spare mattress on the floor where

I can escape when I can't stand being kicked in the back any longer. Ben climbs into it and dozes off. Jacob and Evie are lying horizontally across the big bed, kneeing me in the back, when the phone rings. It's about 5am. At the end of the line I can hear Tim and Chris trying to set up their satellite phone. They are having a mundane conversation about sticking a plug in something. They can't hear me, but I can hear them. Ben wakes up:

"What's happened? Where's Dads?"

I whisper back across the twins, who are breathing deeply through snotty noses:

"I don't know, but I can hear them. He's with Chris. They must be ok. They are trying to plug something in."

The phone rings again. It's Tim. He sounds ecstatic:

"We're in Kabul; I just wanted to let you know. It's amazing! We just walked in. Don't worry! I'm safe. I'll call you later."

It's impossible not to worry. How can they have just walked in? It must be a trap? Kabul has to be the most dangerous place on earth. Ben is lying quietly in the dark:

"What do you think it's like? What do you think Dads is doing?"

"I don't know. I hope he's being careful."

I can't move. Jacob, who has a habit of lying on top of me when Tim is away, is now pinning me down. After he was born, he spent a week in intensive care. Tim was by his side nearly all the time. He bonded with his father and he's Tim's baby. I'm always second best. Now I know what so many fathers feel like when children prefer their mothers. Even if I am not his first choice, now Tim is gone, he wants to make sure I don't go anywhere when he's not awake to keep an eye on what is going on.

Ben's voice breaks through the dark.

"Are you thinking what I'm thinking, Mummy?"

"Probably. What are you thinking?"

I am hoping, on the one hand, that he isn't, as I don't want him to have to contemplate the horrible side of what could happen next but, on the other hand, I hope that he is, because I could do with someone to talk to. We may have fights over why he won't eat his breakfast, what time he comes home in the evening and gets up in the morning but he is also a friend. Silly squabbles don't count. The hours I invested in him have paid off.

"Surely there will be snipers?" He says.

There's a pause, while we both think about it. I want to take an eraser and rub the thought out of his brain but I can't even put my hand out to touch him without risking waking Jacob. That I can do without right now. Ben is a disembodied voice in the dark:

"God! He's so lucky! I wish I was there."

There's a pause and with a jaunty tone in his voice he asks:

"Don't you, Mummy?"

I admit that part of me does. I am however, more taken aback by the matter of fact tone in his voice. It's completely normal for him that Tim should have just walked into Kabul. I feel I was right all along to be direct and not to cushion him from what was happening in the world around him. Now he can appreciate the moment and revel in the excitement.

We lie there in the dark, trying to work out what is going on, until the news comes on at 6am. Life is fascinating. As it becomes clear that Kabul is in fact safe, just as Tim had told me, I begin to feel elated, although slightly guilty that I trust the *Today* programme more than my husband.

We set off for school glowing with excitement as if we are in a porridge oats advert. It lasts through the day. As we drive home we pass the traffic lights where a small Chinese man is selling the *Evening Standard*. Chris, who is writing for them, has his story on the front page. The kids open the windows and wave and cheer at him as we shoot by. He gives us a rather odd look.

The stories that do come out of Kabul in the next few days are all about men going to the barbers and people buying pop music for the first time. It's rather an anti-climax. Unfortunately, rather than going to get his new beard shaved, Tim heads to a photographer to have his picture taken with Chris and their translator. It reminds me of a photo my mother has of my grandfather in Cairo during the First World War. He poses proudly with his best friend. He has a cocky look in his eye. He seems convinced that he'll survive the next battle.

I'm feeling generally relaxed and rather upbeat these days. My mood even survives paying the enormous bill I have just been presented with by the garage for fixing the car. The war has been good for our bank balance. I haven't put my handbag down on the table before the phone rings in the kitchen. The sun is shining.

"This is the foreign desk at the *Evening Standard*," says a chirpy voice at the end of the line.

Why are they calling me, I wonder? I'm not married to Chris. A cheerful young man says:

"I just wanted to let you know that your husband isn't dead. Chris Stephen just phoned to let us know he was ok and asked me to pass on the news to you."

It's the same tone he uses for ordering his tea or thanking someone for a piece they have just filed on a West End show. I'm completely taken aback, even though I have had these bizarre calls before from some journalist in an office who has no idea of the intensity of what is being said and is gone before you get an explanation. I've even had one at 3am from someone on a night shift. These calls always come when you aren't mentally stalking the frontline or running through the latest ghoulish scenario, but while you are bathing the baby or cooking some baked beans or simply asleep. That's why they are so shocking. All I can think is how Tim looks, his smell and what it's like to run my fingers along his back. Do I remember everything clearly enough? I feel I have to be on guard all the time. I often stare at him while he is doing something completely mundane like emptying the dishwasher in the hope that I can capture the essence of him. Waiting at home is truly exhausting. I have learnt to treasure that ball of tension at the back of my mind. It's my link to Tim. I switch it off at my peril. On the positive side, it makes the world seem a sharper more intense place. It makes me feel more alive. It's rather addictive or maybe it is just Tim who is addictive. The flood of adrenalin from the phone call brings the kitchen to life. Even the coffee stains and bits of chocolate cereal on the table seem to pulse with vigour. You can take your husband being alive for granted too easily.

I listen to the news on the radio to find out what has been going on.

It transpires that a group of journalists has been shot and killed on a road close to Kabul. Tim was about to set off down the same road. I panic. I must warn the kids. All I can think of now are those *Evening Standard* billboards. They won't cheer when they see this one. I call the school to ask them to warn Ben and Esti that their father is not dead but can't get hold of any of their teachers. They don't have mobile phones. I'm in a bubble cut off from the real world where everyone is happily going about their business, as if nothing has happened.

When the kids walk in the door later in the day, I can see from their faces that they have seen the headlines. They have an edgy, nervous look about them as they push open the front door.

"It's not Dads, it's ok." I say.

Esti unwinds her scarf slowly and throws her bag down on top of it:

"Phew! I saw the headlines but I didn't have enough money to buy a paper."

I think we should get them for free. All the worries of the day must have been in the scarf. She wanders into the kitchen to make a chocolate spread sandwich and then turns on the telly as if I had just said Tim had popped out to buy some butter. Half an hour later, Ben crashes through the door. He looks rather pale. She shouts from in front of the TV:

"Dads is fine!"

"Thank God for that," he says shuddering slightly. Before yelling:

"Mummy where are you? I'm starving."

19 - The South of France: Forget the Marzipan Fruit

It's a bright, sunny Saturday morning in April 2002. As our Eurostar train shoots into the tunnel, Ray stares at the black window:

"What would happen if someone decided to blow up our train?" she asks still gazing into the void.

I sit there pulling a few odd expressions while I try to think of an answer.

"We'd all be dead! You freak!" shouts Ben.

I blame Tim for this appallingly bleak worldview and am momentarily glad I've left him behind at his desk in the sitting room at home. Ben is in full flow waving his arms, which at times seem too big for his body:

"Gallons of water would gush into the train as the tunnel collapsed. The blast would smash our bodies into a thousand pieces."

Ray giggles with delight at her brother.

Twenty minutes later, we shoot back out of the tunnel at Calais. The kids cheer. Not because we are safe, but because we are back in France. Ben picks Evie up onto his lap. She is wearing her Afghan war pink fairy dress.

"They speak French here," he explains. "Like they do in school."

"We like school, Ben," Evie pipes up.

She always uses the royal "we". She talks for the two of them. It irritates Jacob intensely. He looks infuriated. We rattle south to the sun south to the sun. I am to research my guidebook for families. Sun, ice cream and sand – what could be nicer?

First stop the Camargue, western Europe's largest river delta. It's a vast marshy plain dotted with lagoons and cut off from the sea by banks of sand.

"Flamingos!"

Evie gasps in awe as a pink haze of flapping wings rises up from the reeds in front of her.

"Pink for you Evie," says Jacob, who always wants everything to be just right for his sister. He's delighted that she likes them, as if he had ordered them up especially for her. The louder he shouts the more birds rise up from the murky lagoons. Esti shatters the beauty of the moment with a shriek:

"My God! What's *that*?" She points at the horizon. "That's absolutely disgusting!"

Across the water are the dark and foreboding chimneys of the Fos oil and gas terminal. Large flames flare up into the blue sky. It's like a set from the twenties movie, *Metropolis*.

"Whoever let them put that here? What's wrong with them? What are we doing here?"

Both Ben and Esti regard anything outside Paris with slight disdain and trepidation. Ben is convinced it's full of sinister locals. For them Paris is France and Paris is their Auntie Sylvie's flat. Tim's sister lives in a whitewashed turn-of-the-century apartment, with wooden parquet floors and a view over the rooftops. Nothing is ever out of place and it has a calmness lacking, *chez nous*, in Shepherd's Bush. She also has more gadgets than we do and unlike me is always immaculate in high heels. On one occasion, she took Esti to her manicurist, which Esti judged cost the same as our weekly shopping bill.

We drive on to Avignon. It's not what I was expecting at all. Most of the town is one huge suburban sprawl of ugly blocks of flats which are no doubt home to France's alienated immigrant community. The apartments are surrounded by acres of supermarkets, garden centres and prefab warehouses, most of them selling gigantic swimming pool shells, which are piled high in their forecourts. The kids gaze silently out of the window as I drive around a couple of pointless mini-roundabouts. There's a deep intake of breath as I drive past Toys "R" Us.

After Avignon we drive on to Orange, to check out the famous Roman theatre. One of the endless guidebooks I have in my handbag suggests we buy sandwiches and eat them in the park behind the theatre. It sounds idyllic. It's nothing of the sort. It's a lonely spot, especially on a Monday afternoon. The sky is an oppressive grey and a group of bored teenagers sit smoking on a bench, the back of which is covered in National Front graffiti. There is broken glass under the swings. There's discontent and anger in the air.

We drive south. The coast is flat and boring but I want to see the seaside resort of La Grande Motte, just south of Montpellier. It's famous for its tall, pyramid-style hotels and apartment blocks. When I tell the kids where we are going, Ben waves his hand with a Gallic flourish in my face. It's his turn in the front seat:

"Ah! Yes! I did an exercise on this in geography. You know what's really interesting about this, don't you Mummy?"

I don't but I'm not letting on. I'm feeling rather out of my depth.

"My geography book was full of pictures of the weather patterns in Australia and cocoa pickers in Ghana, you know," I say as a diversionary tactic.

There's some giggling from the back seat. I can't see what's that funny about Ghana. Esti does:

"You're old, Mummy, just face it!"

"No! I'm not old! I'm British," I retort.

"Look! You'll never understand this, unless you listen." Ben's tone is exasperated. He launches into a long explanation about Charles de Gaulle and his plans to build a Costa Brava in France and how the plan culminated in the construction of La Grand Motte and the other concrete, soulless towns along the Languedoc coast. I'm infuriated that he knows more than I do about the place. He's just like Tim. I had no idea that he knew all these things.

Then we turn north and drive to Fontvieille. Reading up over the winter I have discovered a nineteenth century writer, called Alphonse Daudet, who wrote funny stories about the Provençal locals in a book called, *Lettres de mon moulin.* Just outside the village is the original windmill where he set some of his stories. I'm rather impressed with myself. It's perfect for my guidebook. As I pull into the car park however, Ben leans over from the back seat and says dismissively:

"I don't know why you want to see this. He never lived here, but in a big house up the road."

How does he know that? Esti who is hunched in a doze next to me, in the front seat, growls through her scarf:

"I hate stupid Daudet. He makes me think of all those terrible *dictées* (dictations) you have to do at school. Do we really have to see this?"

Ben, Esti and Ray proceed to check notes on which was the worst *dictée*; the one about a little white goat or the miller. Daudet is a mixture of Beatrix Potter and Thomas Hardy. It appears that everyone in France knows who he is and, of course, they do too. I'm left to imagine what it would have been like, if my mother had never heard of Oliver Twist or Scrooge. I'm the mother of five little foreigners. I had no idea how French they were. I thought sending them to a French school would make them bilingual not give them an alternative persona. Some days they seem more Tim's children than mine. They have joined a club which I will never be able to join, however hard I try. Secretly I wish they had never heard of Daudet and we could have just discovered him together. They are at home in France, something I will never be. They speak so fast I can't understand them. Not only do they speak perfect, accentless French, which I do not, they adopt a different attitude and they even stand in a different way when they speak it. They laugh at jokes on TV I didn't even realise were jokes and now I am discovering they know all about a whole world that I have just opened the door to. It is a strangely alienating experience. I thought mothers were supposed to be able to read their children's inner thoughts and not to have to ask for a translation.

By the time we get to Nice things are looking up. The weather is wonderfully warm and sunny. Peter Mayle's Provence must be lurking nearby and I'm sure that I am about to find it. A large jet begins a slow descent across the bay as we sit on the pebbly, city beach, but that doesn't matter. The breeze is balmy and warm. The sea is a brilliant blue.

We walk along the seafront towards the dusky pink buildings of the old town past the luxury sweet shop Auer and stroll on to the market. Sitting next to the ripest fresh fruit and vegetables are marzipan versions – plates of carrots and tomatoes, even some marzipan fish. There are huge piles of colourful, boiled sweets and a lady with big gypsy earrings cooking a chickpea pancake called *socca*. At last I have found somewhere someone might want to come on holiday. Even the kids, who I am finding a bunch of know-it-alls, are impressed.

We buy a picnic and discover that the place is so luxurious that there is even a lift to the top of the Colline du Château, Nice's city park. You don't have to let a long, sweaty hike up disturb your hairdo. Ray is first in:

"Must be all those old ladies! That's why they need the lift," she giggles.

We emerge into the bright sunshine. I take a picture of Ben in front of the broad sweep of the Bay of Angels. He's fourteen and looks so handsome and grown up. I think "that's my son" and more slushy, motherly thoughts along those lines. I forget I'm working. It feels like a holiday. Anyway I have decided to take an hour off to do something personal with the kids. Now is just for us.

We head across the pathways towards the city cemeteries. Doing my research, I have at last discovered something that they don't know about. Behind the park, is a small Jewish cemetery. Inside it is a memorial to the thousands of Jews who were deported from Alpes-Maritimes in 1943. One of them was Tim's grandmother, their great-grandmother.

When the war broke out Tim's grandmother and his aunt were living in Paris, having fled from Berlin in 1933. They soon fled again to escape the German occupied zone and ended up in Nice which, from November 1942 until its capitulation in September 1943 came under Fascist Italian rule and, to the rage of the Germans, a haven for Jews. Mussolini had sought France's most south-easterly province, Alpes-Maritimes, because, until 1860 it had been part of the Kingdom of Sardinia.

One afternoon, soon after the Germans had moved into Nice, Tim's aunt Huguette, who was a little older than Esti is now, came back from school to find nobody was home. Tim's grandmother was by this time en route for Drancy, a suburb of Paris, where Jews were held before being deported east. From there she was put on a train and sent to Auschwitz. The paperwork kept by the Nazis tracks her movements to what must have been the very end. We have it in a file at home. I've always found it amazing that there was any paperwork at all.

Walking in the warm sun, everything that had happened in 1943 seems very remote. The whole visit seems like a courtesy call. I check that Ray has the basic facts of what happened clear. I simply tell Jacob and Evie that we are going to see a memorial that's been put up so we can remember Granny Marion's Mummy. They nod happily and carry on munching on chocolate spread sandwiches. Finding the graveyard however proves difficult, as it's tucked away on the slopes behind the park's enormous waterfall, next to a huge Catholic cemetery crammed with gothic tombstones. In fact, it's beginning to take so long to find, that I wonder if we should abandon the whole idea altogether, when Ben suddenly spots it:

"Look! That's it. It can't be anything else."

At the top of a small slip road is a gate barred by two large police vans. The policemen standing by them are armed, while at their feet are five vicious guard dogs, who are growling and snapping, desperate to be let off their leads. Evie grips her chocolate sandwich, her eyes wide with terror. Her pink fairy dress looks out of place. I explain what we want. The kids say nothing; now I'm expected to do the talking. The police politely open the gate. Inside the small cemetery, it's silent and, between the trees, you can see the blue sea glinting in the sun. The headstones are simple and understated. Jacob, who is sitting in the buggy next to Evie, holding his *Thomas the Tank Engine* backpack stuffed full of trains, looks up bewildered and then stares long and hard at me:

"Why does Granny Marion's Mummy need those dogs?"

I wish I had just stayed in Shepherd's Bush. I always thought it was a good idea to confront kids with whatever the world served up. This time I'm definitely wrong.

Subdued, Ben, Esti and Ray pick up pebbles to place on the memorial. Esti dusts the bits of dirt off the bottom and relights a candle that has gone out. Quietly, the three of them start reading the names on the nearby gravestones, while I stand looking at the small memorial. I realise that this woman, who grew up hundreds of miles away in Germany, must have been only a few years older than me. She, probably, felt just as much a stranger in France, as I do. After all she only came to France as a mother of two in 1933. I've never thought about her before. Suddenly, I feel a deep desire to meet her. What would we have to say to each other? I wonder if she met anyone she knew after she was arrested and how desperate she must have felt about Huguette, not knowing what had happened to her daughter, as I gaze around at what is an incredibly beautiful spot. The sea twinkles in the distance. It's a beautiful azure blue.

The dogs look different now that we are on the inside. They don't appear threatening anymore, but protective. France has the biggest Jewish population in Europe but even then it's tiny at just 650,000, especially if you compare it to the country's several million strong Muslim population. Since September 11th, anti-Semitism has been getting worse. There have been hundreds of vicious attacks on businesses and ordinary people going about their daily lives. Graves have been desecrated and some children on the way to school have even been stoned. Only last month arsonists set fire to the synagogue in Marseille. It was left completely gutted. Synagogues in Paris, Strasbourg, Lyon and Nice have also been targeted. It was out of an academic interest that I followed the reports in the newspapers. Now I realise that they are part of my life. The news seems to have jumped out of the TV and wrapped itself around us and invaded what was supposed to be our private time. This isn't the kind of danger that you can intellectualise and keep at a distance either. This is what my mother was worried about. I look down at Jacob. He looks so small and vulnerable hugging his toys close to his chest, so do Ben and his sisters.

"Those dogs are to make sure no one breaks in and damages things," I say to Jacob. He nods. He doesn't look too sure. I can see he thinks I'm glossing over things. I am. The kids stand in front of the buggy and look at me. Despite all their bravado, I can see that I am, after all, still in charge. It's time to leave.

We start walking along the leafy street back down into town. Then, after a few yards, Ben stops in front of me and opens his hands and fingers wide in exasperation. I pull back surprised. It's as if he had just jumped out of the bushes. In the cemetery he looked rather limp. He seems to have suddenly doubled in stature.

"See! Look! Look at the real France! Forget the marzipan fruits. This isn't just a holiday resort, it's a real place and *I* have to live in it everyday. Racism is a really big issue here."

Has he fallen out of love with France? Is he about to become a rebel and tell me he doesn't like eating "proper stuff" anymore? He's bubbling over with anger. I think he is going to cry.

I don't say a thing, although I can suddenly feel a cold knot in the bottom of my stomach as the day before we set off replays itself in my head. While I was packing, we had a call from the head teacher at school to say that Ben had had a fight with some boys in his year but had refused to tell her what it was about. We were taken aback, as he had known these boys for years. When he arrived home he was very upset, but after a lot of coaxing, he told me that a row had broken out between him and the others, when they had made some anti-Semitic jibes regarding Esti. I was shocked, especially when Esti backed up her brother's story and added casually, that this was nothing unusual.

"I ignored it. He should too," she said with a shrug.

I was in a rush trying to get packed and had decided to do the same. I realise that this was probably a mistake. There are some things that you can't ignore. There's a side to this boy's life I know nothing about. The children aren't know-it-alls at all. In fact they need me to look after them and I need to do that job better if we are ever going to get to journey's end. Identity is, after all, an issue in our family.

Evie has decided to take a nap, something she often does in moments of stress. Jacob is playing with a toy train. He has a serious expression on his face and looks at me steadily. I feel like I want to apologise. I look across at Ben, who is now marching off ahead with his hands thrust into his trouser pockets. I turn to Rachel and Esti who just shrug their shoulders and sigh.

The next day, we drive to Cannes. Ben is in the front seat. The waterfront is a hideous mixture of grey apartments and urban decay.

"It looks like motorway-sur-mer", he grumbles. "Who wants to holiday here?"

As we approach Cannes, the coast begins to improve. There are rocky coves and the sea is blue. It's the Saturday before the first round of the 2002 presidential elections. In the town centre the offices of the National Front, the far right party of Jean-Marie Le Pen on Rue d'Antibes, are festooned with flags; music is blaring out. Esti sees the danger immediately. I decide not to linger and drive up into the Gorges du Verdon, France's answer to the Grand Canyon. On the way Esti notices that Jacob is feverish and has a few watery spots that look horribly like chicken pox. This trip is jinxed.

Cannes seems a million miles away, so do the bad things in life as we follow the winding road along the gorge. The small river below is an extraordinary bluey-green. This looks like the Provence I first read about on my Bucharest balcony. I can't believe I have found it. In good spirits, we check into a small hotel, which is built around an old water mill on the edge of the town of Castellane. We get two rooms in the annex, which is hidden up a dusty path behind the main hotel. Jacob is feeling better and we all have fun in the restaurant, where I order roast lamb for the kids. But after dinner, Jacob throws a high fever and Ben, who is desperate to watch the results of the first round of voting, is livid when he finds that the TV in the hotel lounge is broken.

While I look after Jacob, who by now is covered in spots, Ben and Esti sit in the car, listening to the radio. Eventually Jacob nods off and I step outside on to the balcony to admire the stars with Ray. Suddenly, Esti charges up the rickety wooden stairs outside of the annex. Panting, she blurts out:

"Come quickly! Le Pen is winning! Ben is going mad and smashing up the car!"

I panic:

"What! It's a hire car!"

I run down the stairs barefoot and in my nightie. It isn't quite as bad as it sounded but Ben is sitting in the front seat kicking the dashboard and swearing.

"Ben! Thank God the hotel TV was bust. What is the matter?" I ask in confusion.

Esti hands out the diagnosis:

"Le Pen has beaten Jospin."

Lionel Jospin is the Socialist candidate. Le Pen has polled roughly 20 per cent of the national vote. He will now go on to the second round to challenge President Chirac, who isn't very popular. I can't understand at first. Ben is furious. I can see he's fighting back the tears. I wasn't prepared for any of this. I haven't even followed the election campaign very carefully. I've been too busy reading about honeybees and olive oil.

"If he wins, I won't be French anymore. He's going to strip second-generation immigrants like us of our nationality, the f***ing bastard," splutters Ben.

This isn't something I want to discuss in public, as one thing I do know is that there are too many Le Pen supporters in this part of the world. I bundle him up the wooden staircase and towards our rooms at the end of the balcony wondering when I emigrated to France. By the time we get to the door, his tears have turned to anger:

"I'm not going to just lie down and take it! No one's going to push me around! You know where it could all lead."

"Go to bed, Ben."

I try to coax him. It is difficult to know what to say. I can't change the results or Le Pen's policies. I didn't know he would react like this.

"No! How can I go to bed *here*?"

It takes an hour or more to calm him down. He still refuses to get into bed and in a sort of personal protest, eventually falls asleep lying across the bottom of it. I feel like I don't know him at all. It worries me. I should do.

As soon as he has dozed off, in a panic, I remember Jacob and rush next door to my room.

"Don't worry, Mummy. I've been checking him."

It's Ray. She's in the other bed cuddling Evie. In the dark, I listen to Jacob's feverish breathing and think about all the stories I've read in the press about angry, young Muslim boys, who've turned into suicide bombers. Perhaps they are feeling just like Ben. I feel for their mothers.

Watching your children learn that some people hate them simply for what they are is one of the hardest things a mother can do. Teaching them to learn something positive from it is even harder. My mind drifts to when we first really talked about the Holocaust, one winter's night, in Belgrade. Then I felt confident, when I told Ben, that it could never happen again. But that was a long time ago. As far as massacres and murders go, things have moved on a bit since Srebrenica. In those days, a few carefully chosen words could ease his fears. Now we are in a new ballpark altogether. A quick cuddle won't fix this one.

The next morning, it's on to Monte Carlo, to spend a couple of nights in the luxurious Hermitage Hotel, where we have been given complementary accommodation. Monaco is one of the wackiest corners of Europe. It's the size of a small country town, but has its own euro coins, its own stamps and even its own pin-up princess or two. There are a string of small museums and gardens all displaying Prince Rainer's private collections of everything from model boats to tigers, in which we while away our time. It's the ideal place to recover. It's a toy town city, in a parallel universe of luxury.

A few nights later, we are sitting on the chintzy bedspread eating a picnic supper, in the flowery, Queen Mother-style bedroom. We don't have to pay for the room but I do have to pay for dinner, so we've stocked up at the supermarket. On the TV news, is an interview with Le Pen. The interviewer fawns and nods. I long for Jeremy Paxman to appear and snarl at him but the interviewer keeps on smiling. At the end, he even wishes him a polite "good evening". I'm horrified and, as I offer Ben a slice of the chocolate cake he chose, I remind him that eighty per cent of French voters didn't vote for Le Pen. He ignores me and gobbles up the desert. He bends down and picks up his little brother.

"This *Paris Brest* is wonderful! The filling is just right," he says cutting him a slice. How does he know it is called a *Paris Brest* I wonder? When I was his age there were just sponge cakes or fruitcakes. No one gave them a name. While I think this can't possibly be my child he begins to discuss the merits of various Parisian cake shops with Esti. I can't join in. This is the "proper stuff" I have never got to grips with.

Last stop: Marseille. Esti hates it. She takes her anger out on the pavement, as we walk down the main boulevard, the Canebière, gesticulating at it wildly:

"Look! It's covered in discarded chewing gum, just like outside the tube station at home."

I agree. It's revolting.

"It's perfect!" Ben says to my surprise. "Yes! That's what it is! This is Shepherd's Bush on sea," he declares proudly.

"God! That's just what I wanted to get away from, you idiot," retorts Esti.

"Esti, Marseille is multi-ethnic and home to Zinédine Zidane," he says putting his hand on her shoulder. "Huge crowds on the Champs Elysées cheered him after he scored two winning goals in the World Cup Final, because he was a Frenchman, not just an immigrant."

I'm not sure that Marseille is the answer to France's problems. Neither is Esti who rolls her enormous eyes at him in disgust:

"You know Ben. You and I, we should really be in Paris, at the huge anti-Le Pen demonstration. Then you could go down the Marais and eat a bagel."

The Marais is home to Paris's old Jewish quarter, one of Ben's favourite haunts.

I wish they were both there and then we could all have some peace. Unfortunately, the two of them snipe their way around the sights in the hot afternoon sun.

Eventually, we make our way back to the old harbour side and to what was once the old Panier area of town. In 1943, the Nazis blew the whole of this part of Marseille sky high, because it was a refuge for Jews and the Resistance. Esti looks glum:

"There's no escaping them, is there Ray? Nazis get everywhere. I think Mummy and Ben are obsessed. That's it, obsessed."

I see the attraction of never leaving Britain again. I would like to hide away my family on a wild rugged beach and pretend that the rest of Europe and its wars and prejudices don't exist. I long to be one of the

Cream for Mo
Caniscan

Take phone charger.
Packed lunch   + Blackberry

1 boiled egg

cheese
sandwich

_____

K's PPT
presentation

people who will probably end up buying this guidebook I'm writing, who will come here for two weeks, go home and forget all about it. I want to rent a beautiful villa, swim in the pool, drink wine and eat figs. I feel cheated out of a cosy dream that kept me going through the war in Croatia and the war in Afghanistan. I would like to thump Peter Mayle in the face and shout: "*J'accuse!*" He peddled me a lie. But, instead, we trudge on, until the back streets bring us to the dark, gloomy main road that runs alongside the Panier, up from the harbourside. There are no cars and it's eerily empty and expectant. There are police everywhere. In the distance, I can hear the sound of chanting growing nearer. It sounds ominous. In a few minutes, a long demonstration, numbering thousands of people, files by in a noisy protest against Le Pen. Ben is jumping up and down with excitement on the edge of the pavement. Esti is next to him waving her scarf over her head cheering.

I feel like kissing every one of the demonstrators to thank them for what they are doing for my children. Ray, who is standing next to me turns, and in that sage way that only she can sometimes sum things up, says:

"That's a bit of luck. Now, let's hope he'll calm down."

Evie notices the change in atmosphere and sees a window of opportunity:

"Can we have a biscuit?"

She has noticed that we are standing outside a cake shop. I go straight in and buy a large selection, although once inside, I suddenly realise how a casual observer could interpret my actions. They could so easily think that I am doing this deliberately, as if to turn my back ostentatiously on the demonstration. Things are never what they seem.

"Who cares about what people think? We know the truth. That's enough," says Ray.

As we come out of the shop, Ben runs over. He's smiling alluringly:

"Can we join in?"

Esti is breathless with the excitement, nodding enthusiastically at me, eyes sparkling, trying to get me to agree. I'm about to say: "No, it's got nothing to do with us," when I realise that this is a stupid thing to say. Have I learned nothing? Once this would have had nothing to do with me but now it does. I'm racing to keep up. All the same, I don't want to get involved, as there are plenty of things I need to do before we leave. I compromise. I buy them a Coke and they cheer the demonstration on from a café at the corner of the road. I give Marseille a glowing write-up.

20 - My Ireland...or Yours?

"This is terrible! I didn't expect it to look like this at all."
Ben's head is bobbing up and down between the two front seats. Even when he's in the back, he still manages to have a major presence in the front:

"I thought Ireland was supposed to be beautiful. That's what you told me."

We cruise around yet another mini-roundabout and past a few bungalows set in a boggy, flat landscape, broken only by the occasional clump of spindly trees bent by the wind. We're in Roscommon. My mother's family came from Ireland. After Le Pen, it's time to escape to a windy, wild corner of Europe - my windy, wild corner. Although I happily agreed bring the kids up as Jewish, I did this to please Tim and its left me with the niggling thought that my background has somehow been pushed to one side. Well, my mother's at any rate, she's the one with the Irish Catholic family. My father was an English Protestant but that never seemed to count for much. He wasn't interested in where he came from only where he was going. That left us with only the Irish Catholic bit to identify with.

"This is just scrubland! I can't believe we come from here!" Ben is outraged. "Where did the ancestors live? Where did the Flanagans come from?"

He looks around wildly, as if there will be a notice saying: "Flanagan descendents - This way." Esti gives him a withering glance:

221

"Oh God! Ben! When they couldn't pay the rent, the landlords drove them off the land, even though they were starving. They lived in mud huts that just fell down when they left. They died in the open air. They just dissolved into the grass at the side of the road they were so poor. Don't you know anything about the potato famine? You dork!"

I have visions of my ragged ancestors, de-materialising, *Star Trek*-style, on the tuft of grass just outside the car window. I feel a sharp pang of empathy with them. It's a horrible thought that they have completely disappeared, without trace. I have only a tuft of grass to identify with.

Esti, who is an addicted reader of memoirs and stories about young girls and women surviving terrible hardship, has done her homework. Along with books about Jewish girls narrowly escaping death in occupied Europe, she's clocked up a few editions on starving teenagers emigrating from Ireland to America. Admittedly, I've passed these books her way. She didn't reach for them instinctively in the way she did for Anne Frank's diary, but she has, to my delight, read them all the same. But, she still can't shut Ben up that easily:

"You must know what village they came from Mummy! Call Grandma! Ask her!"

"I don't have an hour and a half to spare, Ben. You know, she'll start at the beginning and by the time she gets to the bit we want to hear about, I'll have glazed over. Anyway, we have to meet Daddy, Granny Marion and Pa at the airport at Knock. We're late as it is."

Esti giggles:

"Come on Ben! What do you expect? White cottages with roses round the door."

"Yes I do!" he replies: "John F. Kennedy's house is still there. I saw it in the guidebook – it's white. Why can't I have one too?"

In minutes, we pull into Roscommon town. My grandmother's family came from somewhere near here. They left at the time of the famine in the 1840s. It's a dreary collection of granite buildings. Ben, whose head is still nodding up and down between Esti and I, lets out an indignant:

"Ughhh!"

"No wonder they left," says Esti.

I'm deeply disappointed. I didn't expect it to look this bad. Irish towns aren't up to much at the best of times but this one is really depressing. I was hoping to impress them.

When I was a little girl and my grandmother came to stay, I would be sent into the sitting room to entertain her while my mother cooked the dinner. Invariably, Gran was watching the news. It was the height of the Troubles in the 1970s and the headlines were always about a bomb or shooting in Northern Ireland. The Protestant leader, Ian Paisley used to pop up on the screen. She would blurt out, sitting on the edge of her seat:

"That wretched man, they shouldn't give him the time of day. Poor Ireland, oh my poor Ireland!"

At that moment my mother would appear and say to Gran:

"Mother! Have another sherry."

I knew the events on the screen had something to do with us but I wasn't sure what. I realised that Gran's Ireland and Ian Paisley's were two different places but I had no idea what was so wrong with Paisley, as no one ever had time to tell me. Maybe that is why I am always explaining things to my children. I try to tell this to the kids, by way of an apology for Roscommon, and maybe for myself as well, but Ben is getting grumpy. He wants to talk about his ancestors, his imaginary ones, not my Gran:

"Oh, not this story again! I've heard it all before. What's it got to do with it, anyway?"

He slumps back and falls asleep.

We have rented a cottage on an island off the west coast that's connected to the mainland by a causeway that you can only get across at low tide. It's a rural idyll all of its own. In fact the kids like it so much that they ask me not to write about it or even mention its name. This is the first time this has ever happened. I hope it has something to do with the Irish in them.

Not much further along the coast from our island paradise is Dan O'Hara's Homestead. It's a reconstruction of a subsistence farm from around the time of the Potato Famine of the 1840s. We are lucky it's there, because it's the only place that we can visit on a rainy day in Connemara and get back from before the tide cuts us off.

After we pay for the tickets, we are in to see a long film, which you are required to watch, before you head up the hillside to see the tiny, stone cottage. We settle down in the darkened room. Dan O'Hara, it transpires, was a real man. There is even a famous ballad sung about him. I've a sneaky suspicion that the whole thing is a bit of a con but don't want to mention it. Dan O'Hara lived on the homestead with his seven children. It has to be seven doesn't it? He didn't own the house he lived in, or the land, but paid rent to the local landlord, just like all the other Irish peasants of the time. To the sound of mournful music, we discover his simple but happy lifestyle growing potatoes came to an abrupt end, when he decided to put in some larger windows. The landlord put up his rent, to take account of the home improvements, even though O'Hara had paid for them out of his own pocket. When he couldn't pay, he was evicted. There was no other employment in Ireland, so he had no choice but to emigrate. He set sail for America. On the boat, his wife and three of his children died. At this point in the story my father-in-law, who is a devoted father and grandfather, starts sniffing and puts his arm around Ray. At the end of the film, poor old Dan O'Hara, ends up penniless, on the streets of New York. He is forced to put his surviving children into care, while he lives by selling matches. It's an Irish version of the Little Match Girl.

Gloom laden, we trudge up the hill, in the drizzle. Ben is running behind me:

"That's amazing, did you hear that? He didn't speak English! My ancestor didn't speak English."

"You're not related to Dan O'Hara, are you? Did I miss something?"

"Come on Mummy! You know what I mean. Grandma's family were all like him weren't they?"

I think of Granny Clarke, with an "e", and tales that Gran would tell me, that we were, in fact, descended from an aristocratic family, who disowned my great-great-grandfather, when he ran away with the serving maid. I'm sure it is all poppycock but I don't want to be a Dan

O'Hara and dissolve into the landscape, neither did Gran. I want to find a castle, called Flanagan Hall, or at least, a whitewashed cottage, not a hovel.

"I feel really sorry for poor old Dan O'Hara," says Ray.

Esti grabs her sleeve:

"Oh! Get real Ray! He was an idiot! It was his fault for putting in the new windows. I'd have been really mad at him, if I was his wife. I could imagine Ben doing something as stupid as that."

Dan O'Hara's house is minute and has just two beds. A fight immediately breaks out about who would have slept in which one. I feel for the man. I imagine having to share a bed with seven children. It's too much for Tim, who goes outside. I ask Esti to pose, so I can take her picture with Jacob, in Dan O'Hara's doorway. When the picture comes out, I can see she is looking sulky. It's clear that she is wishing she wasn't being made to stand there, that she would rather be somewhere else.

At the foot of the hill is a café. There is also a huge gift shop. Tim drinks coffee with his parents, while the kids start rifling through heaps of emerald green coloured teddies. Then they move on to the piles of key rings, each with every Irish surname imaginable on. There are shelves of tea towels, showing where the main Irish clans come from. Fortunately, for my credibility, the Flanagans are shown living in and around Roscommon. I was beginning to wonder if they really existed at all. As last, I have some evidence of my ancestry. My past exists on a tea towel, if not in reality. Now I know why there is so much of this stuff on sale in Ireland. It's all most of the diaspora has left. Ben decides to buy a tea towel and send it to Grandma, in Ilkley. She's delighted and says it's too good to use to dry dishes and she going to keep it in a safe place. Tim is incredulous.

I know Ben has tried hard to find some Irish connection to please me but he and Esti have only managed to identify with Dan O'Hara. It's enough to make my grandmother turn in her grave. You are who you think you are, not what you really are. I was wrong to dismiss identity as irrelevant when Ben was born. It's fascinating. Tim, who is not particularly interested in any of this, rather like my father, jumps ship. He has an assignment in Iraqi Kurdistan. I suppose he knows exactly who he is.

I have just about given up on Ireland when we drive into Belfast. I'm flustered and keep taking the wrong turn. I once worked here as a *BBC* trainee. I was drawn to the place by a desire to find out what was so wrong with Ian Paisley. I haven't been back for fifteen years and I am completely disorientated. The whole town has been rebuilt and tarted up. We cross the motorway that slices through the city and drive into the most interesting part of town, West Belfast. Here are two of the most famous streets in Britain, the Catholic Falls Road and the Protestant Shankill Road. They run parallel to each other and were at the heart of the sectarian fighting of the last thirty years. The two communities live in areas separated by huge metal and concrete barriers, although the back-to-back Victorian tenement slums and hideous sixties housing estates are nearly all gone. Large swathes of West Belfast have been turned into a sea of modern, small, suburban-looking houses.

Cruising down the Shankill, I try to spot the shop, where I once went to interview some members of a Protestant paramilitary gang. Pregnant with Ben, I desperately needed to go to the toilet and was escorted upstairs to a small curtained-off bathroom. There were wooden crates everywhere and I wasn't sure if the gang member, who guided me upstairs and stood guard by the curtain, was there to protect my decency or stop me looking in the boxes. I have never liked the Shankill Road. It must be in the blood.

"Oh what idiots! Look at that Kentucky Fried Chicken!" shouts Esti, as we get near to the end of the Shankill. The outside of the KFC is decorated with a large mural featuring black-hooded gunmen sporting Kalashnikovs. Ben is in a more sombre mood and gets out of the car to walk about. The empty wasteland opposite is littered with the debris of a riot which had taken place the previous night. He comes back with a serious look on his face:

"It's unbelievable! This is Britain, but it looks like those places in Bosnia, where they paint the pavements and hang out their flags to let you know who's who and who owns what. I can't believe that you were right. You always said Bosnia looked like Belfast."

I wonder why he never listens to me. None of the kids try to grab the moment and ask if they can go into the KFC. There's something about the Shankill that doesn't make them feel like lingering either.

We drive on and up to the housing estates, on the very edge of West Belfast, where there is more evidence of rioting. They've been throwing bottles or Molotov cocktails and there is broken glass everywhere. The kids ask to ride around the estate once more. Then we turn down into the Falls Road. Ben and Ray get out to inspect one mural after another. All along the street are huge paintings depicting crucial events in the Troubles. We are sitting in the car in front of a picture of Bobby Sands, who died during the Hunger Strike of 1981.

"What's the Hunger Strike?" asks Esti.

"IRA prisoners in a big gaol near here decided to refuse to eat until they were recognised as political prisoners," I explain. "They said they were fighting a war for an independent, united Ireland. That man there, Sands, was the leader. He was elected as an MP but he died in prison."

"Can't they think of something more recent, it all happened so long ago?"

Ben is getting back in the car:

"Esti, you are wrong," he says. "It's just because you have never heard of the Hunger Strike and it means nothing to you."

She's completely baffled:

"So, it means something to you?"

"No, not really, but it's just like the Balkans here, don't you think? It doesn't matter if it happened long ago. They think it was yesterday. It's like 1389 and the Battle of Kosovo."

She nods. At last they agree on something. He continues:

"I think everyone who lives in Britain, should be made to come here and see what it's really like. I think everyone would be less quick to judge other people in what they consider are far away places, if they saw what we have in our own backyard. See this! You can see British people are no different from Serbs and Bosnian Muslims."

Unfortunately what unites Europe is a lack of brotherly love. It's an impressive speech, but, I'm annoyed that Ireland is described as a "back-yard". Southern Ireland has passed them by without any profound effect. They feel nothing for their Irish past. It's the Falls and the Shankill that mean something to them. How ironic. I have no family ties with the North but here they recognise something they have grown up with, a Europe riddled with conflict and hate. I have passed on my childhood desire to know what was wrong with Ireland and they have decided to apply the question to the whole continent.

21 - Santa's Gift

In Shepherd's Bush there is no escaping the "Diddle e de de de do, diddle e doo" of the *Thomas* theme tune. Tonight Jacob is in a sulk because I don't want to play with his wooden train set. He wants his father but Tim, who was happy to swap the Irish rain for the rugged, dry landscape of Iraqi Kurdistan, is not at home. His application for a visa to visit the rest of Iraq controlled by Saddam is sitting on a desk in Baghdad. A new war is on the way and I have no intention of hanging around waiting to be engulfed by it, playing toy trains. I've had enough of that sort of thing. *Family Circle* has commissioned a feature on inter-railing with kids. It's time for some real trains:

"We are heading up to the Arctic Circle to meet Santa," I announce at supper.

There's a sharp intake of breath.

"I once saw a *Blue Peter* Christmas special about a group of kids with terminal diseases, who were taken to meet Father Christmas," I add as some sort of explanation. I've always wanted to do this, ever since I was a child.

"Brilliant!" says Ben scooping up Jacob. "Santa! Did you hear that we're going to meet Santa?"

As soon as school breaks up for the summer holidays we're off. We shoot across Norway at breakneck speed - the scenery is magnificent but everything is so expensive we can't afford to eat - so we can't linger and enjoy the countryside. As the train rattles into Stockholm, a city that exudes regal self-confidence, an equally poised Ben flaps the *Herald Tribune* with a flourish and smiles at the pretty, pink baby across the aisle:

"According to the *New York Times* they are going to try to take control of key command centres in Iraq. Do you think that's a better idea than mounting a land invasion from Jordan and Kuwait?"

Later I'll be grilled on whether or not I think Saddam Hussein has weapons of mass destruction, while I wonder why Ben thinks I'm likely to know whether he does or not. No one else on the planet does. I'm flattered that he thinks I might. He's yet to recognise my full limitations.

"Where first? How about the military museum?" says Ben as he feigns excessive interest in what the guidebook has to say about the Swedish versions of weapons of mass destruction from the Thirty Years' War. Esti looks at me sternly. I can feel a fight brewing.

I decide that we will catch a boat across the harbour to Djurgården, where the Swedes unwind when the going gets tough. On the island there are acres of green space, more museums, a funfair and more importantly Junibacken, home of Pippi Longstocking, the national heroine.

"Yey! Pippi Longstocking!" shouts Ray, her eyes sparkling. "The Pippi Longstocking centre!"

Ray is a fan of this unruly little girl with orange pigtails and no parents. In fact, Esti has a soft spot for her too. Longstocking spends her time rebelling and breaking rules.

The highlight of a trip to Junibacken is a ride on a small train though the world of her creator, Astrid Lindgren.

It gets off to a good start as we rumble past a scene of Pippi's house and overgrown garden. But things get confusing as we trundle past scenes from Lindgren's other stories. The kids haven't read any of her other books. I have read none of them. Esti is incensed:

"What's all this! What's this got to do with anything?"

"Sssh, Esti! Jacob and Evie don't care. Look." Ben gestures at his brother, who is sitting on his lap engrossed.

We shuttle up in front of a scene of a pretty town with clapperboard houses. A voice on the speaker at the back of our carriage says:

"It was the day I found out that I was going to die."

Ray looks shocked. Esti is livid:

"What! This is a show for kids?"

The mystery voice tells us that the boy in this story is dying of tuberculosis and has just found out that he has months to live by accidentally overhearing a conversation. He doesn't fancy being buried underground. His elder brother tries to comfort him. We are all riveted by the depressing scene being played out on the speakers behind us while we stare at the charming model village in front of us. Suddenly, our hero's house catches fire. Esti recoils:

"I don't believe it!"

The story continues. It's better than a soap opera. The older brother tries to save his dying little brother by jumping out of the window with him in his arms. The eldest one is killed. The youngest however is cushioned by his big brother's body and survives to die another day. This is just too much for Esti:

"What are they doing, putting this in here? These people are completely crazy! This isn't what you come somewhere like this to see."

Death and destruction has its place in real life and should, she thinks, stay there. I assume that is how she has it sorted in her head. The carriage jerks on to the next scene to yet more mutterings of disbelief all round. I find a guide to the works of Lindgren in the gift shop:

"Hey Esti! That story about the boys is famous, it's called *The Brothers Lionheart* and it's supposed to teach children not to be afraid of death."

"Terrify them instead. Can't anyone have any fun around here? They're so gloomy." She marches off, out of the door.

I'm beginning to think she'll never understand Scandinavian culture, when we move on to the Vasa Museum, next door to Junibacken. Inside is a huge seventeenth century warship that sank in the harbour on its maiden voyage in 1628. It's a Swedish version of the Mary Rose.

"Hey! Do you see that Esti? There's a film telling the story of how it was salvaged - Let's watch!" Ben guides his sister into a small cinema.

Ray follows.

They settle down in the dark. The commentary is in Swedish. Jacob and Evie don't want to watch. We set off to explore. I discover that the same film is running in French, in the next room. I go back to tell them.

"No thanks! It's very interesting," Ben whispers in the dark.

Esti waves happily. Ray grins. I wait by the door until it finishes, wondering if I'll ever comprehend them. They can make themselves at home anywhere. I wonder if it's genetic or we have moulded them to be like this. What if I hadn't come to Sweden? I would never have discovered this.

My mobile rings. It's Tim. He has a long list of suggestions about where we should go and what we should do in Stockholm. This is one of those moments when he can be extremely irritating. Is there nowhere he has never been?

It's early August when we finally make it into Helsinki Central station. It's a square, dirty, dark, flat building. It's also solid and grim, like a lot of the Finnish capital. It seems out of all proportion to the city, as if it wanted to be grander, but couldn't quite manage it. Inside, it has a rather sulky atmosphere, which the kids soon pick up. When we arrive at the platform, from where the night sleeper to Rovaniemi is due to depart, there's a dusty, double-decker commuter train revving up. Jacob poses proudly in front of it. He's clutching his *Thomas* backpack.

"Take my picture!" he orders, sounding rather like his big brother.

At this point, the train starts to pull out slowly. His face crumples and he begins to cry. Esti and I run up and down the platform, trying to make sure that we haven't made a mistake and missed the train. Typically, there's no one to ask. Ben, of course, is nowhere to be seen and has disappeared into the newsagent.

"Can we get it to stop, so we can get on?" suggests Esti.

"We can't do that and leave him behind!" I shout over the engine noise.

As the train pulls away, Esti turns around and glares at me:

"You're *so* stupid! You can't organise anything. Now, we've missed the f***ing thing."

"Don't swear! What about Ben?"

"Forget him!"

It's mystifying. Only half an hour ago, they were laughing and joking. Now they are deadly enemies. I check the departures board. I'm on the wrong platform. I panic. This is the highlight of my trip. I'm not sure if Esti thinks this is all a stupid idea or simply that I'm plain stupid. Jacob is snivelling:

"I want Daddy. I want my Daddy."

"Daddy is in Kurdistan. You'll have to make do with me," I snap and immediately feel rotten to the core for being so horrid.

Ray bends down to comfort her little brother. Evie looks pale and a little tense at the sound of my voice. She's sucking yet another chocolate biscuit. Ben saunters over.

"Where have you been?" I ask curtly.

"In the newsagent, I told you. If you wanted me, you should have got someone to come and get me. I want to find out what is going on in the world. Go on shout at me! You'll feel better."

I do. We sit on a bench and wait for our train to arrive, a not very happy picture of family unity.

Tim phones. He has just been to Halabja where Saddam Hussein murdered up to 5,000 Kurds in a chemical attack in 1988. I don't want to hear about this. I want to meet Santa. I hope I don't sound disinterested. He thinks it's ridiculous that I ever thought that we had missed the night train. I suspect things might be a little better organised if he was here. As a result I start bickering down the phone and then hang up. Ben, who is now engrossed in latest edition of *The Economist* groans:

"By the way some field marshal is predicting that the war in Iraq will be a quagmire and will take years to finish."

Horrified at the thought, I call Tim back. It would be so much nicer if he were here. I know he has always wanted to make love on a night train.

When we do finally make it to Rovaniemi, I discover that Santa's hometown is an Arctic version of Milton Keynes, but the kids don't seem to notice. The drive to Santa's headquarters is bleak. We pass a collection of desolate, depressing, empty reindeer pens. On the edge of the car park they are grilling reindeer sausages. Cutesy Rudolph sentimentality hasn't reached this far north. As a result Evie will spend the next leg of the train journey fiddling with the hem of her fairy dress and worrying about why some people like to eat reindeers. It seems like the least of our problems.

"Some people are very odd here, you know. They don't like reindeers and they have them for lunch," she tells Tim down the phone to Kurdistan.

I can hear him laughing.

Santa's office is in a large wooden cabin at the exact point where the Arctic Circle begins. Ben and Jacob are just ahead of us in the queue. Next to them there are piles of books that supposedly contain lists of the names of all the children in the world. Jacob looks up in awe. In front of us are couple of Japanese, a few Italians and some Germans. We watch as they go up to talk to Santa. Esti takes a sharp intake of breath:

"Listen! He's talking to them in Japanese! I just heard him speak Italian, too."

It turns out that he also speaks German. It's a really believable act. Ray, Jacob and Evie are captivated and in a state of awe. Evie holds my hand tight. Ben, who I never thought would stop believing in Santa, is bending down next to his brother pointing out the huge pot of porridge cooking on the stove:

"It's Santa's favourite food, Jakie."

I watch them and realise that hard talking about the bleak side of life doesn't necessarily destroy a child's ability to enjoy the innocent, sweet things it has to offer. Santa restores my faith in humanity. Ben was right to make sure that Ray didn't find out that he doesn't exist.

At last, it's our turn. Santa turns first to Jacob:

"You were naughty the night before you left home. You shouted and wouldn't go to bed. Your Mummy got cross."

Jacob hangs his head. I think he is going to cry. It's true he had a tantrum. A lucky guess, I think. But, then he turns to Esti:

"You have a quick temper and were in a bad mood last night."

How does he know that? I'm impressed. Esti looks astounded but for once doesn't answer back. What does he know about me? He laughs. It's a real belly laugh and he ruffles Jacob's hair as he stands up to shake their hands. He's truly enormous and takes size 56 shoes. He dwarfs Ben who has an enormous grin on his face. I can't believe that, at this moment, my camera jams. The official photographer takes a picture and says we can e-mail it to a friend. A photo of us with Santa wings its way through cyberspace to northern Iraq. Tim is unable to open it.

Four trains and two ferries later, we are back at the heart of things – in the south-western suburbs of Berlin, not far from Potsdam. Until the Wall came down, this suburb was in the East. There are wide boulevards lined with tall trees. There's hardly anyone around.

"We've made it," says Ben with an air of triumph.

I look down the empty street and back to a small crumpled piece of paper with an address on it. In pencil Tim's aunt has written "27 Waltraud Strasse". This was once Granny Marion's grandparents' weekend house. For me and Ben, this is the serious business of the summer.

One evening, a few months ago, we were eating supper in the kitchen watching a TV documentary. The historian Anthony Beevor was putting forward his theory that Stalin was determined to take Berlin before the Allies, because he wanted to get hold of the Nazis' nuclear programme which was being developed at an institute in what was to become East Berlin. On the screen Beevor marched around a large garden and pointed at the huge wall of an old Nazi nuclear reactor. Through the clatter of the dishes, the name of the institute sounded exactly like the one that was built in the grounds of Granny Marion's family's house. Intrigued Tim turned up the volume as Ben spluttered and dropped his fork:

"What! What did he say? Granny Marion owns a nuclear reactor? I don't believe it! History was made in my garden?"

"I only said it sounded like it was there. Don't jump to conclusions. Anyway, it isn't your house," added Tim calmly.

"What do you mean – it isn't my house?" shouted Ben angrily. Esti glared at him in exasperation:

"You are so stupid sometimes. If it's anyone's house, it's Granny Marion's. Geddit? Not yours. Hitler stole it off her grandparents – not you, idiot."

The fact that the Nazis built an institute in the grounds of the house has led to endless legal complications, especially since after 1945 the property ended up in communist East Germany. The lawyers are still wrangling about whether she and her sister Huguette will get any compensation. I think, perhaps we should just send Esti and get her to say:

"It's Granny Marion's. Geddit, guys!" and all would be fixed.

The weekend after we had seen Beevor's documentary, Tim's aunt Huguette passed through London on the way back from Germany to San Francisco, where she now lives. I asked her if there was a reactor in the back garden of the house in Berlin.

"Why, ja! An institute is built in the garden." She replied.

Huguette has a German accent, while Granny Marion has become completely French. This is a great mystery to the kids. I explain that she is married to a German.

"But, she's lived in America for fifty years," says Esti.

Tim adds that when they moved to France in 1933, when she was six-years old she refused to speak for six months and then announced that she was no longer going to be called Inge-Margot, her original name, but Huguette. This was the name of a popular girl at school. She assumed a French identity but now has a German accent. Some things one can never get to the bottom of.

Huguette fiddled about in her handbag and produced a small, yellow note pad and a pencil. She wrote down the address of the house but Ben and I were left none the wiser about whether or not there was a reactor in the back garden. Esti and Tim were disinterested but Ben wouldn't let it drop. I wasn't sure if he was interested in the house, the family or the big political history. When Ben tried to ask Granny Marion about the reactor she just laughed and said:

"Why do you want to talk about these things?"

I was as intrigued as him and felt I had to see this place.

So, here we are outside the metro stop, fumbling with the tiny piece of paper on which Huguette had written down the address. It isn't at all clear where the house is. In the hot August sun, we start trudging along a leafy street. Eventually, we come to a small house with roses in the front garden.

"It must be this one. It says number 27," I say putting the paper back in my pocket. Ben looks aghast:

"It can't be! Granny Marion wouldn't live in that!" It's a pretty little suburban house. She has an elegant mansion flat in Kensington. "That's number 27a. Look! Why haven't you got your glasses on?"

We go further down the street and through the large gates of an institution. Ben marches ahead:

"This is it! It has to be! It's the only institutional building around here."

By the gate is a large, elegant, turn-of-the-century house. It has been converted into flats, presumably for the people who work here.

"I'm going in," says Ben.

I panic:

"You can't do that! They might arrest you for trespassing."

I pull at his sleeve.

"But, this is our house! Come on Mummy! I didn't come all this way not to go in and have a look at, what is, after all, *our* house. Are you coming? What's wrong with you all of a sudden?"

I hesitate and then we follow him. The main door is open and a smell of lunch cooking in one of the flats above wafts down the stairs. We walk through the entrance hall and out of the back door. I look around nervously in case anyone has seen us. The hallway is whitewashed and has a fire door in the middle. It's totally lacking in atmosphere. I blink as we emerge back out into the bright sunshine. Ben is standing in front of me with his arms open:

"Well, is that our house?"

He's expecting a reply. I am completely lost:

"I don't know. How am I supposed to know?"

I want to say:

"Help, how has life brought me here, snooping around a house in Berlin?" But this isn't what is required. He wants me to give him a solid answer but I can't.

"Ask someone, then," he snaps irritably.

"What am I supposed to do? Ring on the doorbell and say: 'I'm sorry to disturb you but was this house confiscated off my mother-in-law's family by the Nazis and then nationalised by the Communists? If so, my son would like it back and you have to move.' Get serious Ben!"

"It looks like the sort of place Granny Marion would live," says Ray. Esti is silent.

"Let's walk about," I suggest. It's a beautiful summer's day.

We push the double buggy through, what is now a disused children's hospital, and round the large, shady, deserted garden. There's no nuclear reactor anywhere to be seen. As we skirt past some whitewashed, 1930s, hospital buildings, I begin to realise that I am in the wrong place. The house, "27 Waltraud Strasse", is on a lake. There is *no* lake. I'm not sure if I should tell them or not. I'm not sure it really makes any difference. I don't think Tim's mother will ever get the house back, so they may never know I've made a complete mess of the whole visit. If Tim had been here this would never have happened but he's not because I'm the one who is interested in this kind of thing and he isn't. He concentrates on the present.

"Oh, no! Imagine what went on here. It must have been a Nazi children's hospital! It doesn't bear thinking about, does it kids?" I say.

Esti has her hands thrust in her pockets:

"No wonder Granny Marion has never been very interested in getting it back. I don't want to own this place!"

I sympathise. The only thing I've ever inherited is a butcher's shop and I am a vegetarian. Ben is jumping around the buggy to block her path waving his arms:

"But, Esti - it's the size of Shepherd's Bush Green! It's stolen property!"

"What are you going to do with it? Move in?" she sneers.

"Hang on guys. Don't argue! We don't even know if we are in the right house." I add.

Esti grins:

"We're not arguing, we are just debating. It's the Jewish way of doing things."

Within minutes Ben realises there is no lake. He is completed flustered.

"Anyway," Esti says, "what does it matter if we are in somebody else's house?"

I feel that she would happily just take this one, sell it and be done with the past. This does, after all, seem to be the way things are done. If someone steals your house, you steal someone else's.

The hospital grounds are hot and oppressive. Searching for the non-existent lake we have ended up underneath some tall birch trees surrounded by high grass and weeds. There are gnats dancing in the air in front of my face. It's a scrubby dead end. I just want to go but I can't. I have a feeling that fate has brought me here. This time I just can't walk away. It was my idea to come in the first place. As I try to work out what to say to the kids I feel angry that Tim isn't here and I am. He has followed other people's stories in a whole variety of wars and civil strife so why isn't he following this one, his own one?

As I dither, suddenly things tumble into place. I can almost hear the ideas and the thoughts rushing past. No one told me when I had Ben, that I would stop being someone who just came from London and had Irish, English and the odd Huguenot ancestor. Nobody warned me that I would end up in the garden of a house in the suburbs of Berlin coming to terms with my children's highly complicated past. The whole debate that everyone but Tim and I were interested in having, centred on superficial things like whether or not Ben would be circumcised or eat pork. Suddenly I realise that I have come to Berlin to find out what really matters when you fall in love with and have children with someone from a different culture or a different religion. Their background becomes yours and visa versa. It's a slow process but eventually you become ethnic gender benders. Tim's background is my children's background, so it's mine too. There's no shirking this anymore. I have been worrying about being excluded from the French club when in fact, without realising it, I have joined the Jewish one. At last I can answer my mother's question. I think we have worked out who we are. The sun flickers between the leaves. The funny thing is that although the kids look the same as ever, I feel like I have just met them. I've lost interest in the reactor.

"Thanks for bringing us," says Esti. "It doesn't matter if we've messed up. What matters is we came." I feel like I am ready to face the world a stronger person.

Tim phones to find out how everything is going. He is in Iran continuing his tour of the "Axis of Evil" while I try to sort out what I think about the headquarters of the former Axis powers. I relate the trials of the day so far. He is rather disinterested as if this is all old news and has a list of suggestions of other things to do in Berlin. The key to survival is clearly not to take things too much to heart. I follow his cue. We opt for some sightseeing.

At Potsdamer Platz, Ben, who is interested in modern architecture, enthusiastically explains to Ray how Renzo Piano designed the masterplan for part of the post-Wall reconstruction of the square.

"You know, I think I could live here," he announces with a flourish. "Look at all this rising from the ashes."

I stare at him. I'm not sure, if he's joking. He isn't. He is the epitome of human nature; robust and irrepressible. I'm beginning to think that I'll never understand my eldest son, when I remember he's just behaving like the Croatian family in whose bed and breakfast we once stayed. They had returned after the war and moved into the house that had probably once belonged to their Serbian neighbours and carried on as if nothing had happened. It is possible to paper over the cracks. It's amazing how a lick of paint can consign something so swiftly to the past. It's been a productive summer. I have learnt that the kids have grown up to be flexible, optimistic and not at all embarrassed by having a bit of fun at the North Pole. Thanks Santa.

22 - War in London

It's a Sunday morning, in late September, a few weeks after the start of the school term. Ray, now aged nine, is sitting at the kitchen table writing her autobiography for the English teacher:

"What shall I say next Mummy?"

I pick up the exercise book. So far she has written carefully, in her new fountain pen:

"When I was small I lived in Belgrade. My father is a journalist, who writes about wars. Some of them are scary, much scarier than *Scary Movie*. My Mummy writes about travelling with children. I've been lucky to go to a lot of places. Last year we went to Mostar, where I saw many people with shell shock and this summer, we took a train to the Arctic Circle to meet Santa. I would like to travel more. Perhaps, I'll go to Africa next."

As the storm clouds gather, the weeks click by uneventfully until there are whoops of joy all round when Tim finally gets his visa for Iraq. Now, it's a question of timing. Tim needs to arrive just before the war breaks out as his visa only lasts ten days. We plot together about when he should leave. If there is going to be an invasion Tim wants to be in the Iraqi capital when it happens.

One day when Tim is out, his mother asks me why he doesn't get a new line of work. She looks frail. His father has just died. Life seems a little tenuous, I agree. One morning my father-in-law was laughing and waving "goodbye" as he walked down the front steps and then two weeks later he was dead. She doesn't want her son to take any risks but Tim loves his job and I can't imagine him doing anything else:

"He wants to be there to tell the world what is going on," I mutter in his defence.

That doesn't cut much ice with his mother. I wonder why I'm having to defend him and why he isn't here to do it himself. I point out to her that our overdraft is mounting and that the war could be very profitable.

"Pah!" she says and flicks her fingers as if she is washing her hands of both of us. There are days when I feel exactly the same about my husband.

Feeling slightly guilty about this, I resolve to show my support for the project by buying him some Christmas presents that might be useful in Iraq. Ray, Jacob, Evie and I go to a local, outdoor equipment shop. I have just found a tourist guide to Iraq when the shop assistant comes up and asks us if we need some help.

"My Daddy is going to Iraq and we want to buy something for him for Christmas," says four-year old Jacob.

The assistant doesn't blink and suggests we buy a compass to stop him getting lost in the desert and a plastic water bottle. The shop is round the corner from the *BBC* and he has probably had hundreds of journalists in here already stocking up. As he shows me a fleece with a detachable inner layer, he adds:

"It's proving very popular. If he's planning to sleep out in the desert, it would be an excellent buy. The desert in Iraq can get very cold at night."

How does he know this? The fleece is £85! My budget doesn't stretch to that. We wrap up the supplies we can afford and put them under the tree.

In January, Tim goes on a frontline training course and, when he gets back, it's an unusually calm and controlled Friday evening for our house. I've even managed to clean the kitchen and there's some soft music playing on the stereo. Jacob and Evie are sitting at the end of the table colouring quietly. At the other end, Ben who's missed dinner is eating an omelette. The girls are leaning with their backs on the sink chatting and laughing. Tim sits down next to Ben. I hand him a bottle of beer. He's opening the large box that's been delivered, while he's been away. It's his chemical weapons protection equipment. It was delivered to the neighbour because we were out. When I told him what was in the box, he didn't blink, but he shook his head with a sigh of resignation. Now the box is open on the kitchen floor. Tim pulls on the gas mask and starts making deep breathing sounds that are something akin to an amplified, dirty phone call. He can't see what he's doing and knocks over his beer. He blames Ben. The kids look at him with bewildered amusement. Ben sniggers, while he sets the beer bottle upright. I'm lost for words but Esti breaks through the amplified deep breathing:

"Dads! I don't think this is the moment! Do you?"

Tim peels off his gas mask and looks around innocently, while Jacob and Evie pick up their pens again.

The preparations continue apace: George Bush, Tony Blair and Saddam Hussein have taken over my life. One afternoon I'm shopping in Sainsbury's for supplies of soap, shampoo and aspirins for Tim to take with him when he calls me on my mobile to tell me to buy rolls of cling-film, so he can wrap up his electrical equipment if there's a sandstorm. It will keep the sand out. I'm amazed. It looks so innocent. I didn't know it had such powers. I pile the cartons of cling-film, one on top of the other, at the checkout. The shop assistant scans them over the barcode reader. My head is buzzing with a tension that I wish I could shove out of the way as easily as I can thrust the cling-film into the plastic bag. I feel like shouting at the people around me, who seem totally indifferent to what is going on in the world:

"Don't you know why I am buying this cling-film? Don't you know that there is about to be a war?"

Fortunately, I restrain myself. They do know. The rights and wrongs of the decision to go to war are rapidly becoming a national obsession. This time everyone knows what is going on. I tell Tim about how the cling-film upset me when I get home. He's picking at a half eaten piece of cake someone has left on the kitchen sideboard. He laughs at me and puts his arms around me. I feel infuriated and foolish.

Eventually, he leaves for the Middle East. He gets up at 5am to pack his bag. When the taxi arrives I'm in a deep sleep. I wake with a jolt as he tiptoes from room to room to kiss the children "goodbye".

"Good luck," mutters Ben from under the covers.

Ray gives him the tiny, green teddy bear she bought at Dan O'Hara's. It looks crumpled up, as if she has been holding it tight all night, waiting for this very moment.

The morning light is hard and the air is damp and cold. I watch Tim loading his bags into the boot of the taxi. He turns to wave happily, his eyes bright with excitement, as Jacob appears at my side and slips his arm round my thigh. He runs back up the steps to give me one last kiss. I give him one of my earrings as a good luck charm. The lucky grey t-shirt I always used to pack was lost years ago. One more kiss and he is gone. I stand there on the front steps staring down the road with Jacob in my arms. Then I realise that my feet are frozen and there is not much point in standing here any longer. It isn't going make any difference to the course of events and turn George Bush and Saddam Hussein into best friends. I have a husband who is addicted to finding out what is going on in the world's most dangerous places and I have to fix the kids' breakfast.

Tim eventually arrives in Baghdad and Ben spends the entire weekend before the war breaks out, working manically, around the clock, on a Russian project. He's just got back from a school trip to Moscow and has to write an illustrated account of everything he has seen. To add to the complication, while part of it is in Russian, the other half is in French. So, while I suppress twangs of panic and try to stay calm, my main task is to correct the grammar and spelling in two languages of a screed that covers an unending stream of A4 paper. It is covered in doodles; fine little pencil drawings of tanks, trees and people with wizened faces and chiselled features. I can't believe 50 pages are required but he is insistent that everything must be perfect for the Russian teacher.

To add to my problems an endless troop of visitors pop round to see us. I cook and serve them up meal after meal. I wish they would just go away and leave me in peace. It's unnervingly similar to the round of activity that follows a death. Journalists get killed in silly, pointless wars all the time. No one pops round when Tim goes to an African war zone although I think they are far more dangerous.

By Monday morning, it's clear that the war in Iraq is about to break out within hours. The sun is shinning and it's exceptionally warm. How can a war break out today? I wonder if my grandmother felt like this on September 3rd 1939. Tim calls to see if everyone got to school on time as if that was the most important thing in the world. He does the school run when he's in London. I don't mention that Ben is still at home. What would be the point of that today? I am completely exhausted, but the project still isn't finished, as Ben writes on and on. He wants to complete it for the class at noon and begs me to let him skip the first lessons. This isn't the moment to argue, so I agree. I spend the time between corrections, writing notes to the kid's teachers to tell them that Tim is in Baghdad. Ben is fidgety. I feel tired.

"What if they realise Dad is Jewish?" says Ben.

"Let's just hope they don't," I reply.

We both know just how dangerous that could be. I'm terrified they might accuse him of being a spy and shoot him.

I am in fact incredulous that no one over there has noticed that Tim has a classic Baghdadi Jewish surname. His father's family lived there for generations until they saw the writing on the wall, about a hundred and fifty years ago, and moved on to India. Over in Iraq Tim is being served classic Iraqi dishes just like the one's his family have always eaten on high days and holidays, like chicken and okra, which is one of Tim's favourite things. He has to pretend he's never tasted them before. In fact, Iraq is like some bad penny that keeps popping up in the family. My grandfather fought there during the First World War and Tim's maternal grandmother's family, the Sassoons were also from this doomed country. Tim is very distantly related to Siegfried Sassoon, the First World War poet. Ben loves shoving this fact down the English teacher's throat: Writing about the horrors of war must run in the blood.

Back at home, there is a second, huge, anti-war demonstration about to be held in Hyde Park. I think the war is a bad idea and that the whole weapons inspection process should be given more time. My mother wants to know why we aren't going to the protest since my father knew Iraq well and went to work there regularly, training and examining Iraqi doctors. We often went with him. We even stayed in the same hotel, the Al-Rashid, where Tim is now staying. I tell her that I just can't think about whether the war is legal or not at the moment. I can't cope with this. I don't want to get involved. I just want to go onto autopilot and survive. I can tell she is disgusted with me.

When I put down the phone Ben appears in the bedroom. It's Saturday morning. He sits down on the bed next to me. He has his mobile phone in his hand as if he has already, or is just about to make a call:

"Everyone from school is going to the demonstration but I told them I couldn't face it. I feel rather bad about it. What do you think?"

I tell him about my conversation with Grandma.

"At least you understand," he says shrugging his shoulders as if to shake off the pressure.

"It must be the same if your Dad is in the army. If Dads is going to be killed in a war at least I'd like to think it was a moral one and was worth it," he says. "Anyway I have work to do."

"I understand," I tell him.

He is bigger than me but not too big to cuddle. He flops on my shoulder. I try to comfort him:

"That has nothing to do with it, really, does it Ben? Someone has to be there to say what happens when the bombs start falling. It doesn't actually make any difference now to the people of Baghdad if the bomb that falls on their head is legal or not. Anyway Dads isn't in the army. *The Economist* and the *New York Review of Books* are paying the bills. He doesn't have to do any fighting."

He gets up with a sigh, paces up and down the room a few times and walks away from me. I decide it's better to leave him to get on with his homework than start flapping about. We've been down this road before. When Tim calls, I relate the day's events but I don't think he knows what I am talking about.

I feel as well prepared as I can be for the conflict. Ben and Esti both have mobile phones now and, in the run up to the war, I have tried to brief the younger three to forestall any misunderstandings. No anthrax cock ups this time. Information overload is my new strategy. Day one of the war is the first time Esti, now aged twelve, buys a newspaper. This is the sort of conflict that I couldn't have hidden, even if I had wanted to. The local supermarket has a widescreen TV over the checkout that is permanently tuned to *BBC News 24*. We have TVs all over the house and, in the morning, while I clear off the breakfast, I watch the bombers take off from Britain and calculate just how many hours we have of normality before the bombs start falling in Baghdad. I don't have to tell Ben and Esti this. They have worked it out for themselves and are home before anything happens.

My friend Sophie is now living around the corner. She comes almost every day to offer moral support. It's like the old days in Bucharest all over again. We are sitting at the kitchen table having a cup of tea. Sophie has married her boyfriend, who was in Dubrovnik during the siege with Tim, and they now have two children. Alec has covered an endless stream of wars, just like Tim, but is now the foreign editor of the *Daily Telegraph* and is spending this one in London.

"Do you remember that conversation we had when they were in Dubrovnik?" she asks me as she wipes smeared chocolate off her three-year old's face:

"I asked you if it got any easier the more times you went through it and you said, 'ask me in ten years time.' Well, do you realise that was ten years ago?"

We agree that it doesn't get any easier. Experience has only taught us that there are a long list of things that could possibly go wrong.

During the first few nights of the war, other journalist friends come to watch the battles on television with us. Chris comes round. He has missed this one as he's writing a book:

"You shouldn't be alone at a time like this Rosie," he says patting me on the shoulder and cracking a few jokes that involve scenarios of Tim being blasted by a cruise missile or besieged in Baghdad for months. We all laugh. What else can we do?

Then, one evening, I watch the news with another friend who covered the Balkan wars. On screen, a young, black reporter is standing right next to some British soldiers firing as they sprint across a street in Basra.

"What do they expect from journalists now?" she asks me. "To die on television so they get better ratings?"

I think she is probably right. I am glad the kids are busy doing their homework. I sit there and think about the families of the soldiers who are firing into the darkness behind him and I wonder if they are watching. You can make out their faces. I hope they aren't killed on screen. Imagine if you saw your husband or son die on TV while you stood in the checkout at the supermarket.

Then, during one news report a few days later, the camera is suddenly splattered with blood. A *BBC* news team have been hit. I jump up off the sofa and turn the television off. I don't want the children to see this. Fortunately, they are all in another room. I wish someone would spare a thought for them, when they decide what they show and when. The whole thing is rather ghoulish, although I'm more addicted than anyone else. I tell Ben to watch the footage online.

One evening a missile explodes in a market in Baghdad. Tim calls me after he gets back from inspecting the damage:

"There were coffins stacked so high they were towering above me," he says. The line is so clear, it's as if he is in the next room. I feel very close to him.

"Many of those who died were the same age as Ben and Esti," he continues. He has seen the bodies and talked to the relatives. He sounds flat and exhausted. I couldn't do this job. There is nothing glamorous about it. It's dirty and unpleasant.

Eventually, we have less visitors dropping by to watch the news. The war is becoming a normal backdrop to everyone's daily life, even mine. One Friday evening, when everyone has decided that they have better things to do than hang out with us, I'm just coming downstairs from putting the washing away in the kids' bedrooms, when I hear the television is on in the sitting room on the ground floor. I pop my head around the door to see who has escaped the noisy basement, where most of our family life is centred. Ray is sitting on the sofa watching a live feed from Baghdad. They are expecting cruise missiles and a bombing raid at any moment:

"I want to watch when it happens" she says calmly.

She isn't ten until May but I can't just turn the set off and pretend nothing is going on, although I suspect plenty of parents would, but they haven't been here. I sit down next to her and hold her hand. She squeezes it tightly. We sit there for a half an hour watching the empty streets of Baghdad, but nothing happens. It's so surreal that I start to laugh and in the end, I have to say to Ray:

"Look, I have to go downstairs and cook supper. I can't just sit here watching an air raid that isn't happening. Will you come down?"

"Call me when it's ready. I'll stay here."

While I throw some potatoes in the pan and turn on the oven, I wonder what is happening upstairs. I am immensely proud of her nerve. *Thomas the Tank Engine* is on down here. The fridge is half empty. Tim has had to take thousands of pounds in cash with him as credit cards don't work in war zones and, as usual, we've had to put up a large proportion of the expenses up front. I'm left with an enormous overdraft. The only things I can afford to buy are on "buy one, get one free" and there is only supersavers sliced bread in the breadbin. Dinner is going to be rather dull.

Ray watches on for another fifteen minutes, then I put on the television news in the kitchen. We eat dinner in front of the grainy black and white image of night time Baghdad. Still nothing happens. Then, live coverage suddenly stops, to make way for *Top of the Pops*. This is, of course, when the action starts. So much for everyone's favourite topic of discussion, the pros and cons of the wall-to-wall coverage of the war. It isn't wall-to-wall at all but I suppose the chattering classes are out to dinner and haven't noticed.

When Tim calls later in the evening, the bombardment is in full swing, but there are only comedies and DIY shows on television. He wants to know how Esti's maths test went. Unfortunately, it's not good news on that score. He tells me to take some money out of the savings to tide us over and wants to know what's in this morning's post. As we talk, I hear a cruise missile crash into the building next door. The hotel is in the centre of the city close to all the top, priority targets. He is in his hotel bedroom, simply waiting for room service. He doesn't flinch. I can tell because the tone in his voice doesn't alter.

Half an hour later, Ben and I hear a report on *News at Ten* on *ITV* that says Tim's hotel has been hit. Fortunately, I'm sitting down:

"I'm shaking Ben. You call. I can't hold the phone!"

He is amazingly composed. He suddenly seems to have become a man. He has completed part of his journey through life. I am glad I was there to be a part of it. He dials the number while I think:

"What am I doing letting him make this phone call?"

It dawns on me that our relationship has just changed fundamentally. He has become a son who looks after his mother. He has taken control of the situation. I think this has a lot to do with they way I have brought him up. Not everyone might agree with what I have done but at least it has prepared him for life.

We get through first time. He puts his hand on my shoulder protectively:

"Calm down! It's ringing."

Thank God for the kids, I couldn't get through days like this without them.

"It wouldn't work, if it was bombed, would it?" he adds optimistically.

I'm not so sure about that. I see images of phones ringing in the wreckage. Within seconds, we get Tim, who is happily eating his dinner. The report was wrong.

"Don't worry! It looks worse on TV than it really is," he tries to reassure me.

"But, you haven't seen the TV! How do you know?" I scream back down the line.

I think it was better when I didn't have such a good idea of what he was up to.

The next day, after we have argued for over six hours, he moves to what I consider to be a safer hotel, the Hotel Palestine.

From now on the days pass by in a blur of cooking, cleaning, homework and watching television - frontline reports that is. I speak to Tim at least two or three times a day. Most of our discussions are completely mundane. I'm worried Baghdad won't fall and there will be a siege. It could go on for months. Then one morning, I am driving back from dropping the kids off at school, when I hear a live report from the Hotel Palestine on the *Today* programme. The US army has arrived in the city centre. There is a loud bang and their correspondent, Andrew Gilligan, who is soon to become famous – or infamous – for his reporting on the programme, says he has to go, as the hotel has been hit. My legs go to jelly and I have to pull over, to recover. I've never had such a shock before. An American tank shell has ripped into a bedroom on one of the top floors and killed two people. Within minutes my mobile rings. It's Tim who tells me he's fine. I've never felt so relieved in my life. I feel terrific.

"What are you doing?" he asks. As if that mattered.

I greet the kids home from school, who have by now got so used to the conflict that they had forgotten their mobile phones:

"It wasn't Dads. He's not dead. The Palestine Hotel was hit, but Dad is ok."

"Where was Dads when it happened?" asks Esti.

"Eating a banana in his room," I reply.

"What! I don't believe him! He's such an embarrassment. How can I tell anyone that?"

She is a war reporter's daughter. Blood and gore are consigned to their place by black humour. Life is momentous and banal all at the same time. What can you do but laugh? That is what is missing on television. Journalists dodge the bullets in front of the cameras but what you never see them do is call home to see if someone has paid the gas bill.

"Great. I want to be a reporter like Dads and see history unroll before my eyes," announces Ben.

"What! Two of you! What will you be eating? Anything but a banana!" shrieks Esti.

"What does he do in Baghdad – nothing but eat?"

"I decided that in Mostar," adds Ray.

"What!? You'll eat a banana. Yes, you would, you fruit freak!"

No, "I want to be a journalist."

She says this with a calm serenity that makes me think she is just like her father, capable of remaining totally normal while chaos breaks out all around him.

"Three of them Mummy! That's too much!" says Esti slumping in the chair.

"I thought you wanted to be a photographer," I remind her.

"Yeah, so I do! But I'm not going to be caught eating a banana in a crisis!"

When the joke is over. Ben gets up off the sofa where he has flopped down and walks over to me. He is taller than me now. He puts his arm round me and gives me a squeeze:

"Come on Mummy! Life is rich. You have to go out and grab it. You shouldn't be so nervous."

One thing I have learned is that I can always rely on the kids to put me in my place.

REPORTAGE PRESS is a new publishing house specialising in books on foreign affairs or set in foreign countries; non-fiction, fiction, essays, travel books, or just books written from a stranger's view. Good books like this are now hard to come by - largely because British publishers have become frightened of publishing books that will not guarantee massive sales. At REPORTAGE PRESS we are not adverse to taking risks in order to bring our readers the books they want to read.

Visit our Website: www.reportagepress.com, the ultimate on-line travel book shop. We not only sell our books but also books, films and documentaries about the places and subjects that interest our customers, with country by country recommendations compiled by regional experts. We also provide travel tips. On the website you can meet and share ideas with like-minded people. You can also download our books in e-format and as pod-casts. 5% of the profits from our books go to charity.

You can order further copies of this book direct from REPORTAGE PRESS. Free UK Delivery!

To order further copies of *Are We There Yet?* please send a copy of the coupon below to:

REPORTAGE PRESS - 26 Richmond Way, London W12 8LY, United Kingdom.

Alternatively, you may download an order form from our website: www.reportagepress.com

Please send me _____ copies of *Are We There Yet?*

I enclose a UK bank cheque or postal order, payable to REPORTAGE PRESS for £_____, @ £ 8.99 per copy.

NAME:
ADRESS:

POSTCODE:

Please allow 28 days for delivery. Do not send cash. Offer subject to availability.
We do not share or sell our customer's details. Please tick box if you do not wish to receive further information from REPORTAGE PRESS. ☐